TRAGEDY at GRAIGNES

Captain Abraham (Bud) Sophian, 1915–1944

TRAGEDY at GRAIGNES

———◆———

The Bud Sophian Story

Margaret R. O'Leary
Dennis S. O'Leary

iUniverse, Inc.
Bloomington

Tragedy at Graignes
The Bud Sophian Story

iUniverse books may be ordered through booksellers or by contacting:

iUniverse
1663 Liberty Drive
Bloomington, IN 47403
www.iuniverse.com
1-800-Authors (1-800-288-4677)

ISBN: 978-1-4502-8329-8 (sc)
ISBN: 978-1-4502-8330-4 (dj)
ISBN: 978-1-4502-8331-1 (ebk)

Library of Congress Control Number: 2011900022

Printed in the United States of America

iUniverse rev. date: 02/17/2011

To the American paratroopers who perished in Graignes, France, June 6–12, 1944, and their families.

Contents

Authors' Preface

The idea for writing the biography of Captain Abraham (Bud) Sophian (SO-fee-yun), Jr., MD (1915–1944) originated in the weeks following the passing of his ninety-year-old brother-in-law, Theodore (Ted) Morgan O'Leary (1911–2001) of Fairway, Kansas. Ted possessed dozens of boxes of old letters, books, and photos, which belonged to the storied Sophian and O'Leary families of Missouri and Kansas, respectively, and dated as far back as the 1860s. We discovered the boxes while cleaning the green-shuttered, Tudor-style house in which Ted and his wife Emily Sophian O'Leary (1913–1994) had lived for more than a half century. Ted and Emily were both writers who cherished the letters they received over their long lives. Hundreds of these letters survive, and several dozen letters were from Emily's only sibling and younger brother Bud, the hero of this book. We began to sort them with the expectation of writing the present biography.

Progress on the Bud Sophian biography initially languished as other priorities cropped up. We today recognize and thank US Army physician Colonel Roy S. Marokus for jump-starting the creative process. How did Colonel Marokus know of Captain Sophian? Captain Sophian was the battalion surgeon and parachute infantryman who Nazi Waffen SS troops brutally murdered only hours after surrendering himself and his patients and medics to them in Graignes, France, six long days after parachuting into Normandy on D-day, June 6, 1944. Colonel Marokus

1

had visited the Graignes War Memorial late in 2008 and noted Captain Sophian's name on the memorial plaque. Colonel Marokus then located and contacted us, because Captain Sophian's sacrifice moved him. Colonel Marokus's compassion for a fellow US Army physician and his effort to reach out to Captain Sophian's descendants inspired us to complete the biography.

Captain Sophian's experience in Graignes emerged belatedly from the shadows of World War II history, when American paratroopers who had survived the Graignes tragedy held stateside reunions and revisited the French hamlet multiple times beginning in the 1980s. Over the next two decades, books and films (see References section) emerged to detail the so-called Battle of Graignes and the ensuing massacre of Captain Sophian, the medics, and the wounded patients under their care.

Gary N. Fox wrote one of these books, which he titled *Graignes* (Fostoria, Ohio: Gray Printing Co., 1990). Fox's book stands out because it was the earliest and drew much of its information from eyewitnesses, such as Frank Naughton, a first lieutenant who survived the Battle of Graignes and subsequently ascended the army ranks to become a colonel. Fox acknowledged in the front matter of his book:

> In the research phase, I relied heavily on Colonel Francis E. Naughton's memoirs which he graciously allowed me to use. I also had the pleasure of speaking with him concerning various events which took place at Graignes, France during the 1989 507 Parachute Infantry Regiment's Reunion in Columbus, Ohio. Colonel Naughton further took the time to read the rough draft of my manuscript and had made precise and helpful comments. Without his detailed memory of events, I could have never attained the degree of accuracy I wanted.

Another surviving officer named Earcle "Pip" Reed also "kindly took the time from his busy schedule to read the rough draft," continued Fox, "and recommended factual changes that were needed.

He gave me further insight into particular events which took place at Graignes."

A third person to inform Fox about the Graignes catastrophe was Captain Leroy Brummitt who answered letters sent by Fox. Brummitt shared with Fox a copy of his June 16, 1944 after-action statement, which he had presented to the 82nd Airborne Division G-2 (US Army intelligence officer at the division level and higher) after his horrendous ordeal in Graignes.

US Army paratrooper officers Naughton, Reed, and Brummitt left Graignes to avoid capture by Waffen SS troops, and they lived. Captain Sophian was the only officer who did not flee Graignes, because he had fourteen wounded paratroopers who needed his care, and he would not leave them. He surrendered to Waffen SS troops as they overran Graignes by waving a white flag at the door of the badly shelled Norman church of Graignes, hoping for fair prisoner treatment for himself, his two medics, and his patients, according to the Geneva Convention of 1929 to which Germany was a signatory. The Waffen SS troops instead committed unspeakable atrocities on their seventeen American prisoners, leaving many of them bloody and mutilated in grotesque heaps. Most of the men died quickly, but some lingered before drawing their last breath.

The International Military Tribunal at Nuremberg in 1945 indicted the Waffen SS as a criminal organization. The tribunal concluded that "units of the Waffen SS were directly involved in the killing of prisoners of war and other atrocities in occupied countries," noted George H. Stein in his seminal work titled *Hitler's Elite Guard at War: The Waffen SS 1939–1945* (Ithaca, New York: Cornell University, 1965, pp. 250–251). However, the proceedings were designed "only 'to identify and condemn,' and declaration of criminality did not empower the Tribunal to impose sentence upon them or to convict any individual merely because of membership," Stein added. Allied military courts tried and convicted a few hundred Waffen SS personnel, including some combat members of fighting formations in occupied countries such as France, but the courts never tried any person for committing the Graignes massacre of unarmed medical personnel and their patients.

Military historian Martin K. A. Morgan expanded our knowledge of the heady, then desperate, experience of the American paratroopers trapped in Graignes in his fine book *Down to Earth: The 507th Parachute Infantry Regiment in Normandy June 6–July 15, 1944* (Atglen, Pennsylvania: Schiffer Military History, 2004). In particular, he obtained and published (p. 258) closely held documents that the US Army generated during its investigation in June 1947 of the Graignes battle and massacre. Morgan said he obtained the documents from Total Army Personnel Command, Freedom of Information Act Office.

The historical record of what actually transpired in Graignes in June 1944 remains incomplete despite the information gathered by the US Army in June 1947 and the remembrances of paratroopers who fled Graignes and who much later told their stories. What is missing from the historical record is the contribution of the soldiers who did *not* survive their fateful Graignes sojourn. Dead people cannot talk, or can they? Captain Sophian, for one, can talk posthumously through books such as this one.

Captain Sophian's judgment and actions during the Second World War were the culmination of the rich and challenging life he led before he was inducted as a medical officer into the US Army in 1942. His life, though shortened, still spanned the First World War, the Roaring Twenties, Prohibition, the Great Depression, and the Second World War. Bud's correspondence with his rambunctious older sister Emily for over fifteen years (1929–1944) and other Sophian and O'Leary family archival materials tell the story of his compelling life. These letters are reproduced verbatim (i.e., word for word, without correcting spellings, word usage, or grammar) in the following text so that Bud, Emily, Estelle, Dr. Sophian, Lucille, Keckie, and other people in his life may speak directly to you and to the historical record.

Bud Sophian's story is but one of hundreds of thousands of stories of young American soldiers who lost their lives in the European Theater of

War during the Second World War. We hope that this book and others like it will encourage families of World War II decedents to publish their loved ones' stories so that present and future generations may appreciate the lives and sacrifice of the soldiers who perished, in addition to the soldiers who survived their punishing ordeals.

We thank the staff of Pembroke Hill School and Notre Dame de Sion School in Kansas City, Missouri; Phillips Academy in Andover Massachusetts; Stanford University in Stanford, California; and Cornell University Medical College in New York City, New York, who helped us in our research of Bud's days at their schools.

As authors, we want this book's treatment of Bud Sophian's life to be fair and accurate, and we would be pleased to correct all errors of fact. If you identify an error of fact, please contact the publisher who will forward your message to us for prompt consideration of text revision.

Margaret R. O'Leary, MD
Dennis S. O'Leary, MD
Fairway, Kansas
October 1, 2010

Chapter One: Family Heritage

Most people knew Abraham Sophian, Jr. as "Buddy" or "Bud," and he preferred these monikers to the more austere "Abraham," which was also his father's name. For example, one of his army physician colleagues wrote to his parents:

> It was with the greatest surprise that I learned of the great loss of your son, Captain Abraham Sophian Jr. in the 7 April [1945] issue of the *Jackson County* [Missouri] *Medical Society Weekly Bulletin*. Please accept my sympathy at this time. Personally, I always remember him by the name of "Bud." He was always a cheerful and courteous fellow.

To distinguish between the two Abraham Sophians in this book, we refer to the son as Bud Sophian, Dr. Bud Sophian, Captain Sophian, or Captain Bud Sophian, and to his father as Abraham Sophian, Dr. Abraham Sophian, or Dr. Sophian. Dr. Abraham Sophian did not serve in the military, so there is only one historical Captain Sophian, i.e., Captain Bud Sophian (or Captain Abraham Sophian, Jr., as the US Army knew him).

Bud's parents were Estelle Felix (1886–1970) and Dr. Abraham Sophian (1884–1957). Estelle and Abraham came from two large Jewish families that immigrated to New York City in the late nineteenth century from Prussia (Germany) and Russia, respectively. The Felix family, which emigrated in at least two stages between 1883 and 1890, was of Greek Jewish heritage, according to Estelle Felix. The Sophian family emigrated from Kiev in southwestern Russia in 1890 and was of Armenian Jewish heritage, according to Dr. Abraham Sophian.[1] The Sophian family fled Russia because of repressive, reactionary, and anti-Semitic policies emplaced by Tsar Alexander III (who reigned from 1881 to 1894) and his ministers and confidants, especially Constantine Petrovich Pobedonostsev (1827–1907), Procurator of the Holy Synod, lawyer, and one of the most chilling and self-righteous anti-Semitic officials ever produced by Russia.[2-4]

The anti-Semitic policies implemented by Tsar Alexander III further restricted (some restrictions were already in place) where Jews could live in the so-called Pale of Settlement and the occupations that Jews could pursue. The Pale of Settlement refers to the region of Imperial Russia along its western border in which tsarist Russia permitted Jews to reside. It extended from the pale or demarcation line inside of Russia to her borders with Germany and Austria-Hungary. The Sophian family likely witnessed the first of three waves of violent anti-Jewish pogroms that swept through Imperial Russia between 1881 and 1884, but escaped the second and third waves (1903–1906 and 1919–1921), because it had moved to America to dwell in safety.[4-9]

Bud's mother, Estelle Felix, was born September 8, 1886, in New York City as the youngest of eight children. Her father was prosperous manufacturer, merchant, and salesman Arthur A. Felix who was born January 20, 1855, in Russia (according to his petition for naturalization filed in the US District Court, New York, New York, on May 31, 1900). Estelle's mother was Emily (Tillie), who married Arthur in 1874. Arthur first came to the United States on August 8, 1883, on the SS *Canada* (according to its passenger list submitted to the District of the City of New York, Port of New York on August 8, 1883), put down roots, and then returned to Russia to retrieve his four older children. He arrived back in New York City with his brood on December 23, 1890, aboard the SS *Servia*. His four oldest children were Sara (born 1875), Pauline (Polly, 1877), Eva (1879), and Josef (Joseph, 1881). He and Emily produced four more children in New York City: Louis E. (1883), Jane (1884), Flora (Floey, 1885), and Estelle (Bud's mother, 1886).

Arthur A. Felix prospered in New York City as he had done in Russia and qualified to become a naturalized citizen of the United States on May 31, 1900, after living at 457 Pleasant Avenue in Ward 12 (located above 86th Street) in Manhattan for the previous ten years. About eight hundred thousand people lived in Manhattan's nine-square-mile Ward 12 in 1910, which calculates to a population density of eighty-eight thousand people per square mile.[10] The Felix family was able to avoid the difficult life facing Russian Jewish immigrants then crowding into the tenements of Manhattan's Lower East Side (according to the 1900 US Census, Manhattan Borough, June 26, 1900).

The Sophian family was economically less fortunate than the Felix family. Dr. Abraham Sophian (Bud's father) was born on January 1, 1884. His parents were lumber merchant Morris Sophian (born 1849) and Dora (born 1855). Both parents were natives of Kiev, Russia, as were their five oldest children: Meyer (Michael, "Mike", 1873, who became a physician), Jennie (1877), Rose (1880), Harry (1883), and Abraham (1884).[11-13] A sixth child named Gussie (Golda) joined the family in New York City in 1893. Gussie Sophian resided in the Hebrew Orphan Asylum for a time. There, in June 1902, she won a silver watch as a prize for a contest she had entered, as reported in the *New York Times*.[14-15]

In 1890, the impoverished Sophian family lived in the tenement at 250-252 Henry Street in Ward 7 on Manhattan's Lower East Side. This densely populated area in 1910 contained some one hundred thousand people who lived in an area less than one-third of a square mile—an astounding population density of about 325,000 people per square mile.[10] By comparison, the population density of Manhattan in the year 2008 was around sixty-seven thousand people per square mile—the highest of any county or borough in the United States.[16]

The tenement occupied by the Sophian family was near the famed

Henry Street Settlement at 265 Henry Street. The American nurse, social worker, and Jewish feminist Lillian D. Wald (1867–1940) founded the Henry Street Settlement in 1893 to improve the plight of Lower East Side tenement dwellers.[17-19] German Jewish banker and philanthropist Jacob Schiff (1847–1920) supported Russian Jews who had suffered in tsarist Russia. In 1895, he purchased and donated the building at 265 Henry Street to the Henry Street Settlement.[20]

The two youngest Sophian brothers, Harry and Abraham, married two of the youngest Felix sisters, Jane and Estelle, respectively. Harry and Jane Sophian and Abraham and Estelle Sophian, with their children in tow, moved from New York City to Kansas City in 1916 and 1917, respectively. The Felix and Sophian siblings and their children remained close throughout their lives.

Bud's father, Abraham Sophian, won a full state scholarship to Cornell University on June 7, 1902 by scoring very high marks on a competitive examination conducted by the State of New York's Department of Public Instruction (Charles R. Skinner, superintendent). Students at the time typically proceeded directly from high school to medical college if they wanted and qualified to become a physician. Cornell University trustees established the Cornell University Medical College on April 14, 1898, as described in *A History of Cornell* by Morris Bishop (Ithaca, New York: Cornell University Press, 1962, p. 320.). Eighteen-year-old Abraham thus applied his state scholarship toward financing his medical school education at Cornell University Medical College in New York City, rather than pursuing undergraduate studies at Cornell University in Ithaca, New York.

After completing medical school in 1906, Dr. Abraham Sophian won through yet another tough competitive examination a coveted place at Mount Sinai Hospital in New York City to pursue his two-year post-graduate medical study (1906–1908). There he trained with physicians who comprise a who's who of early twentieth-century medicine, as described in *This House of Noble Deeds: The Mount Sinai Hospital, 1852–2002* by Arthur H. Aufses, Jr. and Barbara J. Niss (New York,

New York: New York University Press, 2002). For example, one of his favorite teachers and mentors was master diagnostician Nathan E. Brill, MD (1860–1925). Dr. Brill first described endemic typhus (Brill's disease) and learned *his* clinical medicine from another famous clinician Edward G. Janeway, MD (1841–1911). Dr. Brill's quietude, humility, and scrupulous honesty resonated with young Dr. Abraham Sophian.

After his hospital residency at Mount Sinai Hospital, Dr. Abraham Sophian joined the Research Laboratory staff in the New York City Health Department and later affiliated with New York University, where he developed immune sera for the treatment of infectious diseases such as epidemic cerebral meningitis. Prior to the 1940s, no antibiotics existed to treat infectious diseases. In the absence of antibiotics, some physicians prepared and administered immune sera, which contained antibodies to infectious agents that the physicians were trying to contain. Dr. Abraham Sophian manufactured his immune sera by inoculating horses with diseased material. He later collected the horse's blood serum, which now contained antibodies to the diseased material under consideration. He then injected the serum into humans suffering from the disease. The immunotherapy helped more times than not, according to data he carefully collected on the efficacy of the treatment.

Dr. Abraham Sophian's research and clinical expertise in infectious diseases earned him acclaim and a brisk demand for services outside the boundaries of New York State.[21–25] For example, he first visited Kansas City in 1910 to help local authorities contain a meningitis outbreak. In the latter part of 1911, a serious meningitis epidemic erupted in Dallas County, Texas. Senior research physicians at the Rockefeller Institute of New York City dispatched Dr. Sophian to Dallas to work with local physicians to contain the epidemic. In January 1912, the Texas State Board of Medical Examiners granted Dr. Abraham Sophian a medical license. He proceeded to fix up an old hospital to which he insisted that local physicians admit their most serious cases.

During this time, Dr. Abraham Sophian worked almost twenty hours a day caring for the extremely ill patients in the old hospital.

His efforts were successful in reducing the death rate through early recognition of the disease and injection of immune serum that he had manufactured and transported from New York. In addition to caring directly for patients, he held daily clinics for physicians from the surrounding towns to instruct them in the diagnosis of the disease and in the use of the serum. The epidemic lasted about two months. A few days before his departure, grateful Dallas citizens presented him with a silver loving cup, and his new Texas physician colleagues gave him a lovely silver tea service. New Yorkers cheered his successes, as reported by the *New York Times*.[23-24] After his return to New York, Dr. Abraham Sophian wrote the classic book *Epidemic Cerebral Meningitis* (1913), which remains today an important reference in the recognition and treatment of the disease.[21]

During this very active period of Dr. Abraham Sophian's life, he managed to court Estelle Felix, who was working as a schoolteacher in the New York City public school system. They married on April 26, 1911, and moved into a large, beautiful home that they shared with relatives in the planned enclave of Long Beach, Long Island, where few Jews lived at the time.[26-27]

In 1917, Dr. Abraham Sophian moved his family to Kansas City, where he served as the first director of the original laboratory of Research Hospital (also known as German Hospital and German-American Hospital).[28] He also opened a medical practice in 1917 to care for Kansas City residents from every walk of life, including Irish and Russian Jewish immigrants crowded into damp and rat-infested hovels in McClure Flats, and wealthy and powerful men, such as lumber magnate Robert Alexander Long (1850–1934) and Democratic machine boss Tom Pendergast (1873–1945).[29-30]

Harry Joseph Sophian (Bud's uncle and Abraham's older brother) first worked in New York City with realty executive Ringland Fisher "Rex" Kilpatrick (1882–1955) before moving to Kansas City in 1916.[31-32] There he purchased parcels of strategically located land and eventually built two historic Kansas City luxury apartment buildings: Georgian

Court Apartments (400 East Armour Boulevard) and Sophian Plaza (4618 Warwick Boulevard, National Register of Historic Places, 1982). The Kansas City architectural firm of Shepard and Wiser designed the buildings.[31–36] Harry Sophian built a third luxury apartment building also named Sophian Plaza in Tulsa, Oklahoma (1500 South Frisco Avenue).

From 1917 to 1930, the Abraham Sophian family lived in one of the original twenty-four Georgian Court apartments, which then boasted between six and nine rooms each. From 1930 to 1933, the Abraham Sophian family moved to Sophian Plaza, located about a mile south of Georgian Court.[37] In 1933, the family moved into a custom-built mansion on a towering limestone bluff overlooking Brush Creek in what was then unincorporated Kansas City, Kansas, and what is today Mission Hills, Kansas.

Estelle and Abraham Sophian were forward thinking about their identity as Jewish-Americans. They believed with other Reform Jews that Jewish assimilation into American society was appropriate and desirable. Furthermore, they and other Reform Jews believed that intermarriage between Jews and people of other faiths was an acceptable way of achieving that assimilation. Orthodox Jews, by contrast, believed that God had irrevocably separated Jews from all other peoples on earth and to even consider assimilation through intermarriage was an unforgivable act of disobedience (to God).

Estelle and Abraham followed other Reform Judaism practices, such as using English instead of Hebrew at services and discontinuing special diets and rituals such as the *bris* (the covenant of circumcision). They believed that these customs only served to further distinguish and distance Jews from other peoples. The Zionism movement, which promoted the return to Israel of Diaspora Jews of the Hebrew nation, also did not resonate with them.[38–39] Reform Judaism historian Michael A. Meyer described the Reform Judaism movement as the "branch of Judaism which has been most hospitable to the modern critical temper while still endeavoring to maintain continuity of faith and practice with Jewish religious tradition."[39]

Monotheism is the central tenet of Judaism; that is, there is one God, not many gods. To the Abraham Sophian family, belief in God, Jesus Christ as the Son of God, and the existence of the Holy Spirit (Holy Ghost) seemed to imply three gods, or polytheism. The argument that God, Jesus Christ, and the Holy Ghost are three aspects of a single divine unity did not make sense to them.

Dr. Abraham Sophian Family, Kansas City, Missouri, ca. 1925.
Left to right: Estelle, Bud, Abraham, and Emily Sophian.
Sophian Archives.

Harry J. Sophian Family, ca. 1920.
Left to right: Harry, Jane, and Lucille Sophian. Also in photo are
niece Emily Sophian (in front) and nephew Bud (in car) Sophian
(children of Abraham and Estelle Sophian). *Sophian Archives.*

Dr. Abraham Sophian (left) with his patients, lumbar baron
Robert Alexander Long (center) and Democratic political boss
Tom Pendergast (right), in Kansas City, Missouri, ca. 1930s.
Sophian Archives.

Chapter Two: Early Years, 1915–1929

———◆———

Both Bud (April 28, 1915) and Emily (September 28, 1913) Sophian were born in one of the earliest community hospitals in Manhattan and from there were taken to their parents' Long Beach, Long Island, home. Both were healthy at birth.

Bud was one of the "prettiest babies" relatives had ever seen: "He was really beautiful," noted Emily. However, shortly after Bud learned to walk, he developed into a "regular little family nuisance," she added. "He has always taken the greatest delight in pestering both Mother and me – (Even Dad sometimes) – and, were it not for his charming disposition, I doubt very much if any nurse would have stayed with him over a week," Emily averred. She continued:

As a child he was very much afraid of the water and much preferred playing in the sand to jumping in the pool or lake. In fact, it was not until just about a couple of years ago [when Bud was ten] that he overcame his fears and became a good swimmer. He now loves all water sports. However, he is a trouble-maker in the water as well as on land, for ducking people is one of his greatest sources of pleasure. I am almost certain that that is the reason mother cares so little for swimming.

From a beautiful, tho annoying child, Bud has grown into a handsome and still more annoying boy of twelve. He is extremely intelligent, although he does not work unless he has to, and is an excellent athlete, playing a very good game of tennis, golf and especially football. He should excel at the latter, however, for he practices his tackles on me at every available opportunity.

Now, in spite of his many attributes, especially his looks about which everyone comments, our "trouble-maker" remains naïve and not conceited. I think the world of him – (tho he does not seem to think I do) – and do not know how I'd ever get along without him.

Abraham, Estelle, Emily, and Bud moved to Oklahoma City, Oklahoma, for the winter of 1916, possibly because of Abraham's expertise in managing infectious disease epidemics or business investments there (e.g., Sophian Plaza, Tulsa). The Abraham Sophian family then returned to Long Beach, Long Island, for one more summer (1917), at the end of which they packed their belongings to move that autumn to Kansas City, Missouri. For about one year, the family lived in a house on Paseo Boulevard, the major north-south parkway in Kansas City modeled after the *Paseo de la Reforma* in Mexico City, while Harry Sophian was building Georgian Court Apartments. Upon completion of the building, the Abraham Sophian family took up residence there for the next thirteen years.

Kansas City, Missouri, appealed to Estelle and Abraham Sophian for many reasons. Its geography was "neither east nor west nor north nor south," and it provided comforting anonymity in a "gateway to somewhere else, funneling thousands of travelers to the western frontier." Its citizens were "likely to be German or French, black or white, Jewish or Catholic."[40] In addition, Kansas and Missouri experienced many infectious disease epidemics in the early twentieth century. Shocking sanitation and medical practices fueled many of these epidemics. Dr. Sophian felt needed in Kansas City.

Abraham and Estelle Sophian soon joined the Congregation of

Temple B'nai Jehudah, which a group of prosperous German Reformed Jewish settlers had founded in Kansas City in 1870.[41] Temple B'nai Jehudah was fully modern in the Reform sense, e.g., the services were mostly in English, and the rabbi's sermon was the main feature of the service. The congregation participated in responsive readings and hymns, and dropped many distinctive Orthodox Jewish rites and customs, such as wearing prayer shawls and hats. Men, women, and families sat together in pews instead of apart, according to gender. The prayers in the *Union Prayer Book* had undergone revisions to remove references to the restoration of the temple service, dispersion as exile or punishment, and prayers to God to rebuild Jerusalem and bring the Jewish people back to the Land of Israel. American scholar Nathan Glazer declared, "One cannot underestimate the sheer force of the rationalist and progressive position adopted by the [Reform] rabbis, a position all of whose implications they worked out and tried to realize."[42]

Both Bud and Emily Sophian received confirmation in Temple B'nai Jehudah. The confirmation ceremony is "an institution adopted from Christianity where it represented the culmination of a course of study intended to prepare the young person for adult status in the church," explained Michael A. Meyer in his classic work *Response to Modernity: A History of the Reform Movement in Judaism* (1988, p. 39). He continued, "If in the traditional Bar Mitzvah ceremony the young man was to show his capacity to read from the Torah and also often to give a rabbinic discourse, in the confirmation ceremony he was to demonstrate that he had learned the principles and duties of Judaism as a religion." As members of a Reformed Jewish congregation in the 1920s and 1930s, neither Bud nor Emily experienced a Bar or Bat Mitzvah rite, respectively. Indeed, the Abraham Sophian family celebrated Christmas.

Orthodox and Reform Jews differed on the appropriateness of conscripting young Jewish men into the military. Eastern European Orthodox Jewish immigrants in particular repudiated military conscription. This deeply held belief dated at least to the beginning of the nineteenth century when Russian rulers had demanded that Jews living in the Pale of Settlement perform military service as an essential precondition for full equality in the Russian state. "If Jews sought civil parity, it seemed commonsensical that they should be required to fulfill their obligation to the state that conferred upon them the yearned-for privileges. The readiness of Jews to sacrifice their lives for their country demonstrated ... that they deserved equal rights," explained one scholar. Orthodox Jews keenly disagreed, declaring Russian military conscription the "contemporary embodiment of the biblical Joseph, whose brothers sold him into Egyptian bondage."[43]

Reform Jews tended to view military conscription in the United States as a necessary civil service that the country intermittently required to protect the American (and Reform Judaism) values of freedom and social justice. Bud and his family clearly understood and accepted this reality, and he, like most other young men of his generation, willingly responded to the call to fight fascist dictators such as Adolph Hitler (1889–1945) and Benito Mussolini (1883–1945).[44]

Some Orthodox Jewish immigrant families in Kansas City disparaged the Sophian family for leaving the ancient fold to join a Reformed Jewish congregation.[45] At the same time, some of the city's most established Reform Jewish families deprecated the Sophians as Russian immigrant upstarts whose presence debased Temple B'nai Jehudah. The Sophian family thus experienced a measure of antipathy from both ends of the spectrum of Judaism in Kansas City.

Furthermore, members of the Abraham Sophian family weathered discrimination from people and organizations from outside the Jewish community in Kansas City. For example, most private schools in Kansas City during the early twentieth century rejected outright the applications submitted by Jewish parents on behalf of their children. In addition, most Kansas City hospital boards of trustees refused to grant medical privileges to Jewish physicians, including Dr. Abraham Sophian, to care for their Jewish and non-Jewish patients inside the hospital walls. Dr. Sophian's superior New York City medical training and extraordinary clinical experience in places such as Dallas were unequalled in the Kansas City medical community, and few physicians or hospital administrators would dispute his brilliance and compassion as a physician. However, Protestant and Roman Catholic boards of trustees oversaw most of the hospitals in Kansas City on behalf of their respective religious organizations and summarily rejected all applications for medical privileges submitted by Jewish physicians.

In the early part of the twentieth century and before the founding of Menorah Hospital, only one Kansas City hospital—Research Hospital—accepted applications from Jewish physicians for medical staff privileges. The Jewish community of Kansas City eventually privately financed and constructed Menorah Hospital in the early 1930s to provide hospital beds for the patients of Jewish physicians. Indeed, Menorah Hospital provided qualified physicians of all faiths a place to care for their patients who required hospitalization.

Dr. Sophian described the frustration he experienced for more than a decade of practicing medicine in Kansas City in an unusually upbeat letter to Emily during her first year at Smith College (in Northampton, Massachusetts) on April 10, 1931:

Dear Em:
Your Dad was surprised and honored last night by being elected as President (Chief of Staff) of the Research Hospital Staff. It came as an unexpected surprise, was unanimous and many nice things were said which rather made me feel ashamed of the Resentment [Dr. Sophian's personal writing style involved sometimes capitalizing non-proper nouns and verbs] that I had felt so long for discrimination and lack of recognition. As one gets older, one learns however that one keeps on learning and would if one lived to be a thousand years. With the new Hospital [Menorah] to be opened soon, this new office [chief of staff of Research Hospital] will be difficult, but I intend to

21

work hard and do some much needed construction work [for Research Hospital].

Everything else quiet on the Potomac.

Hope things are well with you and Remember this is the last lap for this school year. So go to it Em and show them.

Love from Dad

Kansas City lumber baron and devout Christian Church (Disciples of Christ) member Robert Alexander Long staunchly disagreed with his Protestant denomination's leaders, who ostracized competent physicians from their Christian Church hospitals, only because the physicians were Jewish. R. A. Long and Dr. Sophian first met and became fast friends in 1910. Over the quarter of a century that they remained friends, they argued often and passionately about religion and philosophy. One outcome of these monumental mental marathons was that R. A. Long offered land and money to the Christian Church to build Christian Church Hospital in Kansas City, on the condition that the board of trustees grant medical staff privileges to all qualified physicians regardless of their religious faith.

The board of the Disciples of Christ rejected R. A. Long's request, built the 150-bed hospital anyway, and dedicated it on April 9, 1916. Mr. Long dutifully spoke at the dedication. After Menorah Hospital was completed, Mr. Long received his hospital care there from Dr. Abraham Sophian. Mr. Long died in Menorah Hospital from an abdominal ailment in 1934 at age eighty-four years.[46] Both Abraham Sophian and Robert A. Long were intense, brilliant, quiet, and self-absorbed men who shared a deep friendship and abiding belief in the American values of freedom and justice that transcended their faiths.

Estelle Sophian was the petite but stern and some say humorless matriarch who conducted her family's social, economic, and legal affairs like a prizefighter. Her attention to her children's growth, development, and well-being was evident in the many dozens of letters she wrote to each of them during her life. She was utterly devoted to properly feeding, dressing, and grooming Bud and Emily, and she never let up on improving their speech and manners. Abraham assisted her in disciplining and nurturing Bud and Emily when she told him to.

Harry and Jane Sophian had one child, a daughter named Lucille, who was born in New York City in 1909. Upon arriving in Kansas City in December 1916, she began school at the French Institute run by the sisters of the Roman Catholic Congregation of Notre Dame de Sion. The sisters were originally from Paris and had arrived in Kansas City on October 22, 1912 at the invitation of Bishop Thomas F. Lillis and Reverend William Dalton. The latter was pastor of the Annunciation Church at Linwood and Benton Boulevards in Kansas City, Missouri. Both Bud and Emily would soon join their cousin Lucille at the French Institute.

The sisters of the Congregation of Notre Dame de Sion were well suited to the task of educating the Sophian cousins. The congregation's history dates to its founder Father Theodore Ratisbonne (1802–1884) who was "a native of Strasbourg [France] and a man of exceptional background and education who had forsaken the [Jewish] religion of his ancestors and embraced Christianity only after years of anguished searching for his faith."[47] Father Theodore stressed a deeper understanding among people of all creeds, races, and nations, with a particular emphasis on generating dialogue between Jews and Christians. A Notre Dame de Sion sister (Sister Marie Ida de Sion) penned a history in 1965 of the Congregation of Notre Dame de Sion in Kansas City in which she wrote the following about Father Theodore:

> Some time after his conversion to Catholicism and subsequent entry into the priesthood, in 1830, he was assigned to the famous church of Our Lady of Victories, in Paris, as an assistant. Simultaneously, he was made chaplain of an orphanage run by the Sisters of Charity, in the rue Plumet. It was there that, in 1843, in answer to numerous appeals, he opened a small home for Jewish girls.[47]

In 1847, Pope Pius IX approved the Paris community under the title chosen by Father Theodore: "La Congregation de Notre Dame de Sion." The following year in Paris, Father Theodore founded the order of the Fathers of Sion, which his younger brother Marie Alphonse Ratisbonne (1814–1884) then joined after also converting from Judaism to Catholicism. The swift global expansion of the congregation is described elsewhere.[47]

Estelle Sophian had few options for educating her two children, since existing secular private schools in Kansas City barred Jews from attending and the alternative to a private school was the fledgling Kansas City public school system. For Estelle, the French Institute run by the sisters of the Congregation of Notre Dame de Sion was thus a godsend. She decided to send hesitant six-year-old Emily to join her ten-year-old cousin Lucille Sophian there in September 1918. Nearly five-year-old Bud joined the two girls in March 1919. In 1921, the school boasted twelve boys (including Bud) whom the Sionian sisters fondly referred to as the "Men of Sion," according to *Sion-Sixty News* published in 1972–1973 to celebrate the school's sixtieth anniversary.

Emily Sophian received her entire pre-collegiate education from the sisters, graduating in 1930. Lucille Sophian left the school in 1925 at the age of sixteen years to live independently, though she continued to receive financial support from her parents. Bud attended the French Institute until June 1924 when he (at age nine years) and the other boys in his group were ineligible to continue there in accordance with rules established by the sisters. Bud then transferred to another school.

Dr. Abraham Sophian called his son Bud a "model child" whose personality was "sunny" and "exuberant." Bud possessed the "gift of concentration," which was indispensable for any boy or girl who aspired to the field of medicine, opined his father. Dr. Sophian strongly encouraged both of his children to enter the field of medicine, but only Bud responded to the call and stuck with the arduous preparation required for that profession through college, medical school, and a hospital internship. Dr. Abraham Sophian looked forward to the eventual return to Kansas City of his only son to join his busy internal medicine practice. Dr. Abraham Sophian, at age fifty-three years, had earned professional certification (#1742) in the new specialty of internal medicine from the American Board of Internal Medicine on July 1, 1937, only one year after the board had been incorporated in 1936 by the American College of Physicians and the Section on the Practice of Medicine of the American Medical Association. Bud's letters clearly show that he planned to follow in his father's footsteps not only by becoming a physician but also by specializing in internal medicine.

Bud's family and many relatives coddled him, but he also lived in the long shadows of his mercurial and rebellious older sister and his energetic and peripatetic physician father. Perhaps because of the oversized personalities of his sister and father, Bud developed an extraordinary empathy for his fellow human beings and had an uncommonly large capacity for friendships. Cornell University Medical College Dean Joseph C. Hinsey described Bud's affability and compassion in a letter to Dr. Abraham Sophian in 1945:

April 11, 1945

Dear Doctor Sophian,

We have been shocked by the news we have received about Bud. I have written his wife Dorothy today but I am writing you, not only to express our sorrow over his loss, but also to let you know of his deep love and respect for Mrs. Sophian and yourself. I know that both of you are well aware of this but you will appreciate it as an expression of one who had his full confidence as a friend outside his immediate family. Many times he spoke of how much he admired your accomplishments and ability and was ever striving to measure up to your expectations.

He loved life and lived it to the fullest. He had a great capacity for friendships. He was devoted to his profession and I am confident his future attainments would have been ones about which you would have been just as proud, even as you have been up to now. I sincerely hope that his supreme sacrifice will contribute to making this world a better place for men and women and children to live in peace.

Sincerely,

Joseph C. Hinsey

Bud loved playing and following collegiate and professional sports. He was a very funny person with a quick, quirky, dry, and self-deprecating sense of humor, and he often used his strong sense of humor to mitigate tension and conflict. Bud was devoted to his family, usually doing everything his parents and sister ever asked of him. He thrived in structured organizations, such as sports teams, fraternities, and the military, where he often assumed leadership roles, such as quarterbacking a football team or volunteering as a physician paratrooper. Bud was sincere, humble, and principled; he believed in God, and he adhered quietly but strongly to his Jewish faith.

Estelle nurtured the sibling bond between Bud and Emily. For example, she wrote to Emily the following letter in 1928 when her children were thirteen and fifteen years old:

Monday

Emmy darling:

You cannot imagine how happy I am to receive your letters. I miss you all dreadfully but it is necessary for me to [remain] here for the present. I feel certain that you will always do everything that I expect from you in reference to Bud as well as everything else – that feeling compensates me in a measure for being away from you. It is very strange that Susie omitted you from her party but then I would not let that bother me ... Tell Bud I shall write him soon and in the meantime he might write me as you do – and tell me all about the game at Manhattan. Much love and a big hug ... Mother

Another letter written by Estelle in 1928 demonstrates more of the family dynamic:

> Thursday 16th
>
> Dearest Emmy and Bud:
>
> We arrived in Spokane this morning after a fine trip. We are now in Colville [Washington] where Mr. Reed met us and will take us to the ranch – I have tried to write on the way [in a car from Kansas City] but it has been impossible.
>
> Some few days ago, I sent to Halsey [Gulick, summer camp director] your tickets, a full fare for you and half fare for Bud, also a check for seventy-five dollars which he will cash and give to you. I sent that much in case there is any question about Bud's fares. You will then have sufficient money. Of course I expect both of you to be careful about the amount of money you spend. Remember what I told you that it is vulgar for children to spend money extravagantly. On the train the food portions are very large – one portion is plenty for two and you should order your meals accordingly – and whatever you do, please do not fuss. That would not reflect credit on your family ... [Emmy,] [b]e sure to put your rain coat into your trunk because you will need it on the trip home [from Washington to Kansas City]. It would ruin your good coat to use it in the car as the roads are very dusty ... Bud, be sure to bring your riding breeches and wool hose with you. After you read this letter Emmy, either mail it to Bud or send it to him by Halsey ...

At age four years, as noted above, Bud began his formal education at the French Institute of the Congregation of Notre Dame de Sion in Kansas City. At age nine years, he transferred to Bryant Elementary School at 4747 Flora Avenue (Kansas City, Missouri) for one year while his parents explored options for further private school education.[48]

Bud graduated from Bryant Elementary School one year later and in 1925 enrolled in brand new, private, and non-denominational Pembroke School, which was located at 75th Street and Wornall Road in Kansas City, Missouri. Each school day, Pembroke School drivers wheeled through Kansas City's broad boulevards in shiny black Cadillacs to retrieve students in the morning from their homes and return them to home after completion of their classes and extracurricular activities.

The Pembroke School flourished from its founding in 1925 until 1933. Prior to its founding, the three major private, non-denominational schools in Kansas City were Barstow School (founded 1884), Country Day School (founded 1910), and Sunset School (founded 1913). These three schools tried to duplicate in Kansas City the high quality of education provided by elite independent schools on the East Coast. At the time, that Bud and Emily needed formal education, the three schools did not accept Jewish students.

In 1925, a number of faculty members and students associated with Country Day School separated from that institution to found Pembroke School, which encouraged applications from children of all faiths. However, the Great Depression decimated the savings of the school's major benefactor, causing its financial collapse. In 1933, the Pembroke School merged with Country Day School, and the new school was renamed Pembroke-Country Day School.[49]

Bud attended Pembroke School for the equivalent of the seventh, eighth, ninth, and tenth grades (1925–1929). He thrived in academics and athletics, and he especially loved quarterbacking the Pembroke School Junior Football Team in the eighth grade when he was eleven years old. He published an article about the team's 1926 record in Pembroke School's Christmas 1926 issue of *Blue and White Magazine*, as follows:

The Junior Team's 1926 Season
Bud Sophian, '31

The first game of the season was played against Border Star [Elementary School] on our own field. The game ended in a scoreless tie, but it showed the team its weak points.

The second game was with Bryant [Bud's former school], also on the Pembroke field. The team put up a good fight, but we were defeated 14 to 0.

The third game was with Border Star on their field. When the final whistle blew, we were ahead 19-13. Good clipping on the end runs was mainly responsible for our victory.

We played Bryant for the fourth game on our own field. We were beaten 13-0, but the team made a better stand than before.

The fifth and final game was played against Border Star on the Pembroke field. We won 6-0 in a hard fought battle. Hard tackling by the whole team was the main feature. It looked like Border Star would tie the score at the end of the game when they were on our four yard line, but we held them.

The season ended and our record was fifty percent. (Won two, lost two, tied one.) It wasn't so good, but we hope to do better next year.

The lineup in most games of the season was:

Nichols—Center.

Lunsford—Right Guard.

Murphy—Right Tackle.

Fisher—Right End.

Jennings—Left Guard.

Downey—Left Tackle.

Mann—Left End.

Twiford—Left Half.

Crouch—Right Half.

Green—Fullback.

Sophian—Quarterback.

Substitutes:

Dyson—Right Tackle.

Brundrett—Left Guard.

White—Left Tackle.

Norton—Right End.

Alley—Right Guard.

Lathrop—Left Tackle.

Platt—Right End.

Deichmann—Left Tackle.

Daniels—Left End.

Sender—Fullback.[49-50]

Bud first tried golf during the summer of 1927 at Lake Walloon in Michigan where the Abraham Sophian family owned a summer cabin. Dr. Sophian often remained in Kansas City to care for his patients while the family vacationed in Michigan. Emily saved three letters from Dr. Abraham Sophian to Bud that date from the summer of 1927, when Bud was twelve years old. The first reads as follows:

Dear Bud:

Had your Racket and 4 Balls sent on yesterday.

Glad you are having such a good time. We have been having wonderful golf weather here for the last 48 hours, hope it continues. Played last nite with a very fine player at Indian Hills [Country Club, Kansas City], and held my own very well; so must be improving.

Going to Tulsa tonite, and am going to try to get in a little golf this afternoon.

Love from Dad

Dr. Abraham Sophian and other physicians of his era often prescribed golf to their patients as mental and physical therapy. Dr.

Sophian sometimes accompanied his patients on Kansas City's private golf courses, such as Indian Hills Country Club (founded in 1919), to which he otherwise was denied admission.

The second letter (dated July 20, 1927) from Dr. Sophian to Bud at Lake Walloon follows:

Dear Bud:

Received your letter and it gave me much pleasure. I am glad you are having such a good time.

I don't particularly approve of your playing golf with the boys, because that is the way to develop bad golf faults. Instead would suggest that you get regular lessons from some one at the Club.

Have been playing once a week, but hope to get in an hour twice a week additional from now on. My golf this year has been steadily improving, and recently has been quite good for me. I was called to see Harris Ward, brother of James Ward the other day, and met Jamie. He is not heavy built, and does not give the impression of the fine athlete he really is. But he practices a good deal, and takes lessons right along, proficient as he is already. Feeling well.

Love from Dad

The third letter dated August 9, 1927 reads:

Dear Bud:

Glad you are having such a good time, and that your game is improving so much. Wish there were some way for you to get some good lessons however.

I notice your friends the Blues [baseball team] are slipping— what about it?

Have a line on a pretty nifty farm—but hope it doesn't go the way of all of the other farms.

Feeling fine and weather for most of the summer has been wonderful.

Love from Dad

On July 3, 1927, twelve-year-old Bud received the following letter from Walloon Lake summer friend Robert M. Hoover, whose parents had sent him instead to Culver Summer Naval School in Culver, Indianapolis:

Bud:

I have been at Culver for some time now and like it a lot. We drill to lunch and drill out and know our onions on "squads night." The officers are always telling us to "pull in the old guts," and I expect to be either a perfect specimen of manhood or a complete wreck when I get home. When we pass a commissioned officer we must salute him. The rules are very strict here and we are all in uniforms.

Two days ago it was hotter than the equator here, now it is colder than the northpole. The grub is good here for a place that serves over one thousand boys and a hundred or so officers and instructors at every meal. Such is Culver.

I have not seen you for some time and wish you are well. If it is as cold at Walloon Lake in comparison to here as it is here [*sic*] you will freeze no doubt. There is no heat in our rooms. Guess I'll sign off now.

Yours, Bob.

For two months of the summer of 1928, thirteen-year-old Bud attended the all-boys Camp Timanous and fourteen-year-old Emily the all-girls Camp Wohelo near South Casco, Maine. Dr. Luther Gulick (1865–1918), who blazed the iconic Camp Fire Girls movement, founded both camps, which were run by his nephew Halsey Gulick (1892–1993) at the time Bud and Emily were there. On June 28, 1928, Emily and Bud travelled by train from Kansas City to Chicago, where they ate lunch with relatives at Marshall Field's department store, saw the play *Excess Baggage* at the Garrick Theater (demolished in 1960), and stayed overnight at the Morrison Hotel at Clark and Madison Streets, according to Emily. She also noted in her letter to her parents that she was passing the time on the train by reading one of Bud's discarded detective magazines. She wrote, "By the way, the first thing that guy [Bud] did when he saw me was to borrow two dollars."

The following day Emily and Bud took a "terribly sticky and hot train all day" from Chicago to Boston where they transferred to yet another train that took them to Portland, Maine, where they arrived around five o'clock in the morning. Emily wrote, "Bud is on this train and is already the center of a bunch of noisy kids his age. He's really awfully cute but is acting more or less like a gentleman so you needn't worry." The siblings arrived at their respective camps near South Casco in time to hear a bugler summoning campers to breakfast.

In mid-July 1928, Emily sent a letter home to her parents that reported she had hiked with friends into South Casco to buy some ice cream and, while eating it outside the store, suddenly looked up to see Bud riding into town on a horse! Bud was "sunburned" with "curls all over his head" and had come into town for ice cream, too, she explained.

On August 20, 1928, the Camp Timanous boys held a special circus for Camp Wohelo girls. Emily wrote home, "I had more fun – all the *little* boys were so cute. Tumbling was first … The next event on the program was some exhibition horseback riding. Bud sure sits a horse well. He did himself proud in the Roman riding where he came in standing up with one foot on one white horse, and the one foot on the other. I was awfully proud of him."

Emily expressed disappointment with her parents in another letter because they sent copies of the *Kansas City Star* to Bud, but not to her. They replied that Bud depended on receiving the newspaper to stay current on the daily sports statistics.

Each camp took its campers on a daylong field trip to swim and sunbathe at Higgins Beach about six miles south of Portland, Maine.

Bud's future wife was born in Portland, Maine, in 1918 and lived there for eight years.

When camp ended on August 28, 1928, Bud and Emily sped by train from Portland, Maine, via Chicago to Spokane, Washington, where they joined their parents on a visit to the Upper Columbia Orchards then owned by Dr. Abraham Sophian in Marble, Washington. Marble is about ten miles south of the Canadian border and about twenty miles north of Colville, Washington. Bud's experience at Camp Timanous in Maine and travelling with his sister independent of their parents prepared him for the next big challenge in his life: living away from home at a renowned New England boarding school.

Two-year-old Bud Sophian on toy bike
ca. 1917, Kansas City, Missouri. *Sophian Archives.*

Estelle Sophian with son Bud (left) and daughter Emily (right), Kansas City, Missouri, ca. 1922. *Sophian Archives.*

Bud Sophian with golf club, ca. 1927, around 12 years old,
Lake Walloon, Michigan. *Sophian Archives.*

Bud Sophian, ca. 1929, around 13 years old.
Sophian Archives.

Georgian Court, Kansas City, Missouri, built by Harry J. Sophian, ca. 1917-1918. Photo dates from 2010 following Georgian Court refurbishment. *Photo Credit: M. O'Leary.*

Sophian Plaza, Kansas City, Missouri, built by Harry J. Sophian, ca. 1922. *Sophian Archives.*

Chapter Three: Phillips Academy, 1929–1932

In 1929, fourteen-year-old Bud Sophian matriculated at the then overwhelmingly white, Anglo-Saxon, Protestant, all-boys college preparatory school Phillips Academy in Andover, Massachusetts, some twenty-five miles north of Boston. Merchant, manufacturer, and American patriot Samuel Phillips, Jr. (1752–1802) founded the academy in 1778 during the uncertain days of the American Revolutionary War; his good friend was General George Washington (1732–1799).

The importance of responding to the call of duty in the hour of their country's need was a hallowed value taught to young men at Phillips Academy. During the First and Second World Wars, Phillips Academy lost seventy-seven and one hundred and forty-two "heroic dead," respectively. Bud belonged to the latter group. The school remembers its fallen heroes in two tomes titled *Phillips Academy Andover in the Great War* by Claude M. Fuess (New Haven, Connecticut: Yale University Press, 1919) and *Phillips Academy, Andover in World War II* by Leonard F. James (Andover, Massachusetts: Andover Press, 1948).

From his room (#11) in Taylor Hall at Phillips Academy, Bud wrote regularly and devotedly to his sister Emily, beginning in autumn of 1929. Emily somewhat belatedly had decided to live on campus at Notre Dame de Sion School during her senior school year (1929–1930). Bud's first missive to Emily was a pre-printed form in which he identified adjectives to describe various realities at Phillips Academy, such as the quality of the food he was served. This form letter is not reproduced here. However, he refers to the pre-printed form letter in his second letter, dated October 27, 1929, which he wrote by hand and mailed to "Miss Emily Sophian at 400 E. Armour Blvd. Kansas City, Mo.," before she moved on campus. This second missive, reproduced below, is Bud's first known handwritten letter to his sister. No previous letters exist, because the two siblings had lived together continuously either at Georgian Court or at their Lake Walloon cabin, or very close to one another at the Gulick camps in Maine, for all the previous years of their young lives. Bud's handwriting was legible and neat:

Saturday
Dear Emmy,
Its been a long time since I've written [the first letter was the form letter] but I've been awful busy. How are <u>all</u> your admirers? Have you heard from friend "Bob" lately? You know I wrote both Jean and Amelia those printed letters. I heard from Amelia the other day, but her writing was so terrible I couldn't read most of it.

I hear you're going to board at the convent. Tough break. Well, don't work too hard.
Lots of love
Bud.

On November 24, 1929, Bud wrote a letter addressed to "Miss Emily Sophian, Notre Dame de Sion, On Locust Street, Kansas City, Mo.," as follows:

Sunday
Dear Em,
Please excuse me for not having written for so long but I've been awful busy making up what I missed.

I'm glad you like it at the convent even if you don't exactly relish it. You probably get better food than we get up here.

Has Bob been writing to you regularly. You know he made the Princeton varsity soccer team. Thats pretty good isn't it? Your old friend Skinny came up to see me after the game yesterday but he was in quite a hurry <u>seeing he had a girl friend waiting for him in his car</u>.

The game yesterday was real good only it came out the wrong way.

I'll sign off now

Loads of love

Bud.

P.S. I got my numerals

On January 20, 1930, Bud addressed the following letter to "Miss Emilie [the French spelling of Emily] Sophian at the Notre Dame de Sion campus":

Dear Basketball Captain [Emily was elected captain of the basketball team in her senior year] –

Will you please send me your autograph at the bottom of a page of paper covered with hieroglyphics known as the English alphabet derived from the Phoenician alphabet (Don't' take me seriously, all I want is a letter).

Well hows the kid and her admirers. Mostly gentlemen.

By the way pardon the angle of these lines of blank verse, but I'm writing this in a hurry.

I'm working like a son of a gun and I don't like it. Hope you're not, for your sake. I suppose your basketball team is sweeping aside all opposition (some phrase or what?) Here's hoping your lovers keep on loving you.

Love from that person who is known as Bud Sophian – Bye.

On February 24, 1930, he wrote:

Dear Em.

I hope you'll pardon your pater fatus (m) for not having written sooner but he's been quite busy. I'm glad to hear you're back on the basketball team – how are you making out. I was sorry to hear you got sick and glad to hear you got well.

It won't be long till I come home if the folks let me. Try like he— to get them to let me, please.

How are all your admirers? Still attentive I hope?

Well it's time this thesis was brought to a close

I remain

Sincerely yours with

Lots of love

A (Bud) ~~Sophian Jr.~~

Fifteen-year-old Bud began his second year (1930–1931) at Phillips Academy at the same time his sister began her first year at nearby Smith College where she lived in the fourth floor suite of Tyler House. Bud wrote the following to her on October 12, 1930:

Dear Em:

Evidently you dont intend to write so I will. Well baby – hows the kid. I've been working very hard – oh very very hard. Day before yesterday I spent from 6:30 to 12:30 on some darn history.

Honest to God etc. I have very little time to do anything I want. The only time I have to myself is Saturday and Sunday.

As soon as the first rating comes I want to meet you in Boston some Saturday and we can do something. I hope you have plenty of money because I am getting rather low and a trip to Boston would be beyond my means.

Listen baby – I want you to come up here for the Exeter game and the tea-dance afterward. The game is on the 15th of November [1930] and I will be very disappointed if you can't come. I would want you to be here by one o'clock standard time and the tea-dance wouldn't be over until about seven or seven thirty. If necessary you could spend the night here but as there will be an awful jam I think it would be better if you could get back the same nite. At any rate let me know what's what at the earliest opportunity you have.

Good Lord I'm so hungry and tired I can hardly write. The food here is vile.

By the way we won our first game last Wednesday 6-0 and baby your brother broke into print. In the *Phillipian* [school newspaper] it says that Sophian starred in the late football game.

Well – you'll have to pardon this letter as I'm in a daze.
Lots of love
Bud.

Bud played on the Second Football Team at Phillips Academy. On October 26, 1930, Bud wrote:

Sister Mio!
Good lord I hope that isn't a cussword but it sounds pretty good anyway.

I just slept through chapel and got up at the ungodly early hour of 1:15 P.M.

As to where I procured this stationery [simple blue-lined paper], I imported it from Bulgaria – pretty good isn't it. [Bulgaria is a country in the Balkans; Bud would meet Balkan natives in German uniform in 1944.]

Now let's get down to facts – I think you're leading altogether too wild a life – I would advise you to settle down and refuse any further invitations. You should be in your room studying by seven every evening – Oh hell don't mind me, I can't help it – Pardon this scribbling but I'm in an ungodly hurry – Mrs. Diven is here and she asked me over to the [The Phillips] inn

45

for lunch – I don't know how I'll manage to break away from the dear old beaney but I'll try to be brave.

Now, how are you situated financially – I just ain't – If you expect me to meet you on Thanksgiving I'm either gonna have to rob the bank downtown, shake some gold off the family tree or you'll have to lend me some. At present I wish you'd send me about $5 as soon as you can – if you can't spare that much send me as much as you can.

It must be great sport going to all these football games and whatnots but I can hardly say I envied you yesterday if it was half as cold where you were as it was here

I made out surprisingly well in the first rating – I got a 93 in German, an 88 in Latin, an 82 in history and a 72 in English –

Our football team is so far, by the grace of God and all that rot, undefeated. Our luck can't keep up much longer tho and we'll probably lose the next game on Wednesday –
Well I must be toodling
Lots of love
I remain your brother

The next letter from Bud was dated October 30, 1930:

Meine Schwester [My sister in German]:
Say baby I'm sorry I borrowed your last chunks of gold – I thought you said you had so much mayo in the bank. How do you intend to pay the $100 worth of bills. Thanks a heck of a lot. Just the same I appreciate your noble sacrifice.

My God – you should see me now. I got my face stepped on the other day in practice and all the skin is off my nose. I look very nice all decked out in mercurochrome.

What year English are you taking at Smith? Also what year French? I hear you got a hag with your English teacher – some fun – How have your grades been? I think the family will kill you if you don't crash them with some good grades –

When does your Christmas vacation start and end. Ours begins on the 18th of Dec and ends on the 5th of Jan.

Say how would you like to come up to the senior prom. It's about the 23rd of February – I'm not altogether sure of the date however –

Glad to hear that you had a good time with Russ Wilder – have you got him on your chain solid or has Mike got him? Have you heard from Heaps? If you haven't I guess I'm breaking open an old sore. I certainly wish I had some of your old themes here – I'm just hopeless when it comes to writing those darn things – If you've got any good ones laying around send them to me for God's sake.

How do you like the stationery – got it with compliments from the Inn. Oh yeah –

Well it's about time for me to rest my weary self.
Loads of love,
Bud
This writing is the nuts isn't it. Don't mind it tho –

On November 14, 1930, Bud wrote:

Dear Em:
I honestly would like to take this friend of yours but it is really impossible. In the first place I ought to [be] on crutches as my hip is in awful shape and in the second place as I was named on the all-club football squad and shall probably have to practice after the game.

I guess these two reasons sort of cross up but all we'll have in football is signal practice while dancing would require quite a strain on my leg. However, I'm going to avail myself of this friend or another for one of the coming teadances – So be on the lookout for a nice pretty one who is not <u>too</u> old. You don't need to tell her how old I am [fifteen]. You mentioned something about your plans for Thanksgiving. I thought we were going to have dinner together? How about it?

I don't know how I'm going to do this next rating – All I can do is pray.

I haven't got any more time so I'll have to end this so-called letter.

Lots of love

Bud

On November 24, 1930 (Thanksgiving Day was on Thursday, November 27 in 1930), Bud wrote:

Dear Em:

Just got out of the infirmary. I'm feeling fine now, tho. I got hit on the head and kicked on the nose a few times in the Exeter game so I felt pretty rotten – The only trouble with me now is my nose which is still a little swollen.

I've put in a little over 8 hours today on history and I'm not quite caught up yet. This letter is being written in a big hurry so don't mind the writing.

I made out all right last rating – Honors and no flunks. However, I didn't get an honor in German which ain't so rosy.

I want to see you in Boston Thanksgiving. I can meet you anytime and anywhere on Thursday. That is anytime after 10:30. Please write or wire immediately just what is what.

I've got lotsa work left so I gotta sign off. Please write or wire. Toot suite [pun on the French phrase "toute de suite," meaning "immediately"].

Lots of love

Bud

P.S. We lost to Exeter 19-0. I played the whole game – maybe it would have been better if I hadn't. B.S. –

Bud and Emily succeeded in meeting up for Thanksgiving in Boston, much to the delight of their mother, who was worrying about their well-being from Kansas City.

On December 4, 1930, Bud wrote to Emily:

Monday

Dear Sister:

Hello! How are you and what not? I'm in Latin class and I just woke up so that I'd write. God is this an interesting class! Wow!

Who gives a damn what's the subject of sollicitatos or something like that.

I made my train with fully 15 seconds to spare. When I got back what do you think I found? About a whole nite's work ahead of me. Got to bed at about 3 A.M.

The whole dorm got put on room pro. The prof didn't seem to like the idea of our throwing his bed out the window – damn funny these profs.

Good god I'm going nuts if this damn class doesn't end soon. I didn't have any breakfast and I'm hungry – I got a lousy German exam this afternoon – Who cares? (Folks will when they find out what I get).

My nerves are worn to a frazzle – my constitution is shot – I'm a complete wreck – just hanging on and hoping to shove off from this hole soon.

Thank God the bell's ringing. I'll write again tomorrow if I wake up soon enough before the class is over

Well, daughter of my father's wife, goodbye.

Lotsa love

Bud

P.S. I get out early Wednesday morning so I won't be able to go home with you [for Christmas vacation] Love Bud

After Bud and Emily had returned to school in Massachusetts after Christmas vacation, Bud resumed his letter writing to Emily on January 6, 1931:

No, I don't want any money – not yet – [written across the top of the letter]

Hello Sister:
Palpitations and what not. Andover is enjoying my presence again – Gee they get all the breaks here – I'm busy as the devil now so I'll try to write more in latin tomorrow.
Love, love and love
Bud
P.S. Great stuff – there's a foot of snow here, it's colder'n hell and to top it off it's raining like God almighty Love Bud

On February 9, 1931, Bud wrote a long letter to cheer up Emily who was depressed at Smith College:

Hi Sis!
What the hell's wrong with you babe? The folks write you're in the pit of depression, in a horrible state of gloom, and to put it mildly, in the dumps. Buck up beautiful – you know life is only a stage and we are but a bunch of lousy actors etc …

Folks say you're thru with exams and I'm getting 'em thrown at me from on and from all sides. The ratings are this week and God only knows how I'll make out –

"Grumpy" was given last nite for our benefit and it wasn't so bad [*Grumpy*, directed by George Cukor, is an American drama film released in 1930]. "Beggars can't be choosers" or words to that effect – You get me don't you kid.

Be sure to write me <u>immediately</u> – in other words <u>pronto</u> when you find out whether you can come to the prom cause I got to make arrangements – I hope like hell you didn't go on registrars [probation for undesirable academic performance at Smith College]. You know the prom's on Friday nite – the 20 of February. You'd want to get up here about four or five or six that afternoon. What would really be bad is if the folks refused to cough up the necessary funds – It's gonna cost over 20 rocks – that isn't counting your fare – Write a letter full of sob stuff to the pater and mater and express your great desires to come up here. Do this right away as there's only two more weeks.

I've gotten many letters from Natalie but am <u>very</u> doubtful as to the success of my conquest – After all 3 years is quite a [word?]. However, I'm holding up my end of the correspondence with 9 or 10 of the female sex –

That's right kid – take Russ for a ride – set him up and then knock him down.

Had quite a lecture in chapel this morning on the evils of gambling. Yes goddam it [Bud enjoyed gambling] – As you notice from the writing I'm in a big hurry and my haste increases as I approach the end
Love, love and love
Bud

Bud wrote to Emily again on February 17, 1931, on Isham Infirmary (Phillips Academy) stationery. The names of Dr. P. S. Page and head nurse Miss M. M. McKeever adorned the top left corner of the stationery, and the infirmary's telephone number "Andover 183" the top right corner:

Monday
Heh Em!
I'm dying – It's terrible. I just got back from my weekend and what a hang over I had. I got back to find out I flunked English and didn't get an honor in history. God! The folks will love that. I was badly in need of a rest so I came down here [to the Phillips

Academy infirmary]. They refused to take me unless I had some temperature so I put the thermometer on the radiator – It went up to 110 and popped. They gave me another thermometer and this time I was careful and took it off the radiator when it reached 101. They'll probably throw me out tomorrow – hope not – I need the rest. I'm in a most awkward position to write as you have probably figured out – you old detective.

Don't want to seem ungrateful but I just can't come down on the seventh. In the first place the Exeter basketball and swimming events come off then, in the second place the folks wouldn't let me after these marks I got and in the third place I would be far too young and out of place. Not having any more places I shall desist. I'll make a point of paying you a visit next month Oh yez I will.

Be sure to notify me about "registrar's."

The Prom is on Friday, February 20 – thats this coming Friday. You want to get here Friday afternoon about 5 or 6 o'clock. The prom is that nite – formal – and the breakfast dance is the next morning – informal. This dance comes about 10 or 11 o'clock and after it's over you clear out or do whatever we decide. Bring one formal dress and one smooth informal like you'd wear to an afternoon tea-dance or something like that.

Please write back as soon as you find out for sure that you can come and also make your train reservations coming (and going if you have the money). Tell me when you'll get in Andover so I can meet you.

Here comes some medicine and I'm not sick. God! That was close but I managed to throw it out the window.

It's ten o'clock and time to go. Hope you like my little show.

Loo-loo! Loo-loo!

Bud

On April 21, 1931, Bud wrote:

Monday nite
Hi Beautiful!
Cheer up – I'm too busy to write now. I just wanted to let you know I was thinking about you. Don't let anything worry. Buck up, laugh etc.… At least I can give you something to look forward to I'll write you a nice long letter Wednesday.
Mucho Amo
Bud.

As promised, Bud followed up with this letter postmarked April 22, 1931:

Sister dear,
No doubt you are at this point in possession of the unfortunate document which it was my lot to write a day or so in the past [see letter immediately above]. As you might have gathered time was scarce and the rest of my public was crying for me – ain't it awful.

With that sad epistle in mind I guess I'll write you a nice long letter – damn nice of me even if you don't think so.

After receiving letters from all over the state from fair damsels asking me to take them to the tea dance Saturday I picked out Natalie as the most logical person to receive this honor – Ahem – … for God's sake don't tell the folx as they think that more time should be spent by this toiling youth on the fundamentals of latin etc … Nuts! But anyway don't tell them.

Among my great collection of fan mail I note several letters from Johnny and even a couple from Editha – oh of course I have about 5 from Natalie. Ain't it awful the way these women fall for me. I have to beat 'em off with a club. Tsk, tsk …

My sadly overestimated ability in golf took an awful jolt when I found myself rated as no. 17 on the squad. It was no. 8 last year. I think that I can work up with little difficulty.

Paul was very disappointed that he hadn't got to talk with you when you called – He was right there but I didn't hear him ask.

I'm not working too hard at present and I'm quite fearful my grades are going to show that fact – I'm so worried – ha, ha, etc.

I'm really awful hungry and altho I like you very, very much (you're such a sweet little girl) I like to eat also – damn funny I calls it.

Mucha de love

Bud.

Two to three weeks later on May 11, 1931, Bud wrote:

Hi Seester –

Good lord it's so cold in this damn place I am afraid it's gonna snow. But that is beside the point.

From that last statement one is led to imagine that there is a point in this letter – don't get so excited there isn't.

Went into Boston yesterday, to see the Harvard Interscholastics. Exeter beat us but [name?] Brown, that tall dandy fellow who paid quite a bit of attention to you broke the <u>world's</u> interscholastic pole vault record. He vaulted 13 feet 4 5/8 inches – Not bad for an amateur – He also won the high jump at 6' 2".

I did surprisingly well last rating. I got 3 good high honors and I passed <u>English</u> with a 73. That gave me an honor-roll average. Smart guy I am.

My feminine public is coming along pretty well – Editha ranks as a possible one – you know all I need is a little encouragement – she writes quite regularly. Johnny's O.K. and Natalie – I've gotten about 20 letters from her this term already. Dish me –

My Syracuse public [Dr. Abraham Sophian's sister Golda's family] is demanding I pay them a visit. I think I shall gratify their wish on my way home this spring.

I'm not at all sure I'll ask Paul. However, even if I do I don't know whether he'll come.

I must reveal to what depths of depravity I have sunk and admit that instead of that remark about "fruitiness" instead of passing over my head caught me squarely in the eye. Sister, I am ashamed.

Poor Russ – but just think of the pleasure the present recipients of your admiration are receiving. About your snaking Dot's brother from somebody all I say is "Kitty, kitty."
I'm so hungry.
Bud.

As his second year at Phillips Academy drew to a close, Bud initiated a betting caper with a classmate, as he explained to Emily in a letter postmarked May 17, 1931:

Hey Sister:
I've got a bet on with a fellow that I'll get more letters than he will this week. Now, he's awfully good at getting letters and I suspect him of underhanded tricks (I wouldn't pull anything crooked on him for the world, oh no!). The fact is if I lose this bet my financial standing will be uh rather low to say the least.

What I'm driving at is – will you drop me many letters this coming week – about 3 will be enough. You might even get some of your girl friends to do likewise. But for God's sake get me some letters.

Gotta go – I'll write you a smooth letter one of these days – Remember I've got to get all the letters before next Saturday.
Much love
Bud.
I'd die for dear old "Bankroll"

The following day on May 18, 1931, Bud wrote (in pencil):

[No greeting]
For Christ's sake sister – I'm four letters behind. I'll need at least seven from Northampton [location of Smith College] but be sure they're not all in your writing. Please attend to this pronto. Your little brother is hard up – Imagine I'm 4 behind already. Remember I'll need at least seven letters and I could use as many as 10.

Thanx lots – Be sure to attend to this immediately as I've got to have 'em before this Saturday
[No signoff]

Three days later on May 21, 1931, Bud exclaimed in a letter to Emily:

Seester,
Your plan failed miserably altho I do not doubt your intentions were good. You sent five letters all in one mail. Now if that isn't the most suspicious thing I've ever seen what is. Consequently to appease the wrath of my opponent and all the side-betters (you see I'm not the only one who is betting – nearly everyone in the dorm has money on it) I had to count all your letters as one – all your future letters aren't to count. However, by the grace of god I'm only 2 behind now and when the Tyler House [Emily's house at Smith College] bunch arrive I ought to push into the lead – Good Lord, if I get about five letters from Northampton tomorrow I'll be killed – Tell any one who hasn't written not to bother to do so – I've gotten too many letters from Northampton already –

I wrote Marvin [his cousin] in Syracuse to send me some letters and if that brat sends a whole bunch in one mail, my body will be riddled with bullets, knives etc. ... I'm scared to death

I'll get so many letters it will look suspicious. Moral – "Write
No More" – for a while anyway – gotta some sleep tonite.
Much love
Bud.

On May 25, 1931, Bud announced to Emily the outcome of the bet.
He used stationery from the Phillips Inn in Andover, Massachusetts:

Dear Em,
Thanks lots for your kind cooperation. Thanx to the efforts
of Smith I received 44 letters last week and won the bet by 18
letters –

I don't know whether I'll be able to come down to see you
as the only week-end I have left is that of June 13 and I'm afraid
that's too late –

I'm completely bushed altho I got 17 hours sleep last nite –

I can't see why you should want to go to Columbia
Journalistic School [Emily was considering transferring
to another college]. What is this awful mess you've gotten
yourself into? Are you in danger of getting canned or some
such thing? I hope not for your sake – The folx would bite
your head off.

By the way, how do you like my paper – They were kind
enough to let me have it over at the Inn – You see I just rate
around here – To be truthful with you I crooked about 100
sheets of the stuff and got caught in the act. As a result I got
kicked right where I live and only escaped with about 50 sheets –
I don't get the breaks.

Since I've only got one page left I'd better devote it to
thanking the girls of Smith – Beautiful and kind ladies, allow
me to express my heart-felt thanks for your kindness in helping
a fellow-human out of a bad hole – in fact out of one helluva
hole – No kidding those letters came in awfully handy and

saved the Sophian fortunes. As you see I'm running out of paper – Thanx again
Much love (that's for the sister)
Bud

On May 27, 1931, Bud wrote again using the Phillips Inn stationery:

Dear "M,"
Your dear friend V. B. Hagenbuckle just gave me hell the dirty ----. I felt like slapping his face – he's getting altogether too snooty lately. If he's gonna keep his drag with me he'd better watch his step.

What do you know sister mea – I was pledged to a fraternity last nite and I'll probably be initiated next week – It came as quite a surprise and was certainly good news.

My golf game is going from bad to insufferable. I get worse daily – and the Exeter match is a week from tomorrow

Pardon the writing but I'm laying down – (by the way that ought to be "lieing down" [Bud is joking]).

My grades are getting better as time goes along. I can't seem to make mistakes in German – it's a joke. In English I'm making a comeback and whereas I was flunking it last term I'm pretty near getting an honor now.

By the way – that last letter of yours was pretty cruel – I most certainly appreciated your kind cooperation in helping me win my bet – don't think for a moment that you're not appreciated –

Well give my best to every one – my public is crying and I must write them a few letters
Mucho amo
Bud.

On June 19, 1931, Lucille Sophian responded to a letter from her cousin Emily, who had just returned from Smith College to Kansas

City for summer vacation. Estelle had reminded Emily that she should write to her cousin, and Emily complied. Lucille had moved to Southern California (1826 Whitely Avenue, Hollywood), and her apparent joy living in the carefree culture of California, even as the Great Depression loomed, piqued the interest of Estelle and Bud. Lucille gushed to Emily in the following letter wherein she mentioned her favorite haunt, Cocoanut Grove, and a newcomer crooner named Bing Crosby:

Hello darling [Emily] –

All is forgiven (accompanied by soft lights – sad music) – Gee it was swelegant hearing from a close relative (oh yeah) out of the dim but pleasant past. An' 'cause its you and you really do want to hear all news (thereby letting yourself in for plenty!) – you'll have your way, as Emmy usually does, but "Just One More Time" (as Abe Lyman plays it!) [Abe Lyman (1897–1957) was an American bandleader 1920s–1940s].

But really, sweet, when I say dee-lighted – I mean it was actually grand being reminded of a gal like you still being in the family (for a time you'd almost let me forget that – such a thing!) Now if Papa Einstein could work out the shortest possible distance between the given points of Calif. and Maine that would be accomplishing something and then I could be the 12th wise guy to understand his theory – Geometrically this is slightly cock-eyed – but the idea is that oh how grand it would be to have you here – Emmy darlin' – you'd simply <u>adore</u> it – I often wonder how I possibly ever managed to live elsewhere or was I really there? – So perfectly remote does it all seem and how complete everything here is.

Continued – (about 3 wks later)

Darlin – I'd started this letter ages an' ages ago – so it being that I don't over-write myself any – I decided to include this just to prove I've really been thinking of you.

Continuation [Lucille wrote this]

First of all – welcome back to K. C. [Kansas City] 'tho why you're giving that town a "break" is beyond me – wish it was to California that I was extending all welcomes – by the way what are your summer plans – hows for looking us over out here – After all, baby, would we have fun on a grand scale!! In fact that's all I've been doing is just going to smart places and doing interesting things with loads of clever people – its just a continual and constent round of interesting events and how I do love it! –

My "pet place" is still the Cocoanut Grove – we do most of our "dancing dating and romancing" there. They gave Herman Platt [businessman and philanthropist in Los Angeles (1909– 2005)] his farewell party there for 20 of us last Fri. nite – lovely affair. – Incidentally the Platts leave here tonite on the Santa Fe Chief for N.Y. – will be passing thru K.C. Fri nite – am going to ask the boys to call you up – use your own judgement about being at the [train] station – think it would be awfully nice if you can arrange it – they're great youngsters. –

Have been doing lots of swimming both at the beach and at Platts pool. – Some riding and lots and lots of dancing – in fact besides the [Cocoanut] Grove we divide time between the [Hotel] Roosevelt Blossom Room [site of the first Academy Awards presentation in 1929] that re-opened with a grand formal affair the nite of my birthday so they gave my party for me there – they took pictures of the whole thing for "The Voice of Hollywood" (short subject) so watch for it (or ask your neighborhood dealer) –

George Olsen's Club [George Olsen was a big band leader 1920s–1940s] too has been coming in for its share of popularity. Enough for this "California Hollywood Reporting" – tell me about you and yourself and why. Or are they're any "why's" at this moment?

As for me – I'm playing a large and rather interesting field – here's for some of the "line up" –

Lester (of the Ambassador Frank's) who is house-broken and responds to kind treatment.

Charlie Vander – or "he who got shepped" by Abe Lyman – clever publicity man and theatrical writer – and only because he "amuses" me.

Herman Platt because he's a darlin' and a real pal – swell kid and safely "about to be married"

Maurice Kunstler (the hot 'n heavy lover of the yesterdays) – hasn't been of such particular interest and incidentally he's now out in the wilds of Nevada working on this Boulder Dam Proposition [also known as Hoover Dam].

Another one of my pet "ex's" (only "ex" because he's out of town) is Abe Lyman – swell boy taken with or without his famous drum-sticks – Always did go big for him (do y'remember?) to say nothing of his perfect music which Hollywood has lost to Chicago for the present and speaking of music – I'll deviate from the ever-interesting subject of "the boy-friends" just long enough to ask you if you've gotten the record of "One More Chance" as sung by Bing Crosby of the 3 Rhythm Boys – as he warbles it here at the [Cocoanut] Grove its simply swell.

Plus all "local talent" – there's a rather charming newcomer (labeled "from New York") on my list – Larry Mayer by name and possessor of an adorable N.Y. pent-house and aside from that has many other "worthwhile" qualities – really very clever fellow (incidentally damn sweet) and we've been having lots of laughs and fun going places together.

Guess y'know Mother [Jane Felix Sophian] hasn't been at all well – but is home again and getting along pretty well. Dad [Harry Sophian] and I are both fine.

We've a very nice apt. beautifully located and nicely furnished (a complete upper duplex) – have had two of my closest pals Viola and Dorothy Samson – cousins of M.H. Hoffman (picture producer) living here with us – Viola being grand at managing things – etc. – They're precious girls – all our friends and groups being mutual means we always have great times together.

Well darling – feel pretty sure I've covered most all the news – if not satisfactory kindly send all questions and queries to this department where they shall be answered or postage promptly returned – (maybe!)

So with the very bestest love of your most favorite cousin always.

P.S. – Also want to thank you for your sweet birthday wire – it was adorable and added a big thrill right along with the other flowers – candies – wires – calls and doo-dads – [word?] for bigger better and more frequent birthdays.

Love to all

Emily waited until 1933 to visit Lucille in Los Angeles and instead spent a portion of the summer of 1931 with a Smith College friend named Elizabeth Bossett at Grey Gables Ocean House, an inn overlooking the Cape Cod Canal in Bourne, Massachusetts. The inn, grounds, and waterfront originally belonged to US President Grover Cleveland (1837–1908). The Cleveland estate was famously used as his summer White House from 1888–1896 (Cleveland served two non-consecutive terms, 1885–1889 and 1893–1897). It was converted to an inn in 1920, but it burned down in 1973. On September 8, 1931, Bud, who was still in Kansas City for his summer vacation, wrote a letter on Sophian Plaza stationery, which he air mailed to Emily, "care of Miss Elizabeth Bossett at Grey Gables":

Seester--------!

At present our mother (yours and mine) is laid up with an infected hand – Nothing very serious but enough to lay her up and prevent her from writing. Therefore I was drafted to write you a letter to tell you how every one misses and pines for you.

In about 10 minutes I'm off for a very ---- evening – I'm escorting one of the sisters of your first love – Marion I think they call her. I'm so excited – Nuts!

It's hotter'n hell here and I'm gonna try to ditch the party and go swimming

Had a date with Bernie last nite – poor girl's fallen for me – Also I have a new flame who is googenuts over me – Marjorie Benswanger –

Ted Lieberman won everything in the tennis tournament at the club – Gert and I also played in the Scotch foursomes this afternoon.

Gotta go – should never have started another page. Such extravagance.
Mucho de amo
Bud.

Four days later on September 12, 1931, he again wrote to Emily, "care of Elizabeth Bossett at Grey Gables," as follows:

Em my dear –
Just a note to let you know you're in hell plenty with the folx (that makes two of us) – better write and smooth things over – real dutiful and obedient daughter stuff, you know.

Also Mother says you failed to send the remaining portion of your railroad ticket.
Toodle doo.
See you in a few days [Bud was returning soon to Phillips Academy].
Bud

On September 28, 1931, sixteen-year-old Bud telegrammed Emily to wish her a happy birthday (her eighteenth). He was now living in Foxcroft Hall at Phillips Academy. He sent the telegram to her at "43

Forest Circle, New Rochelle (Westchester County), New York," care of Carol Thomas, another Smith College classmate. Apparently she was ill and the Thomas's were taking care of her. Bud's telegram said: "I don't know whether you will get this or not but happy birthday anyway It would have been roses but I held too many duces in a bridge game Love Bud."

Two weeks later, Bud addressed his next letter, postmarked October 12, 1931, to Emily at Smith College, indicating that she had recovered from her illness and returned to school. He wrote it on the flyleaf torn out of his Latin textbook:

Friday

Dear Em –

I hope you feel honored – I am writing you on the only flyleaf I have left in this Latin Book –

It grieved me to the core to learn of your illness – seriously I have been getting up nights worrying about you – ain't love just grand. Oh by the way I'm taking it for granted that you are well by this time – otherwise I would refrain from this frivolity –

This Latin class is god-awful – It lasts only an hour in reality but it seems like an age – If I didn't write letters during it I don't know how I could stand it.

My roommate just recovered from some sickness or other – Shucks! Now I'll have to pray to God for him to get sick again – God knows that's the only way I can get rid of him –

Oh my oh my – will I ever be broke if Saint Louis [Cardinals] doesn't win tomorrow's ball game – I'll be so low that I could walk under a snake's belly with a high hat – tsk, tsk.

It's gotten quite cold here – far too cold for little me – all of which makes me realize that when I get out in the cruel, cold world I shall be a gentleman of leisure (with what, I don't know but who cares) and shall spend my winters on the Mediterranean or some such place –

My fan mail is pouring in – my feminine public may be taking me for a ride but they should know what I'm doing to them (your influence, seester mea).

No more room.

Lotsa Luv Bud

P.S. Envelope by courtesy of Phillips Inn.

P.P.S.S. Met Dop Anderson who came up here with Harvard Fresh yesterday. Look for Sophian's name in papers Sunday morning

Bud sent a Western Union telegram to Emily on October 30, 1931, which read: "Miss Emily Sophian, Tyler House, Smith College, Northampton, Mass.: Sorry I cannot come am playing football tomorrow Love Bud."

A week later, on November 8, 1931, Bud wrote:

Friday

Dear Em:

Apologies no end for not writing sooner – just haven't had the time, you know – All our dear parents have been writing me about is my reformed sister who is working very hard – Congrats old dear! but don't let it get you down. This studying is a tough racket – I made out best ever last rating – 4 honors and an average of 90 1/3 – God only knows how much longer I can kid these old profs along – it's great sport not doing any work except before exams.

In about 20 minutes I'm going down to Abbot – the local girls' school – where they have a half hour dance every Friday nite. Hot show! Paul got me on some hag's calling list – I don't even know her name much less what she looks like – Have I ever been making time with Natalie! I tell you – She's quite a girl – Came up to the teadance last Saturday. We're quite thick at this point – Nothing serious, I assure you, just thick.

As far as Thanxgiving is concerned it looks pretty good. Is there anywhere I can spend Wednesday nite? (besides in a dorm – tsk, tsk) – I'd like to come down – see if you can talk the folx into it.

Ha, ha – doctor business [referring to his father] is picking up or fur prices are going down. It looks like a raccoon [coat] for me – <u>Maybe</u>. Feed the family the old line about how I need one – O.K.!? [Raccoon fur coats were *de rigueur* for the times.]

Football's O.K. I've played in every game but one – You know we're undefeated up to this point – Ahem – God I hope I get my [varsity] letter – don't think I will tho [he did not].
Nuff said.
Mucho amo
Bud.

On November 14, 1931, Bud wrote:

Hi Kid:
How the hell are you? I'm busy as the devil and tired of working – God! I hate to get up in the morning –

I'm going down to Pine Manor [in 1930 an independent junior college for young women in Chestnut Hill, Massachusetts] Saturday so write back real quick – just a note – what is Nancy's and Elise's address because I'm gonna give them a big break – also gonna see Natalie. Whoops.
Love, love and love
Bud.

One day later, on November 15, 1931, Bud again sent a quixotic note to Emily:

Seester –

Am feeling lousy at this point – (mentally) – so this will be naught but a note.

I don't know for sure about Thanxgiving till Mother writes me – you see I gotta have her permission to get out of here. I'll let you know as soon as I find out –

We lost to Exeter yesterday 15-12 Damnit!

That's all there is for me to write in the state I'm in

Toodle doo

Bud

You should see the letters I do get from Natalie – Not bad – quite a change – yes quite a change –

Two days later on November 17, 1931, Bud wrote:

Seester Mea –

Rejoice! I shall be with you over Thanxgiving if the money holds out – Reserve me a room for Wednesday nite anywhere decent – not too expensive tho times are very bad – I may be able to get Paul to come along – doesn't know yet, tho.

That's all –

Love

Bud.

When two more days had passed, Bud again wrote to Emily (November 19, 1931):

Thursday

Dear Seester –

No football game up here Thanxgiving Saturday. Our season ended last week –

Paul can't come but I'll be down sometime Wednesday – I'll let you know when via Western Union –

You're probably sick of this kind of letter but it's all I've time for – busy man, you see.

Love, ma chere petite ["dearest little one" in the French language]
Bud.

On Sunday, November 22, 1931, Bud sent a letter by special delivery
to Emily, which cost twelve cents in stamps versus the usual two cents
per letter. His letter arrived Monday morning and said:

Dear Em:

I've gotten permission from the folx to come down but besides that
we gotta have an invite to the place we're going so you either write
or telegraph – according to the time there remains – so as I receive it
by 10 o'clock Wednesday morning [November 26, 1931]. O.K.?

I think I told you that there wasn't a game here Thanksgiving
Saturday – also that Paul is definitely not coming.

I wasn't here when your telegram from Bridgewater came so
I didn't get it till about 10 P.M. tonite (it's now 11:30). I didn't
think I'd better call – awfully sorry.

I'm going out to Wellesley tomorrow I think – just to pay a
call to a friend of mine – you know.

Lotsa love
Bud.

On November 20, 1931, Estelle shocked Emily (and Bud) with the
following letter:

Friday
Dearest Em:

Again no letter from you – What can be the matter? Perhaps I'd
better come and find out. Since I must be in Chicago Monday
on business I decided to go on and spend Thanksgiving with
you and Bud in Northampton – I am so anxious to see you I
hope nothing happens to spoil my plans the last moment –

If I do not have to return to Kansas City immediately after my conference, I'll see you sometime Tuesday [November 25, 1931].
Much love
Mother –

On November 25, 1931, Bud wired Emily the following: "Arriving at three ten I think & hope Love = Bud." Estelle, Bud, and Emily shared the Thanksgiving holidays in 1931 together in Northampton, Massachusetts.

On December 7, 1931, Bud wrote the following to Emily:

Em darling (as our N.Y. cousin would say) [Lucille Sophian]
I was quite convinced that I'd never get around to writing my "charming" sister although I had every inclination of doing so much, much sooner –

I'm not dragging it out of here till a week from Thursday – that's the 17th of December – I'm taking the Wolverine out of Boston that P.M. methinks.

Had a tea dance yesterday and who do you think I took? I just know you can't guess. None other than my friend Natalie. Had a marvelous time – uh, huh I did. Say I'll let you in on a big secret – I'm kinda fearsome that I'm a gonna fall for that winsome wench if I'm not careful. You women – tsk, tsk –

Working like hell at this point. You know we have finals in a week. I can't quite make up my mind whether studying or praying will do the most good. What I'm afraid of is that they're both futile.

Give my best to Betty – I think she's swell – and write the little brother soon.

Das ist alles meine liebchen (ha ha ha!) ["That is all, my sweetheart" in the German language.]
Bud
I'm having a 2 minute oral exam as a final in German – Oh

what a drag I got with that guy – truth is I played golf with him a week ago 'n I think he's trying to make me keep my mouth shut about his game – it ain't so hot – in fact its pretty poor –

After spending Christmas vacation (December 1931–January 1932) with his family in Kansas City, Bud nearly missed his train back to Phillips Academy, because he went to see a movie. The train was the last one to depart from Kansas City to Chicago that night. Estelle Sophian wrote to Emily about the chaotic scene at Kansas City's famous Union Station, as Bud raced to catch his train:

[Bud] insisted on going to a movie and raced into the station over a minute before the train was scheduled to leave. To add to the excitement the handle of his bag (a brand new one) broke off completely and his golf bag proceeded to shed golf balls and wooden tees all over the station. Besides all of the ado, Bud got into an argument with one of the guards who tried to stop his progress to the train. I did not hear all he had to say except that it wouldn't hurt this man to be a trifle more courteous in the future and that he (Bud) really ought to give him a punch in the nose. Really it was a panic! Shame you had to miss it.

On January 31, 1932, Bud wrote to Emily, who had left Smith College to return to home earlier in January, because of recurrent illness of unknown cause:

Em darling –
That's too damn bad about your having to go home. I'm awful sorry but no doubt the rest will do you lots of good – You didn't tell me whether Betty was going to be operated on or not and if so where – I'd like to send her a little something (if I have the price).

As far as your being griped about not being able to go see me wrestle [Bud was a good wrestler] calm your anger – the meet was postponed till Feb 20 on account of the fact that the whole tops team was sick. Chances are – by that time I'll no longer be on the first team so you didn't miss a thing.

Wrote Natalie quite a letter the other day – asked her what the hell was the matter (knowing all the time that nothing was) and in reply I got two specials and a telegram. Wow! I got a new girl friend now – Young (15) but [word?] hell – She's the most popular girl at every tea dance up here and I got her under my thumb – I still like Natalie the better but who can tell?

You took me wrong about that picture – quite the opposite. I like it immensely – It's a swell picture – just makes you look awful old but we've all gotta grow up sometime, I guess.

I'm kinda afeared I'm not agonna get such good grades this term – I'm really working hard but the exams aren't agreeing with me particularly well – no, not so well.

It's just about midnite now – we had Thomas Meighan [famous motion picture leading man] in Skyline [1931 movie] here tonite and then had a late meeting afterwards – I'm all in, what I mean, we had a big rough house down at the house and what a job they did on me – It's lots of fun if you can stand it. I don't think I can.

We're reading a swell French book – I'll send it to you after we finish it – It's a bunch of reflections from Andre Maurois [French author] – very good stuff and swell reading (in French, bien entendre).

I'm so sleepy I don't know what I'm writing so I'd better stop before I let out something that should be kept secret.

Goode night beautiful – my best to Mr. Navran [William Fletcher "Bill" Navran, that "John Bolesish" suitor who runs into ditches [Bill was dating Emily and ran his car into a ditch while they both were apparently intoxicated; no one was hurt].
Write soon baby,
Bud.

On March 8, 1932, Bud wrote to Emily at Sophian Plaza:

Seester Mine –

Pardon me for being so negligent – couldn't be helped, tho – I've been busy as hell of late – still am – first I was in the infirmary for a while when I hurt my wrist and I'm still trying to make up the work I missed.

Hope your side's much better now – wait till I get home I'll fix you up – Say babe – pretty dirty trick to toss friend Navran over – he lasted longer than I thought he would tho.

As you may judge this I just wrote a note to let you know I still love you – haven't time for more –

Mucho amo

Bud

P.S. The family thinks I'm spending too much dough – speak up for me, little one.

On April 29, 1932, Bud was nearing the home stretch at Andover Academy. He wrote to Emily (who was still in Kansas City) on Phillips Inn stationery (J. M. Stewart, Proprietor), the following:

Em darling –

Your air-mail special delivery was received and duly noted – appreciations no end for your kind thoughts of me – deah, deah –

No seriously I was very pleasantly surprised to hear from you – thanx lots for the advice about watching my step as far as letters to Miss McKenzie are concerned –I've been doing fairly well as far as that party is concerned. Her letters are full of childish devotion if you know what I mean – By the way what do you mean by a "bow trifler"? I've never heard the expression before.

The somewhat undecipherable script is due to the fact I am sun-bathing in front of the dorm – don't mind it dear sister –

As far as your golf game is concerned don't get too discouraged – I too am in a terrific slump – can't hit a thing despite the fact that I'm playing no. 3 man on the team – I played fairly well for a while after I got back from vacation but that soon stopped – 'nother day 'nother dollar who gives a good goddamn anyway? I got spring fever 'n I got it bad –
Pardon the brevity in view of my ailment, will you darling –
Lots of love
Bud.

On June 28, 1932, Bud received mention in the *New York Times* article titled "Morrow sets pace at golf with 78: Choate player leads for first qualifying round of Eastern Interscholastic test; three bracketed at 80." After the first round, Georgetown Prep led with the low of 341 while "Lawrenceville was second with 343 and Choate and Andover were tied at 348. Peddie had 349, while Hotchkiss, team champions in 1928 and 1929, had a total of 384." A student from Choate led the opening qualifying round with a score of 78 (39 and 39); Bud's score was 90 (49 and 41), which placed him fortieth among eighty-seven entrants. The worst score produced by an entrant was 117 (60 and 57).[51]

Bud performed very well during his three years at Phillips Academy. He played ferocious football, wrestled, and golfed for Phillips Academy against Choate, Lawrenceville, Hotchkiss, Georgetown Preparatory, Phillips Academy at Exeter, and other similar East Coast schools. He earned his letter in varsity wrestling but not in football. Bud also became proficient in Latin, French, and German, the latter two of which he would use during his military service in the Second World War. He won the Ancient History Prize and qualified for membership in the school's Cum Laude Society. The Cum Laude Society in 1932 was a scholarship society similar to the Phi Beta Kappa Society in colleges and universities, which recognized high scholarship in preparatory schools. Students became members in the Cum Laude Society by invitation based on superior scholarship in all subjects during the senior year.[52] Of the one hundred and eighty-five seniors in Bud's graduating class (class of 1932), about twenty young men received this honor. Bud graduated from Phillips Academy one month after turning seventeen.

Senior class members at Phillips Academy rated one another on a variety of attributes, such as neatness, athletic ability, modesty, eccentricity, wit, and good-naturedness. The results were reported in Phillips Academy's 1932 *Pot Pourri* yearbook. The one hundred and eighty-five members of the class of 1932 voted Bud the third "handsomest" in their class. He garnered thirty-six votes compared to the first place winner (seventy-nine votes) and the second place winner (sixty-three votes). Bud also earned the second highest number of votes in the "brightest" category, attracting forty-two votes compared to the winner's seventy-five votes.[52]

Of Bud's senior class, eighty-four members went on to college at Yale University; thirty-five, Harvard College; nineteen, Princeton University; thirteen, Dartmouth College; nine, Massachusetts Institute of Technology; seven, Leland Stanford Junior University; three, Williams College; two, Amherst College; two, University of Michigan; one, Bowdoin College; one, University of Minnesota; one, US Naval Academy at Annapolis; and one, Syracuse University. Seven students were undecided. Bud chose Stanford University for unknown reasons. Perhaps he wanted to experience the relaxed California culture and warm weather described by Lucille Sophian, as well as to join the university's new golf program.

Many of the students at Phillips Academy adopted nicknames. Bud's nicknames were "Soph," "Bud," and "Les." Bud's yearbook is filled with notes and signatures from his peers. The notations include:

- "Don't bend the bushes, Bud—Lef"
- "Here's for better days at Wellesley—Pete"
- "Best of luck in Golf—Dave"
- "Yours for better pool games—Whale"
- "Look out for the California babes. You Les ... Cliffe"
- "May the Plaza prosper—Ring"
- "Hey, you, stay away from my women!—George"

- "May you live long and prosper—Webb"
- "You fearful Lesbaby—Johnny"
- "From one duffer to another—Bob"
- "Heh, Les Baby!—The Wolf"
- "Good luck at Stanford—Herb."

Bud's instructors in chemistry (James Chandler Graham) and religion and modern life (Alfred Graham Baldwin) signed his yearbook.

Bud spent the summer following graduation from Phillips Academy at Lake Walloon. On August 17, 1932, he sent a special delivery letter to Emily, who was aboard the SS *Champlain*, Pier 57, North River, West 15th Street, New York City, awaiting departure for France to spend her junior year abroad under the auspices of the Smith College Study Abroad program. Bud's brief note said:

> Emmy dahling –
> What an awful [word?] you turned out to be! Was I ever ashamed of you!
> Seems that our mutual parent – the female one – became angered at me on the home trip from Bay City – I made it to Boyne City in 2 hours 'n a half despite the fact that I took the wrong road out of Elmira and went 10 miles before discovering it whereupon I had to retrace my weary way.
> Audrey [a girl friend] awaits so I must be off – just a couple of words of advice – keep your bowels open 'n your mouth shut and for Christ's sake don't drink out of any strange toilets.
> My best to Mussolini.
> Dein lieber Brooder ["Your loving brother" in German]

On August 24, 1932, Bud was involved in an automobile accident in the Lake Walloon area. Estelle shared the news with Emily in France in a letter dated August 25, 1932:

Wednesday

Emmy dear:

Your brother's luck held yesterday or he would not have been here to tell the tale. He was in a pretty bad wreck judging by the appearance of the car and he escaped without a scratch – Nothing short of a miracle – He was on his way to meet me in Petoskey [Michigan] and took the hill road from the club – He was climbing a hill and when he got to the top there was a big Lincoln [car] coming at him at a terrific rate on his side of the road – Bud had to ditch the car and then hit a tree – The driver of the other car ran away but some witness got his license number and the sheriff is hunting him – The sheriff went over the scene and completely exonerated Bud from all blame – It will take a week to get the car fixed so we are staying on [at their summer cabin at Lake Walloon] – I am so thankful that Bud was not hurt. I can think of nothing else – His spirit is chastened too – He's so attentive and considerate and defers to my wishes without his usual arguments –

On Tuesday, August 31, 1932, she noted to Emily, "Em dear: You note we are still in Wildwood [Michigan] – The parts for the car have not yet arrived and Lord only knows when they will."

On Saturday, September 3, 1932, Estelle wrote:

Still no car ... Your brother and Bill got up at five o'clock yesterday morning to go fishing – They returned here for breakfast at about ten and said they had caught eighty-seven fish but they dumped them back into the lake. A fine fish story thought I but it really proved to be a true tale – fearing they would be called upon to clean the fish they decided to get rid of theirs – Well! I'm getting used to seventeen! [Bud's age]

Dr. Sophian, caring for his patients in Kansas City and awaiting the return of Estelle and Bud, mentioned the car wreck in a letter to Emily in France on September 9, 1932: "You know Bud had a accident in the Plymouth (he was <u>not</u> injured in the slightest degree) but the car was demolished, so that Mother [Estelle] and Bud are not yet home. They expected the parts a few days ago, and should be home this week.

However, on Tuesday, September 13, 1932, Estelle wrote to Emily:

Emmy dear:

Aren't you surprised that we are still in Wildwood? When the car was wrecked, the garage people promised to repair it in a week. To-morrow will be exactly three weeks and if we're lucky we may get it then … We hope to get away Thursday morning. Bud just said he did not believe we'd have the car till Saturday – Just now he is engaged in a game of Solitaire [card game for one person]. He was expecting some girls to visit him this evening – So far they have not put in an appearance –

Bud has been working about the place – He took in the dock, chopped down dead trees for fire wood etc etc – He is keeping his own time and charging me at the rate of 30 cuts an hour. I leave it to you. What chance do I have?

More when I get home

Heaps an' heaps of love

Mother

On Monday, September 16, 1932, Bud and Estelle had were finally back in Kansas City. Estelle wrote to Emily, "Bud is leaving Wednesday morning. We shopped all day. He had a letter from [name?] asking Bud to drive up with to Stanford from Los Angeles."

Postcard of Phillips Academy, Andover, Massachusetts.
Sophian Archives.

Bud Sophian around fifteen years old at Phillips Academy,
Andover, Massachusetts, ca. 1930. *Sophian Archives.*

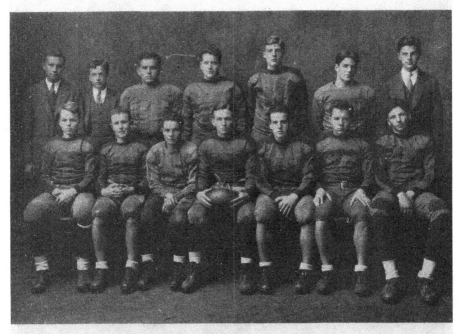

Back: Vye (*Mgr.*) Jenney (*Mgr.*), Harris, Dwyer, F A. Peterson, R. Sears, Linkroum (*Mgr.*)
Front· Platt, Vorse, Noble, R. L. Howard, ·Sophian, Harper, Fry

SECOND FOOTBALL TEAM

Second Football Team, Phillips Academy, Andover, Massachusetts, 1932. Bud Sophian is in the front row, third in from the right. Phillips Academy *Pot Pourri* Yearbook 1932. *Sophian Archives.*

WRESTLING TEAM

Wrestling, 1931

Andover	16	Browne and Nichols	13
Andover	19	Yale Freshmen	8
Andover	24 1-2	Milton	6 1 2
Andover	9	Taft	14
Andover	6	Harvard Freshmen	23

The Team

D. BROWN, *Captain*   J M. CATES, JR., *Manager*

G. T SHALLENBERGER, 115 *lbs.*   U D. E. WALDEN, 155 *lbs.*
J A. C. KENNEDY, JR., 125 *lbs.*   A. SOPHIAN, JR., 145 *lbs.*
B. SMITH, 135 *lbs.*   D. K. BROWN, JR., 165 *lbs.*

D. H. NORTHRUP, 175 *lbs.*

Wrestling Team, Phillips Academy, Andover, Massachusetts, 1931.
Bud Sophian is in the front row, second in from the right. Phillips
Academy *Pot Pourri* Yearbook 1932. *Sophian Archives.*

"BRAD"

207 Park Avenue, Yonkers, N. Y

Born December 7, 1913   Yonkers, N Y
Entered Andover 1931   Yale

Π Δ Φ   Football Squad

Wrestling Team

SHEPHERD FITCH SMITH

"SHEP"

Stonington, Conn.

Born February 19, 1913   White Plains, N Y.
Entered Andover 1931   Undecided

Choir   Winter Track

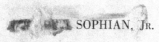 SOPHIAN, JR.

"BUD" "SOPH" "LES"

Sophian Plaza, Kansas City, Mo.

Born April 28, 1915   New York City
Entered Andover 1929   Stanford

Φ Λ Σ   Winning Club Football (1929-30)
All Club Football (1929-30)   AAA Football (1931)
Winning Club Wrest'ing (1930)   Varsity Wrestling (1932)
2nd Team Golf (1930-31)   2nd Honor Roll (1 term)

DAVIS BRYSON STANLEY

"DAVE"

2874 Woodbury Road, Shaker Heights, Cleveland, Ohio

Born June 7, 1913   East Cleveland, Ohio
Entered Andover 1929   Stanford

Η Δ Φ   Winning Club Baseball (1930)
                    Varsity Baseball Squad (1931)

62

Senior picture, Phillips Academy, Andover, Massachusetts, 1932. Bud Sophian is the third photo down from the top of the page. Phillips Academy *Pot Pourri* Yearbook 1932. *Sophian Archives.*

Chapter Four: Stanford University, California, and Leah Ray, 1932–1938

Bud left by train for California on the morning of September 21, 1932, according to his father who conveyed the news to Emily in Grenoble, France, with the quip, "We certainly stretched you [two] far apart." Estelle wrote to Emily on September 24, 1932, saying, "Bud left Wednesday morning looking like a million in his new polo coat – He is furious at you for not writing him. His address [is] P.O. Box 1591 – Stanford University – California."

During his freshman year (1932–1933), Bud lived in the university's all-male, four-story Encina Hall, which American railroad tycoon, California governor, US Senator, and Stanford University founder Leland Stanford, Jr. (1824–1893) had modeled after a favorite Swiss resort. Encina Hall was considered the grandest college dormitory in the United States at the time it opened in 1891, and three hundred young Stanford men moved into its spacious 280,000 square feet. Traditions of rowdiness, vandalism, and violence, including severe freshmen hazing, soon developed. University officials expelled some students for their behaviors.[53]

In 1923, Toyon and Branner dormitories opened for upper classmen, and Encina Hall became a freshmen-only dormitory. Despite the separation of the older from the younger collegians, the freshman residents of Encina Hall continued the boisterous and disorderly ways that had earned the dormitory its original notoriety. Former head yell leader Jim Triolo, Stanford class of 1935 (a year ahead of Bud), remembered Encina residents "winding fire hoses through stair balusters. When they turned on the water, the hoses inflated, sending balusters flying." Triolo also recalled the time a student dropped a water bag from an upper floor during a Mother's Club tea in the Encina lobby. "It hit Mrs. Herbert Hoover [i.e., the wife of President Hoover, who was a Stanford alumnus], and the perpetrator got the maximum work penalty at the Convalescent Home."[53] This acceptance of bad-boy behaviors may help explain why Bud ended up spending a night in the San Mateo County Jail in nearby Redwood City, California, in December 1932.

While seventeen-year-old Bud was adjusting to college on the West Coast, Emily was studying at the University of Grenoble in France. As always, Bud remembered to telegram her on her birthday, September 28 (her nineteenth). The surviving telegram is torn and incomplete: "Happy Birthday No more money no more ..."

Two days later, on September 30, 1932, Estelle wrote the following to Emily: "Bud took his college aptitude exam Monday also a physical exam – His physique was declared perfect – you will be pleased to learn – He took a bus back to Los Angeles and had to sit up all night – He knows we cannot send him more money – He does not have to register until to-morrow and there was no one at the school – He plans to drive back with Don to-morrow."

On October 9, 1932, Estelle brought Emily up to date on Bud's adjustment to college: "Bud is continually complaining about being in a fog about his studies but according to himself, he is the mainstay of his floor – helping everyone who is taking languages and doing Davi's French regularly."

On October 18, 1932, Estelle told Emily: "Bud's letters are one long and continuous cry about how very difficult his courses are and how hard he is working – It may interest you to know that Natalie had a letter waiting for him when he arrived at Stanford – He says they are just good friends believe it or not." She added, "A letter from Lucile yesterday is all excitement about a job she found for herself to do a column in the Ambassador Magazine – She will no doubt write you about it."

On October 24, 1932, Estelle wrote again to Emily, declaring that "Bud speaks of the superior girls in that part of the country, also that he has been secretly bid to all the very best fraternities including the Dekes – Freshmen are not supposed to be approached until the second quarter ..."

On November 2, 1932, Estelle shared with Emily further news of Bud: "Had a long letter from Bud yesterday – He seems to be well pleased with his school but is having a very bad time with his chemistry – You would be amused at his account of the girls he has met and their amazing pulchritude – He has made many wonderful friends and there is not a week-end that he is not invited by at least one boy to go to his home."

On November 9, 1932, Bud found time to write to Emily, who he believed was still in Grenoble. However, Emily had already left Grenoble to move to Paris for the next portion of the Smith College program. Thus, his letter made an additional trip from Grenoble to her, care of "Madame Kann, 78 Avenue Mozart, Paris XVI." Affixed to the envelope were five one-cent stamps depicting the image of Benjamin Franklin. Bud wrote:

Em darling –
I'm so goddamn mad right now I can hardly see – I just spilled an extremely large bottle of ink all over my clothes, bed and shoes – all of which does not tend to improve one's disposition.

The child prodigy [referring to himself] of the Sophian family is encountering no end of scholastic difficulties here – practically flunking chemistry but my sunny disposition has managed to enable me thus far to inveigle passing grades from my prof – the rest of my subjects are quite all right except possibly history which is quite hard – the whole trouble seems to be the fact that all of these subjects require work and to this point I haven't been able to spare the time from my outside activities for this process.

Women out here are rather disappointing – a couple of really good ones tho and I'm not kidding –

Ettlinger and I get along quite well – he's got a car but does me no good as he'll never let me use it – however, I've made lots of awfully good friends here and am not suffering – fraternity rushing starts tomorrow although no pledging allowed till next term – I got 8 invitations for 4 meals from some of the best houses on the campus, Dekes [Delta Kappa Epsilon] included – that doesn't mean much tho – they just want to get a line on you – I'm looking forward to it.

Got a letter today from my pal Audrey – didn't write her but got one anyway – hear from [name] Rigg and Feldman too every once in a while – got a letter from Paul yesterday – He feels very badly about his missing you when you sailed [to France] – he left unexpectedly for their summer home in the White Mountains and had no way to reach you – he wanted me to apologize – said he didn't dare write – you know he's down at Yale –

Really sweetheart you'd better cut down just a little on the rot-gut [poor quality whiskey] – I don't want to preach but it's really pretty bad when overdone. Sorry you're held in – we've got no regulations here [Encina Hall] – perhaps it would better if we had –

By the way what fraternity is Eddie in – Delta (what?) – didn't think he'd last very long – damn fine fellow but aren't they all?!

My golf is quite good of late – I'm on the frosh golf team at present – not for long I'm afraid but who can tell? [Bud joined the freshman golf team coached by amateur golfer Eddie Twigg. Coach Twigg would take the Stanford golf team to five national collegiate titles (1938, 1939, 1941, 1942, and 1946) during his fifteen-year tenure at Stanford University.]

I'm awfully sorry to hear about [Carol Thomas's sweetheart] – if Carol's still there tell her I send my deepest sympathy – It's an awful tough break – tell me tho what did she mean by that note she put in your letter about "her little one" – are my fears justified?

Gotta go little gal – Morpheus [Greek god of dreams] calls – hope you understand my note in French – really I think my German is better than my French [word?] so anyway – but do you know I do about 4 peoples' French for 'em every nite – Don included – and what's more I may be not quite a little angel but I'm not the rake Ettlinger made me out to be – not quite – Yassuh, yassuh and yassuh

Good nite darling

All love

Bud.

On November 16, 1932, Estelle wrote to Emily: "Had a letter from Bud this morning – he is still yowling about his work – Says he has little or no time for regular correspondence but that he wrote you recently – He thinks he will join the Phi Gamma Delta fraternity. They want him to sign a pledge at once. He is still holding off."

On November 21, 1932, Estelle alerted Emily, "Bud has been ill and in the hospital with flu – He missed [word?] exams but in three other courses he got A's so all his moaning was for naught – As usual he says he was lucky in his exams." She concluded her letter by saying, "I'll be missing you plenty at Thanksgiving and Xmas – We hope you'll have happy ones. Bud's going to Los Angeles for Thanksgiving and he'll be home for Xmas – Heaps n' heaps of love, Mother."

On November 24, 1932, Estelle waxed nostalgically in a letter to Emily, "A year ago to-day you, Bud and I spent Thanksgiving to-gether [in Northampton, Massachusetts] – I wonder when this family of ours will be united for Thanksgiving celebration – I hope you are having a very happy day – we drank to you last night at the club party." She added near the end of her letter, "Bud has a date with Dot Allis today … His latest rave, however, is a blond co-ed of rare charm and beauty I am anxious to see her – I wonder if his taste has improved."

On November 28, 1932, Estelle expressed her worry to Emily that "Bud spent the week-end and Thanksgiving in Los Angeles – We have not heard from him since his return to school." Two days later (November 30, 1932), Estelle, relieved to have heard from Bud, told Emily, "Bud had a grand time in Los Angeles. He was very much impressed with a beautiful blond – seventeen – and a vocal entertainer at the [Cocoanut] Grove. I can almost hear you howl – He states that she absolutely has not gone Hollywood and that her mother accompanies her every evening to the Ambassador [Hotel]."

On December 13, 1932, Bud sent a second letter to Emily, care of Madame Kann in Paris. He wrote this letter on stationery from the Langham Hotel and Apartments, a famous celebrity-filled hotel of the era located on Seventh Street at Normandie in Los Angeles. In his letter, he mentions a young woman named Leah Ray (full name: Leah Ray Hubbard, 1915–1999) with whom he was clearly smitten. Lucille undoubtedly introduced Bud to Leah Ray at the Cocoanut Grove where she was singing with the Phil Harris Orchestra. Leah Ray later acted in about a dozen Hollywood motion pictures. Bud also mentions the menacing events transpiring in Europe.

Em darling –

I'm awfully sorry to hear you're not well – I just found out this morning – I'm sure you'll be better by the time you get this – I've intended to write you for weeks but my power of concentration as well as my ambition of old [becoming a physician] has deserted me – signs of approaching age I'm afraid –

By the way, I pledged Beta Theta Pi nite before last – that's the one Fred's in. It's a heck of a good house out here – rates first on the campus and they got a swell bunch of fellows – I got a bid from the Deke house which gave me greatest pleasure to refuse – They're a swell house but all my close friends are going Beta so I did too. There's only two Jews on the campus in fraternities all of which makes me feel overly important –

Listen darling don't let my rooming with Don bother you a bit – I've got enough sense to take care of myself. I hope – anyway. I'm never seen around with him – we have entirely different friends and the only time I see him is at nite or when we're studying. Sorry you feel as strongly about it but don't need to –

Finals start Friday – I'm setting right up now – I got a straight A average on my midquarters but I'm plenty afraid for the outcome of these examinations they're gonna feed us in a few days –

California and inhabitants went wild yesterday – after several days of intense cold, it broke out with a blizzard yesterday – a real one too – most of the people out here never saw one before – acted like idiots – all I did was act cynical like and freeze my darn self to death –

Got a few new women out here – they're really beautiful – what I mean – of course some of 'em have nothing but beauty but some have a little sense – I'm right in there with a plenteous number – believe me it's a job feeding a lot of women in the same school a terrific line – I still remain immune and unaffected by their charms. Right now my main interest is a gorgeous brunette who sings for Phil Harris in the Cocoanut Grove – she's a little southern girl – only 17 – cute as hell and absolutely unspoiled and nice as can be – But sad to say I don't rate so much – only met her Thanxgiving and haven't seen her since –

Got a letter from Ginny Schroeder today – send's her best to you – I've also heard from such people as Fred, Dick, Paul, Kitchel. Millard's not to be omitted or Steward – the latter one receiving little or no attention and bien entendre, no reply – Oh yes, I hear from Gertie Rigg – I answer her – also from Audrey quite regularly but I never answer her – I've gotten 5 or 6 letters and haven't written yet – she wants to marry me or something equally crazy – I stepped out of my class when I met her – she's about 10 jumps ahead of me and God knows I'm trying my damndest to keep up with the time – Johnny and Dot Allis are still around – Dot is awfully cute and much too nice to me – I treat her very badly – Johnny is stepping up – you know she's at Skidmore and they're giving her liberal education, I do believe – The nicer for me when I get home Xmas – save me any further instruction perhaps – who can tell –

And now my dear sister what are your views on the foreign situation? I personally don't know anything about 'em but I'm willing to learn – anyway – forget it – I'm sorry I mentioned it –

As you've probably deduced by this time I'm writing with extreme speed – why, I don't know, other than the fact that I'm two months behind in history and I gotta catch up before next Monday –

Well I hear all good things must come to an end – not that this letter falls in that category but I imagine along that same line all impossible things also must finish sometime und so meine liebe ich muss gehen ["my dearest little one, I must go" in German] – get well real quick –
My bestest love
Bud.

On December 19, 1932, local law enforcement authorities arrested Bud and Stanford classmates Roderick Pearson and Monroe Rubin for absconding with Christmas trees in Redwood City, California, about seven miles north of Stanford University campus. The three freshmen took "[t]rees ... from downtown streets where merchants put them to stimulate the holiday spirit," blasted the *San Mateo Times*. The article concluded, "The students, facing a petty theft charge, were released yesterday morning on their own recognizance." They had spent the night in San Mateo County jail in Redwood City.

While Bud was in jail overnight, Emily was in a car accident in Paris. She cabled her father, who responded on December 19, 1932, as follows:

Dear Em:

Just a short note before Christmas to wish you a most Merry Christmas.

Just received your Cable about your auto accident. You should Remember in cabling to be a little more specific – When you say "not very serious," it doesn't tell me anything except that you are trying not to worry us – which of course I appreciate, but can't help thinking the worst.

Suffice it that I shall be glad to get you home again, and keep you <u>home</u> for a while.

Everything else is quiet.

Bud will be home the 22nd. A Rather quiet Christmas here ... Good luck and love to you and mother [Estelle travelled to Paris to be with Emily]

Dad

Dr. Sophian dashed off another letter to Emily on December 26, 1932, as follows:

Dear Em:

It is needless for me to urge you to be courageous – I know you will be.

You've had a tough break, and I am grateful you slipped thru as you have, and that we still Love you, intact.

Everything will come out alright Old Dear, and this will be just a memory.

You know we're pulling for you, and thinking of you all the time, Rather in a befuddled sort of way I am afraid.

I am anxious to get you home as quickly as possible. I know we can make you happier and also more comfortable, and maybe a little more happy ourselves.

Cheerio – Good luck and Hope to see you Real soon.

Much love to you, dear –

Dad

Emily had sustained injuries when the taxi in which she was riding collided with a car driven by one Monsieur Lecoq of Dordogne at the Rond Point des Champs-Elysees on Saturday night around midnight, December 19, 1932. The French orthopedic surgeon fitted her with a full-body plaster cast for possible back injuries while she was hospitalized at the American Hospital of Paris. Estelle travelled immediately to France to assess the situation and accompany Emily home.

Upon returning to Kansas City around January 17, 1933, Emily was admitted under her father's care to Kansas City's brand new Menorah Hospital. Subsequent testing showed that her injuries were not serious. Nevertheless, her father kept her hospitalized for six weeks of convalescence, a time during which she grew increasingly restless and frustrated with her life.

On January 14, 1933, Bud sent a letter to Emily in Paris, care of the American Hospital of Paris. He wrote the letter while travelling back to Stanford following his Christmas vacation in Kansas City with his father. He mailed the letter from Stanford. The letter did not reach Emily, however, before she and Estelle had left Paris to return to Kansas City. The letter finally reached Emily at Menorah Hospital on January 23, 1933. In his letter, Bud responded to an earlier letter sent by Emily from her Paris hospital bed in which she complained that he had not shown enough interest in her since her accident. Bud's letter read as follows:

Em darling –
I guess I've [been] awfully inattentive and unsympathetic but honest I have been thinking about you no end – I've been kept perpetually busy answering questions about you and your condition – everyone in K.C. is interested and worried – the phone is perpetually ringing as people try to gain the latest reports –

You probably are at the moment accusing me of gross exaggeration but the fact of the case is I am under-rating the interest taken in you if anything –

When we found out you'd been in an automobile accident

I could see all the K.C. gossips immediately saying that you'd been in a drunken auto accident so I told every one that your taxi had smashed up – it's a good story anyway – even if the other may be truer – memories of Bill Navran and ditches and stuff –

K.C. still holds little in the way of good looking women as far as I'm concerned – the west coast presents a far more attractive display – I'm not doing so badly for a little fellow out there –

I was going to attempt to tell you all the people who told me to say hello to you but the task is too gigantic – just consider that every one you ever knew or heard of in K.C. sends their best wishes – even little Buddy – 'ats me –

The Bellerive [fine hotel at 214 East Armour Boulevard, Kansas City] is operating full blast – enormous crowds there all vacation – lousy orchestra, methinks, however. Kay Kyser the leader is the most awful specimen of a man I ever saw and its pitiful to see him try the personality stuff – the Muehlebach [legendary hotel in Kansas City] is very beautiful these days – fairly good orchestra too –

This train is really terrific – but almost all of them are – God! How I hate the darn things –

I tell you, sistah – I'm very drowsy and consequently may attempts at writing are more feeble than usual –

I shall try again anon

All love

Bud –

On January 23, 1933, Bud wrote to Emily at Menorah Hospital professing his love for Leah Ray.

Em darling –

Please excuse me for being so damned inattentive and selfish for the past few weeks – honest I've been thinking of you 'n awful lot 'n wishing there were something I could do to help.

Not a darn thing new with me since my return – I've only gone out once 'cause I've been awful busy making up a little back work.

I say there is nothing new but I'm lying – something has happened – I've fallen very much in love – I got it real bad this time but I will say in my defense I picked a real good one – she's very beautiful, young (17), sweet, unaffected 'n everything – name is Leah Ray Hubbard and she sings in the Cocoanut Grove – has been for about four months prior to which she never had appeared anywhere in her life – hails originally from Norfolk, Virginia – what more can I say about her than that she's just what you wouldn't expect to find in a singer – her mother is down at the Grove with her every nite and will not let her go out unchaperoned. I rate pretty well, I think, but not as well as I might. I sure hope you all come out this spring [1933] so you can meet – you'll love her – so different from my last selections, need I mention any names, as day is from night. I think I sent you a picture of her – I've got a couple more really good ones but you'll have to wait to see them.

Hope you feel an awful lot better – I'll try to write more often.

All my bestest love
Bud

On February 1, 1933, Bud again wrote Emily at Menorah Hospital. She had sent him a wristwatch as a gift.

Em darling –
You ought to be mighty nigh onto all well by this time – sure hope so anyway – just think how you can talk about your

broken back [this diagnosis was never established] after you get well – that's better n' any operation by a darn site.

Say that watch is probably the finest thing I've ever gotten in my life – if there's any one thing I wanted more than anything else that was sure it – and what a watch – it's a knockout everyone wants one like it – they all think it's the smartest, most practical one in existence. I sure agree with 'em with a vengeance –

I'm still aslavin' away believe it or not – the place would be a push-over if it weren't for this chemistry subject – it sure has me baffled, tho and how!

I'm still in love – very much so – this gal sings over the radio with the orchestra and is the most popular vocalist on the coast – never knew I had so many friends till everyone learned I knew her and now she got signed up by Paramount to play the second lead in Maurice Chevalier's new picture [*A Bedtime Story*] – she's so tickled she doesn't know what to do –

I've gotta get to bed before this whole nite's over – more soon
All love darlin'
Bud

On February 23, 1933, Bud again wrote to Emily at Menorah Hospital about meeting band singer Betty Grable at a San Francisco nightclub:

Em darling –
I'm awfully sorry to hear that you've been laid up – it's about time you started getting some breaks for a change –

I've been working like a mad man around here getting next to nothing accomplished. I don't go out anymore but still I get worse grades than when I didn't study at all. I don't understand this business at all –

Lee Norton [big band vocalist] is playing up at the Mark Hopkins nowadays. I saw him the other night 'n he asks to be remembered to you – said he'd write or something but don't let it bother you – he's a dumb guy if I ever saw one but they got a little girl singing with the band who is pretty much all right – name's Betty Grable [future movie star] 'n we get along mighty well – nothing serious at all but it's really a relief to go around with some one that understands a little after having been on a strict diet of Stanford women for so long you could scream.

Leah Ray in spite of all that's come between is still the queen I'm afraid – suppose it's rather stupid of me but I find myself being unable to help myself – it's been mighty good lately – I'm fooling around with several of the girls around school but there's nothing serious about it at all.

Can't understand what's come over me – had a swell chance to go to Carmel for five days 'n at the last minute I turned it down merely so that I could catch up on some of my studying – I'm ashamed of myself but I just hadda do a lot of studying – I've got so many term papers piled up on me I hardly know where to start.

Gotta go – hope you're much better real soon.
Loads of love
Bud

Emily headed to California to visit Bud and Lucille upon her hospital discharge in early March 1933. She stayed at the Gaylord Hotel on Wilshire Boulevard in Los Angeles, where she received a heartfelt letter from her worried father dated March 28, 1933:

Dear Em:
I was happy to receive your letter. Happy for several Reasons. Your Restlessness, your dissatisfaction with Kansas City, made me wonder just how much we really meant to you. I am convinced that in your true inner consciousness, we do mean much to you, but maybe you have just taken us for granted, and not stopped to analyze or think, or I believe you would not

only have given us ready cooperation to our requests, but also in making your daily plans, possibly planned a little for us also.

I am writing this way in Response to your letter, which I say has made me happy because it has a little something in it, which I have been looking for. If I am Right, and I believe so then it is fair to you to let you know my sentiment.

You have now Reached an age of maturity, where sane planning and living, in which pleasure for yourself plays a wholesome part, but not all, and in which happiness to us, a small part, should be allowed for.

I was glad to see your changed Reaction to your friend Knox. After all there was no personal reason for antagonism, except for the Realization that he was just a no good, parasitic bum, and it was just too bad, that one with your possibilities should waste yourself on any trash like that. I am thrilled at the development at M. U. [University of Missouri]. It is a real opportunity.

Much love

From Dad

On April 7, 1933, Bud and Emily clubbed together at the Cocoanut Grove in the Ambassador Hotel in Los Angeles, where Phil Harris, Leah Ray, and Xavier Cugat and his Tango Band were performing. Xavier Cugat, known for drawing caricatures, sketched Emily wearing a huge smile. She enjoyed this memento all of her life.

The summer of 1933 Bud returned home to Kansas City, which was ruled, more or less, by gangsters at the time. He was promptly held up at gunpoint on June 22, 1933, and relieved of the wristwatch sent to him at Stanford by Emily. Estelle told Emily about the holdup in a letter to her in New York City where she was visiting Estelle's brother Louis E. Felix at 160 West 95th Street, New York City.

Bud called Louie Sunday afternoon and was held up that very

8

evening. At the point of a gun he was relieved of the watch you sent him together with everything else in his possession. Johnny was not with him and the two of them [Bud and Louie] joked with the gangsters and tried to talk them out of taking the car away from them but did not succeed. They were compelled to drive to 81st and Wornall Road and there were forced out of the car. Imagine the state of my mind when he telephoned to us around midnight. It certainly was a relief that they were not hurt because as per usual Bud showed fight. The police recovered the car shortly after all this happened ...

On October 1, 1933, Bud found himself heading back to Stanford for his second college year (1933–1934) on the California Limited sleeper train operated by the Atchison, Topeka and Santa Fe Railway. The California Limited connected Chicago with San Francisco via Los Angeles. Bud took one train from Kansas City to Chicago, where he visited friends, including his old flame Natalie. He then boarded the California Limited on which he wrote a letter to Emily, who had transferred to the University of Missouri in Columbia to study journalism. She lived at 810 Hillcrest in Columbia. Bud used the train's "en route" stationery.

Em darling,
I tried to call you a couple of times before I left, but I'm afraid I didn't get ya – I was awfully upset when mom told me you didn't get my wire – I figured that I would probably be a little delayed 'cause I didn't know your address but I thought sure you'd eventually get it –

Don't know when I've ever been so thoroughly bored in my life – this train ride is an awful nuisance with never any one interesting aboard. All I do is sleep 'n read rotten detective stories –

I had quite a time up in Chicago – much better than I dreamed of – first of all I called friend Natalie up who came

running down to see me – she's an awfully good kid 'n believe
me I've got her right where I want her now – as a matter of
fact I now have her right where she had me a year ago last June
[1932] – believe me I fed her plenty – revenge or somepun, says
me – but as for Leah Ray she still has me on the spot. She's lost
a good deal of weight – only weighs 116 – and is more beautiful
than ever. I'm kinda afraid I love that girl more 'n its healthy
for me – incidentally she was just made radio queen of America
1933 – she makes no pretense of being in love with me but I'm
convinced that she likes me more than anyone else – in a way
I guess she's got a lotta sense – there's really very little sense in
professing mad devotion at our ages – it's so damn long before
we could do anything worthwhile about it but it seems like in
spite of that I keep right on professing it –

This all sounds like the confession of an unrequited love or
somepun but I'm never in very good shape after I've been with
that girl –

I'll probably be a couple of days late arriving at that asylum
of learning up there in Palo Alto [Stanford] – I still don't know
when I'm or was supposed to be there – from the looks of things
at home I'm afraid I'm gonna hafta do some pretty heavy work.
Ouch! You go and get the family all steamed up with your fiery
enthusiasm over your new-found work – it looks like an awfully
tough winter for little Buddy –
G'by now – drop me a line some time if you can tear yourself
away from your researches in the libraries 'n places –
Love aplenty
Bud

Bud wrote to Emily on November 16, 1933, about carousing in Los
Angeles with actor Clark Gable the previous weekend. He wrote on Beta
Theta Pi stationery, as follows:

Em darling –

Right now I'm comfortably entrenched in the Stanford Men's
Rest Home trying to recover from the past weekend in L.A. – It
seems that we won a football game down there last Saturday 'n
what a game it was! We all nearly went crazy – tore down the
goal posts 'n everything – The celebration started right after the
game Saturday 'n lasted till very late Sunday nite – and now for
the big surprise – I went 'n got drunk – I had to drink two big
glasses of straight gin to do it but I finally put it over. Don't be
sore or worried about it – I won't do it again cause I hate the
taste of the stuff 'n it's like drinking so much medicine – I didn't
get sick or pass out or anything but I got awful drunk 'n had
a wonderful time – I even went so far at the instigation of one
of the Babes in the party to go over to Clark Gable's table who
incidentally was awful drunk too and induced him to come
over to our table – he 'n I got to be swell pals 'n when his wife
came over to get him I went with him and spent the rest of the
evening 'n his party –

For God's sake Em don't keep this letter 'cause the folks
might get hold of it 'n I'm awful afraid they wouldn't realize
the circumstances and it would upset them something awful if
they thought I drank 'n since I see no cause to upset 'em – please
don't keep this letter –

I saw Deadeye – same old slinking deadeye – also Dorothy
Lee [American actress and comedian] who remembered me –
big surprise! Also Geler Allis who is sick with the flu. She's
prettier than she used to be methinks – so's Dot incidentally –

Somewhere in the course of that hilarious Saturday nite I
found a fancy babe whose name I don't know to this day 'n what
a time we had until her husband (ouch!) found us – he wasn't
very sore; just nearly tried to kill me but I got away unharmed –

I'm getting reports of Leah Ray's engagement nowadays but
she says absolutely nothing about it – I know this guy Lewis

she's supposed to be going for but never suspected anything serious – I'll let you know as soon as I find out definitely –

I'm working like the devil now and getting nowhere fast – I'm very liable to flunk two courses –the family'll be furious but I'm doing more work than I ever did in my life.

That date for New Years Eve sounds all right to me unless Natalie decides to accept my invitation to visit me Xmas vacation. Don't tell the family – I want to surprise them but I don't think she'll come so it's all right –

Rosebud's still in love with me despite a complete lack of encouragement – I gotta go dear – write soon 'n don't work too hard. By the way just found out I got elected into the "Scalpers" – an honorary society of some sort – [Scalpers was the Sophomore Men's Honorary Society at Stanford; twenty-four sophomores earned this recognition the year Bud received the honor.]
Lots and lots of love
Bud.

Bud wrote to Emily again on November 28, 1933, from the Beta Theta Pi House at Stanford. He told Emily about the San Jose (California) lynching of two men who had admitted to the murder of a local person named Brooke Hart. The two men had not yet had a trial when vigilantes strung them up on trees before a throng of people numbering in the hundreds.

Dear Em –
Just heard that you haven't been feeling so awfully well – that's a darn shame. I figure that by this time you should have just about run out of things that could happen to you –

An awful lot's been happening around the generally quiet town of ours – we seem to be football champions after some wonderful games – it's really a kick to see 85 to 100 thousand people jammed into a stadium week after week – we've got the nomination for the Rose Bowl but I don't guess I'll be able to see it –

Saturday nite every one was celebrating the win over California but the evening ended in an awful way – Two fellows from school and their dates hit another car head-on at 60 m.p.h. while coming home and three of them were killed. I knew them all awfully well – in fact I sat next to two of them at dinner Saturday nite – it's an awful thing –

You must have read about the dainty little episode [the lynching] down at San Jose Sunday nite – we went down to it and arrived on the scene in time to see the bodies dangling from the trees – those fellows deserved the lynching they got but it was certainly awful to watch – I'd met this Brooke Hart several times when I was down with Don – he was an extremely close friend of Edward's. [Brooke Hart's father owned the successful Hart's Department Store in San Jose. On November 26, 1933, two men abducted him in broad daylight only yards away from his father's store and then murdered him. Police apprehended the two men who admitted their crime but never received a trial because a mob lynched them first. Police found Hart's body in San Francisco Bay.]

We were just about getting back down to normal last nite when a committee raided the house for intoxicating liquors – great was their surprise when the Beta house was found not to contain so much as a ginger ale bottle – I'm doing all right out here this year [1933–1934] but not nearly as well as last. I'm working like a fool but just don't seem to understand anything. I've got a couple of very fine women on the string although I rarely go out –

Say have you got a lot of dough? If you have will you lend me some till next quarter – It's O.K. if you can't spare it but if you can God bless ya!

Got a wire from Leah Ray the other day emphatically

denying her rumored engagement – well, she isn't married yet
anyway –
Gotta go eat about now
Loads of love baby
Bud.
How do ya like my new stationery? (embossed with Stanford's
seal)

In 1934, Bud and Emily were studying at their respective universities while Estelle and Abraham Sophian moved from Sophian Plaza to their new custom-built home in an unincorporated area of Kansas City, Kansas, overlooking Brush Creek on 63rd Street and Wenonga Road. The unincorporated area subsequently became Mission Hills, Kansas.

In addition to playing golf for Stanford, Bud continued his wrestling career. A February 1, 1934, article in the *San Mateo Times and Daily News Leader* titled "Title Bouts at Card Pavilion" announced the wrestling card, as follows: "The wrestling card: 135 pounds – Ben Barbour vs. Kenneth Reynolds; 145 pounds – Carl Eitnier vs. Bill Metulell, 155 pounds – Dave Cooke vs. Bud Sophian; 105 pounds – Bob Moore vs. Sam Glenn; 175 pounds – Wid Coffin vs. George Lenvens; unlimited – Jim Hay vs. Ted Geissler."

Bud is mentioned in the *Oakland Tribune* on April 20, 1934, in connection with playing golf in the quarterfinal round of the Northern California amateur golf championship. He was paired with J. M. Hunt in the Director's Cup play at 9:30 AM in Orinda, California.

Bud spent his junior year (1934–1935) at Stanford immersed in his studies, sports, and helping to run the fraternity house. In the spring of 1935, twenty-year-old Bud learned that his twenty-one-year-old sister's life in Kansas City had taken a dramatic turn. The *Kansas City Star* had hired her as a reporter for its society page, a job that interested her and brought her great happiness, according to a letter she sent to her friend Nancy Gallagher in May 1935.

While working at the *Star*, she met eligible bachelor and newsman

Theodore Morgan O'Leary, a University of Kansas men's basketball All-American selection (1932), former head coach of the George Washington University basketball team (1932–1934), and son of University of Kansas English Professor R. D. O'Leary and Mathilda Henrichs O'Leary of Lawrence, Kansas. The two reporters were immediately smitten with one another. Bud was curious about the new man in his sister's life. He wrote to Emily the following letter on June 3, 1935:

Em darling –
Awfully sorry to hear you've had such a rotten go of it lately – you're sure not getting the breaks on this health deal –

I ought to be shot for not writing sooner – can't make any excuse for it either except that I've been so blessed busy the last ten days I'm nearly crazy – I'm on every kind of a committee ever invented as well as having no end of work to do around the house, to say nothing of my own school work which has me going pretty successfully – I've had exactly 10 hours sleep since Friday morning and I haven't so much as got to a movie in that time – just lots of work – sounds pretty unusual for me but for some unknown reason I seem to be enjoying having lots to do and continually worrying about things in general –

I wrote the family this morning in hygiene class and I'm writing you now outside the dean's office. I've got to see him about an interfraternity council matter –

You kinda sprung a surprise on the people [parents] with this O'Leary racket, didn't ya? Hope everything keeps turning out all right –

Please pardon the awful [word?] – it's even worse than usual – I'm writing on a newspaper in a rather odd position –

It's hotter 'n hell out here – has been for three days now

but I'm really grateful for it as my neck limbers up swell in this kind of weather –

Goodbye for now darling – hope you're all well by this time – Loads of love
Bud.

Bud remained in California at least part of the summer of 1935, as evidenced by his participation in the Fourth of July invitational golf tournament at Orinda Country Club (Orinda, California), where he earned a spot in the championship bracket. An *Oakland Tribune* article penned by Lee Dunbar on July 8, 1935, mentions Bud, as follows:

The jinx of the Madison Square Garden fight bowl on Long Island has a local duplicate in the annual Fourth of July invitational golf tournament held at Orinda Country Club. No champion has ever won at the Eastern fight emporium, and no champion has ever repeated in the big Orinda event, as Dan Moser found out to his sorrow yesterday as he was defeated by Tome Telfer, 3 and 2 in the 36-hole final.

This tournament, which annually attracts many of Northern California's best golfers, has never been won twice by any person. Moser, last year's titlist, started out like a sure winner yesterday, shooting birdies on four of the first six holes to take a four up lead. Telfer, however, kept whittling away and Moser was only two up at the turn. This lead was dissipated along the route and Telfer was holding the whip hand by the slim margin of one up as they sawed off for lunch. The steady golf of Telfer put him three up at the end of the afternoon nine and he held this advantage, ending the contest on the 15th hole. In defeating the defending champion Telfer medaled 76 in the morning as against 77 for Moser. The winner was one over par for the afternoon journey while Moser was going four over the card.

Tom McCormick scored a 3 and 2 win over Jake Wellman in the 18-hole final of the Orinda flight which was made up of the 16 players defeated in the first round of the championship bracket. First flight honors went to Carl Goemmer with a 4½ and 4 victory over Dr. E. H. White. D. Chalmers defeated Dr. Q. O. Gilbert, 2 and 1 in the final of the second flight while third bracket victory went to Bob Woodyard with a one-up over Bud Sophian ...

Emily accompanied her parents on a long car trip to Canada for the month of July 1935. She spoke to them of her love for Ted O'Leary and that she wanted to marry him. They approved, much to her surprise, and even offered financial assistance so that Emily and Ted could afford a suitable place to live after marriage. Upon her return to Kansas City around August 1, 1935, Emily announced to her closest friends that she and Ted were engaged to be married. They set no date.

Then, in a move that surprised many people, Emily Sophian and Ted O'Leary eloped on August 15, 1935 to Liberty, Missouri, where they were married by a Justice of the Peace. Bud was still in California when the elopement took place. When he heard about his sister's actions, he sent a telegram, which he addressed to "Mrs. Ted O'Leary, care of Dr. A Sophian, 6315 Wenonga Road." The telegram was brief: "Looks like you took a long jump – Love and luck to you and Ted = Bud."

Bud returned to Kansas City soon after and for unknown reasons decided to take a year off from college (1935–1936 school year) to work on the Sophian family farm in Dexter, Missouri. While Bud was living and working in southeastern Missouri, he was involved in a nonfatal auto accident near Jefferson, Missouri, on April 28, 1936, which the *Daily Capital* in Jefferson, Missouri, reported, as follows:

Injured Severely in Auto Accident –
Mr. and Mrs. Alfred Ward hurt in collision on wet pavement

Mr. and Mrs. Alfred Ward, 405 Locust Street, suffered severe injuries Sunday night in the collision of two automobiles on the wet pavement of Highway 50 near the Country Club. The driver of the other car, Bud Sophian of Dexter, Mo., was only slightly injured. Mrs. Ward received a gash on her forehead, a cut lip, a fractured right arm and several loosened teeth. Her husband was bruised about the knees. Sophian told police he was driving east during Sunday night's rain and slapped on his brakes when a truck, lumbering along without a tail light, suddenly loomed before him. His car skidded across the highway into the path of the Ward car which was going west on the highway. Ward applied his brakes but could not stop. Mr. and Mrs. Ward were treated at the office of a physician here and removed to their home.

On August 14, 1936, Bud sent a long, typed letter (single-spaced) to Emily via special delivery from Dexter, Missouri (return address: Box 113). It was the only typed letter he ever sent to her. Many journalists in the 1930s, including Emily and Ted, pounded out their stories and letters on manual typewriters. It is likely that Emily had typed her letter to Bud. In his letter, Bud described life on the farm, his feelings and thoughts about Communists, and his deep loneliness.

Bud earlier had sent a letter to Ted in response to a letter Emily sent to him (Bud). This letter has not survived. Emily apparently responded to Bud's letter to Ted, declaring that Bud was treating her like a nonentity. Why didn't he address his letter to Ted *and* Emily? Bud's response follows:

Em dear
From all reports you are rather angry at me for my failure to acknowledge your letter of a few weeks ago. I'm really very sorry

as I had no intention of arousing your displeasure – as a matter of fact I rather thought you would consider my letter to Ted as to both of you much after the manner that I consider my letters to Dad for Mother as well, even tho I do not mention her – I've been so darn busy I haven't had a minute to myself – the past few weeks I've been working about 14 hours a day in the field which together with cooking my own meals and keeping up with necessary business correspondence has kept me very busy – it's impossible to do anything after dark as the bugs well nigh devour a body whenever you turn on a light – but enough of this –

Your letter was really quite amusing after I had partially succeeded in translating it. I am rather inclined to believe your slight acquaintance with the Noric languages [continental Celtic languages] have done much to impair your coherence. My brief stay on the farm has rather dulled my mind and I experience a little difficulty in making sense of most of your note – I guess it must have been some of this new fangled literature we read about in the paper and hear about on the radio if you can read a paper or have a radio to listen to.

Your comments on Dickie Stern were most enervating – they served to bring to mind a class of people with whom I had occasional contact [Communists in Hollywood in the 1930s?] before my voluntary retirement to the peasant class – namely the intelligentsia – you are quite right about him – he has an insufferable complex that reeks with superiority over we minor humans. I believe brilliance to be a most admirable characteristic in any one unless the possessor continually attempts to make every one conscious of his superior mental equipment (end quote). And such a person is Dickie – he has, however, his redeeming features if you are willing to overlook his eastern affected intellectualism.

I would like very much to accompany you and Ted on your trip east – it could serve as a sort of rehabilitation for my former self after many months of exile among the backbone-of-the-nation-group. If you can talk the family into letting me go it would be very fine – we could take my car and save the wear-and-tear on your new one – after the use mine gets around here a trip of several thousand miles on good roads would be a real rest – incidentally Wesley has had my car on his trip so my method of transportation has been the truck – and so in view of its habitual one-lung performances I haven't dared to venture far from home, all of which goes to show I haven't been anywhere to speak of other than Dexter for quite a while. Let me know all about it soon – I hate to ask Dad if it's all right for me to go even tho I'm quite sure he won't mind – strictly speaking I should have enough sense not to ask him in view of the fact I am supposed to be a working man and up to the present I have inserted into my daily routine numerous capricious trips with the inevitable result of a desultory performance to date – however, the past month or so has been pretty darn trying – I nearly went crazy when we had all those sick hogs, what with nobody knowing anything and everybody claiming to have complete understanding – as a matter of fact my guess as to the cause was correct from the beginning even tho it was just a guess backed up only by what I could derive from text books and bulletins on hand. I really feel that it would do me a lot of good to get away for a while as I really need a bit of a rest – it's pretty tough working in this extreme heat day in and day out and it takes a lot out of you – besides I think it would be a good move to keep me from going sour on the job as it's very lonesome here – I haven't had a date in months, not because I haven't wanted to but because of the complete absence of even a likely prospect.

And now let me wish you and Ted congratulations on this – shall I tritely say – first milestone of your nuptial career [first wedding anniversary] – I think it's all very fine and, were I better fixed financially, would make a more concrete manifestation of this feeling but since my pecuniary status is very poor I shall have to let my good wishes suffice – they're free, you know, but often times are more sincere than sparkling diamonds – honestly tho I do congratulate you and Ted and wish you many more happy ones.

In view of the fact that this letter is rapidly reaching proportions closely akin to a manuscript I'd better stop – besides my noon siesta period is past and I've got to get to work – by the way we siest every day for two hours during the worst heat – start in on mornings at four – work till eleven – siest till one or one thirty, then on till darkness welcomely arrives.

Let me know real soon about the trip as I have to make plans.

Best love and congratulations to you both

Bud.

The day after he sent this letter Bud sent a telegram to "Mr and Mrs T M OLeary = 6315 Wenonga Rd, KSC =," which read, "Congratulations best wishes and love = Bud." It is unknown whether the vacation trip with Emily and Ted took place, as Bud had hoped.

Bud returned to Stanford in fall 1936 to complete his academic studies. He continued to live in the Beta Theta Pi house and earned a place on Stanford's varsity golf team, which was growing in fame for its gifted collegiate golfers. His name was listed for play to begin at 10:30 AM with Tom Cox and Bob Dreyer in the 32nd annual Northern California amateur golf championship held April 16, 1937, at the Lake Merced course in San Francisco, according to the *Oakland Tribune* on that same date.

The 1937 Stanford yearbook, *Quad*, says this about the eighteen-member 1936–1937 year varsity golf team (p. 292):

Golf is essentially a one-man game. Team play is secondary. Thus at Stanford the golf squad is made up of good golfers who can pile up honors on their own and play together once or twice during the year. At Pebble Beach [California] in February [1937], eight Stanford golfers swang around the difficult course to a Pacific Coast Intercollegiate Championship. Bill Oneal won the second flight, and Jack Wallace was runner-up in the finals. Entering on their own, but under the Card [Stanford Cardinals] banner, Stanford golfers invaded the Sacramento Open, San Jose Open, San Francisco City, and the Northern California Amateur Tournaments to place high in every one. At the National Intercollegiates in Chicago last summer [1936], the Card team lost only to Yale. Playing California in April on a home-and-home basis, Card men won by a heavy score, after previously trouncing Pomona. Wallace, Manning, Halaby, Cannon, Boyd, Wiet, Edwards, Oneal, Davis, Crable, Wyeth, and Hyman all earned letters.

Bud and five other varsity golf team members did not earn letters. Meanwhile, Bud Sophian and Leah Ray remained a reportable item. In 1937, their names appeared together in print in the *San Antonio Light* (June 22, 1937), as follows:

Snapshots of Hollywood collected at random: Anne Nagel, pretty widow of Ross Alexander, and Eddie Sutherland together at the Hawaiian Paradise; Townsend Netcher out on a sight-seeing tour of the town with Adrienne Ames. They were chaperoned by Cary Grant and the Allen Tomblings; ... Later they were at the Hollywood fights as were Joe E. Brown, the Harpo Marxes, the Hal Roaches and many other movie folk; Leah Ray stepping out with Bud Sophian at the Famous Door [restaurant]; Dick Arlen and Vic Leming getting all the paraphernalia for deep sea diving...

At about the time the one-liner above was printed, Leah Ray was filming *The Holy Terror* (1937), starring child actress Jane Withers.

The film tells the story of the daughter of a Naval Air Service officer stationed at a naval air force base in Southern California, and includes subplots of German espionage, fixed-wing biplanes flying in tight aerial formations, and parachutists jumping to drop zones, eerily presaging Bud's future.

Bud Sophian graduated from Stanford University in 1938 with a baccalaureate degree in biological sciences, even though he had already matriculated at the Cornell University Medical College in 1937. The reason for the delay in receiving his baccalaureate degree is not known.

Bud Sophian at age seventeen years, Stanford University, 1932.
Sophian Archives.

Freshmen Golf Team, Stanford University, 1932. Bud Sophian is center, front row. Legendary Stanford University golfing coach Eddie Twigg (in hat) stands directly behind Bud Sophian. *Sophian Archives.*

Swimming group, Stanford University, 1932. Bud Sophian is in the front row, second from the left. *Sophian Archives.*

Bud Sophian around twenty years old, Stanford University, ca. 1935.
Sophian Archives.

Postcard of Cocoanut Grove, Los Angeles, California, ca. 1935.
Sophian Archives.

Leah Ray publicity photo, ca. 1935. *Sophian Archives.*

Dr. Abraham Sophian home ca. 1933, Wenonga and 63rd,
Mission Hills, Kansas. *Sophian Archives.*

Chapter Five: Cornell University Medical College, Marriage, and Hospital Internship, 1937–1942

In the summer of 1937, Bud Sophian matriculated at Cornell University Medical College in New York City. Cornell University Medical College was his father's alma mater medical school (class of 1906). Bud benefited from the lavish new buildings and equipment of the New York Hospital-Cornell Medical Center whose gleaming white, alabaster columnar architecture towered over its Upper East Side neighborhood. Head architect Henry Shepley based his design on the Palace of the Popes in Avignon, France.[54] Bud first rented an apartment at 139 East 71st Street, not far from the medical school.

Bud progressed successfully through the first two years of medical school studies, which covered the basic sciences: anatomy, bacteriology and immunology, physiology, biochemistry, pharmacology, and public health. Two years of clinical training in medicine, surgery, pediatrics, obstetrics and gynecology, and psychiatry followed the basic sciences. Bud planned a standard two-year hospital residency after medical school.

Meanwhile, on January 28, 1938, Emily gave birth to her first son Dennis Sophian O'Leary (Bud's nephew). On March 25, 1938, Bud wrote from New York City to Emily and Ted the following letter, in which he acknowledged his nephew's birth and expressed his painful loneliness and desolation over Leah Ray's decision to marry someone else:

Friday

Dear Em and Ted –

I imagine it's about time I wrote to inquire about my nephew's health as well as both of yours – Mother sent me some pictures – the kid [Dennis] looks fine, I guess –

I've been working so terribly hard I can't believe it – certainly hope the results are not disappointing – this week of vacation has been terrible – seen a lot of plays and things but I've been lonesome as hell – no one in town to do anything with – then yesterday I learn that Leah Ray is getting married Sunday here in N.Y. – I didn't like that very much – as a matter of fact it was just about like having some one stick a knife thru me – went out last nite all by myself and got pretty drunk – went everywhere in town and spent an awful lot of money – felt better tho – didn't even have a hangover this morning.

Marjorie [Emily's Smith College friend] and Norman [Bloch, her first husband] have been pretty swell – they just got back from the Coast as you know.

Saw that picture of Francis on *Life* – it's a fright but tell her she can snake my way anytime she hasn't anything better to do –

Drop me a line if you have the time –

Love to the whole family (I mean yours)

Bud.

The *New York Times* published a brief announcement on March 28, 1938, about Leah Ray's marriage, as follows:

Leah Ray Hubbard Married

Miss Leah Ray Hubbard, daughter of Mr. and Mrs. Joseph Edward Hubbard of Norfolk, Va., was married to David Werblin, son of Mrs. Simon A. Werblin of Essex House and the late Mr. Werblin, yesterday in the Waldorf-Astoria by Municipal Court Justice John J. Sullivan. The bride, a movie actress and a singer, is known professionally as Leah Ray. Mr. Werblin is vice president of the Music Corporation of America.

On May 9, 1938, Bud wrote Emily a long doleful letter about medical school, Leah's marriage, and his bleak life in New York City:

Dear Em –

Looks like I'm finally getting around to writing – have really meant to do so for a long time but never seem to acquire the mood for it –

Things are pretty grim around here – I'm so fed up with school I could scream. This year's [his first year of medical school] been pretty tough and has contained very little of interest – just lots and lots of work on fundamentals that has worn me out. I continue to dislike this town with a hate that grows but I'm afraid there's very little to be done about it. Never go out surprisingly enough – maybe I'm afraid if I try it I won't stop for a few weeks –

Saw the Giants play a couple of games – one with Brooklyn and one with Boston. They look pretty good but they're still the luckiest ball club in the majors for my money – They've been winning so many games on their fluke "Polo Grounds" homers it smells. Saw Mungo [Van Lingle Mungo, Brooklyn Dodgers] pitch against Hubbell [Carl Hubbell, Yankees] and the former looked much the better of the two – however, after about so many errors and boners behind him he gave up –

I received a bunch of postal cards which I believe are from Francis – however, I couldn't be certain as the written matter on them is just a bit on the incoherent side – if they are from her please convey my deepest gratitude – the thought was a touching one and served to fan to new highs the flame of love – incidentally, little Mother, we must plan on a little relaxation program sometime during my stay in Kansas City. I have an intense desire to get very drunk and that looks to be my earliest opportunity. I should be home around June 12th or 13th [1938].

I seem to be bearing up under strain of my recent bereavement [Leah's marriage to someone else] as well as to be expected. I was pretty mad for a while though – the entire situation was so hard to figure out – something was wrong somewhere. I had a letter from her on her honeymoon which presented rather an enigma. Her mother and father are on the verge of making legal the separation that has been actual for some time – funniest part is, I think Zeinie (her mother) is in love with me – figure that one out if you can –

I saw cousin [Lucille] at the wedding reception – big as life and twice as ugly. She tried to be very nice but as intoxication became advanced I got awfully tired of her drivel and am afraid I lost patience – You might be interested to know that she has informed every one along the line that she is the *Kansas City Star's* special N.Y. correspondent or some such thing. She is an integral part of the organization of [Arthur] Lyman, [Xavier] Cugat and others (Cugat and Carmen both asked to be remembered) – As far as I can determine she is also making the sleep of numerous ham and egg show people about town happy (?) – Saw her and Polly [Felix, Estelle's older sister] walking down 5th Avenue the other day but fortunately I was at sufficient distance to pass unperceived. As regards Lawrence [Dr. Lawrence Sophian, Abraham's nephew and Bud's cousin] I know nothing – haven't seen him in months. However, the rumors of divorce might logically be true. Minna seemed to be a rather nice sort of person even if a bit on the stupid side while he is getting more conceited than ever – seems that he and Sinclair Lewis [American novelist and playwright] have become buddies and Lawrence runs around a lot with that long-haired, pseudo-intellectual outfit that knows quite definitely what's wrong with everything with never a reflection as to themselves –

Picked up a few dollars on the [Kentucky] Derby (don't tell the family!) – sadly enough it was just a $2 bet but the prestige gained among the neighborhood louts was terrific –

Saw that picture of Francis in *Life*. I'm afraid I thought it looked terrible but what's in a picture?

Haven't seen Marjorie or Norman for some time – business was far from good last time I saw them –

You'll have to pardon it if I seem to reflect a rather fuzzy condition in this letter but it's very late and physiology etc does wonders to induce just such a condition – My very best to Theodore, Dennis and Francis as to you – "parva mater."
My love
Bud.

On July 9, 1938, Bud returned to Stanford University for unknown reasons, possibly to complete a requirement for his baccalaureate or perform a medical externship. He wrote to Emily the following letter while he was there:

Dear Em –
Have a favor to ask and hope you'll comply – Phil Harris and his band are playing a week at the Tower Theater [a popular Kansas City theater in the 1930s and 1940s] starting July 14th [1938] – I saw them for a few minutes on my way thru L.A. this trip. I'd certainly appreciate it if you'd call Phil up and invite him and his wife out to the house [Wenonga and 63rd Street] for dinner – I wrote the family about it, however, if they don't approve of the

idea maybe you and Ted could meet them for a few drinks or something – at any rate you could take Mascott (Phil's wife) and Stub Raemmle (one of the men in the band's wife, she manages the band) out to lunch or something. I'd certainly appreciate anything you can do as they've been awfully nice to me. I told Phil you'd call him. At any rate let me know what's up –

School's really pretty much of a joke – it's not too much fun however, as most of my friends are gone and have been replaced by a bunch of 17- and 18-year-olds. The chances look pretty good for my getting there [Kansas City] about August 20th although I can't be sure yet – probably know this week –
Regards to Francis and Ted
Love
Bud.

On August 8, 1938, Bud again wrote from Stanford University:

Dear Em and Ted –
Just heard about the big operation – hope all's in good shape by now and that it didn't cause too much trouble – also hope that M.B. Lehman, insurance salesman, has not been too attentive since the decision –

Mother wrote that you looked up Phil [Harris, singer and bandleader] and Mascott [Phil's wife] – thanks very much – hope you like Mascott although I'm not terribly optimistic – she's a very strange person, extremely selfish, but really nice when you know her –

This summer has been far from truly disheartening. I thought right along I would be able to get away from here on the 19th or 20th but it looks impossible now – earliest date is the 22nd with the 24th more likely.

I met Dr. Knudsen from K.U. [University of Kansas] – he seems like an awfully nice person although I haven't had much of an opportunity to talk to him – there's also a Dr. Davis out here from Lawrence.

Hope the operation doesn't prevent you from going to Michigan [Boyne City and Lake Walloon]– drop me a line if you get a chance –

Love

Bud.

On September 25, 1938, Bud was back in New York City at medical school. He wrote:

Em darling –

Pardon the pencil and the letter in lieu of a wire but I expect to be broke by Tuesday so this is the best I can offer –

Happy Birthday, little Mother – hope you're all well by the time it [Emily's birthday] arrives –

I'll write you at length when events have filled up sufficiently to make one interesting –

Loads of love to you and Ted

Bud.

P.S. I thought of this myself

On November 23, 1938, Bud in New York City wrote to Emily and Ted in Kansas City:

Hello –

Hope all goes well with the O'Leary's – I'm working like the devil – anybody who gets to be a Doctor ought to be put on a pension for getting there to my way of thinking –

Happy Thanksgiving!

Love

Bud

On January 9, 1939, twenty-three-year-old Bud wrote Emily and Ted a detailed letter about the cruise to Bermuda he took with Abraham and Estelle, who astonished him by encouraging him to marry. Earlier they had cautioned him against marrying before he completed medical school. He wrote:

Dear Em and Ted –

A belated Xmas and New Years Greetings! I know I'm well in the dog house about this time but things have been happening so fast the past couple of months I'm still baffled – in the first place I've been working unbelievably hard and I haven't been too well – seems that I caught a cold Thanksgiving which stayed with me almost to Christmas and with many exams on dish I found myself full to the brim with dope – net loss of 15 pounds. Then vacation and I was so glad to get out of this damn town and away from the books for awhile I didn't think of anything –

I'm quite sure I'll forget to wish Dennis a happy birthday so here it is – hope he's quite fit – the folks tell me he borders on the sensational –

Incidentally they [Abraham and Estelle] got away all right – Dad was bored to death with N.Y. but seemed rather amused by it all – Mother was buying out all the stores while feigning perfect sales resistance at all times – I only saw them in the evenings – so they probably wrote we saw *Abe Lincoln in Illinois, Rocket to the Moon, Hellzapoppin* and *Oscar Wilde*. I liked the first three quite well although *Rocket to the Moon* collapses after the 1st act. *Oscar Wilde* was wonderfully done by this gent [Robert] Morley but seemed to get a bit more than little draggy – *Abe Lincoln* was very fine – *Hellzapoppin* was pure slapstick but very funny –

I called Marjorie tonight to invite myself to dinner but no one was home. Mother got in touch with them before she left –

My latest ailment which I neglected to mention is a bad neck obtained by hitting the side of the pool on the boat [to Bermuda] while in swimming (and sober) – it's giving me a little trouble but it's getting better now – managed to get a few more x-rays tho –

Bermuda was very nice but a bit too communal for my plebian tastes – the weather was mild but no sun. The crowd was mostly older people. I met quite a few Englishers during the golf tournament and enjoyed them immensely – they had quite a struggle understanding my language – in the final match we had a rather large gallery, mostly all English and they treated me fine – they use adjectives I thought existed only in books – This chap I played was the local schoolmaster newly arrived from England – very superior sort but nice – I, far less than any one else, was able to explain what happened to me in that tournament. I expected to fall apart at any minute but continued to have the most phenomenal luck right up to the end. I think I was 3 or 4 under par when he beat me – Mother and Dad were a picnic New Year's Eve – I got about 4 drinks down the Doc [Abraham] and he was dancing like a dervish. They were doing square dances and everything else – never saw them have more fun. I got quite drunk before the evening was over and despite that handicap had a fine time – you know I didn't have a drink of hard liquor from the time school started till I got on the boat – and I'm back on the beer wagon now –

I bought two suits and a dinner jacket in Bermuda – all very fine – total cost of the three was about $90. Dad bought a polo coat which I think is very good looking – They also bought lots of sweaters and things. Dad had his eye on a Vicuna coat and nearly broke his heart when he found they couldn't get one that fitted him properly –

I don't know whether the folks told you but the marriage bans are down or up or whatever you call it – out of clear sky on the boat they both agreed or rather suggested that it would be all right with them if I were to get married before I finish school – and me without a sign of a girl or any prospects of nabbing one – developments should be interesting, tho –

Nothing much more of news except that I escaped when the axe fell Saturday – warnings were sent out at that time to those students who were low in their work – if my luck holds out I may last another year after all –

Incidentally you should see Lawrence [Sophian] now – he's really completely changed and a very swell guy – he's coming out to visit the folks without beehive. Dad is very, very fond of him as is Mother –

Please excuse me for not writing before but I'm really on a merry-go-round and never seem to do anything except go to movies and study

Love

Bud.

In January 1939, Bud moved to a new apartment located at 208 East 69th Street, New York City, which was even closer to school. He wrote to Emily and Ted the following quick note as school resumed:

Dear Em and Ted –

Just a note to assure you that your letter arrived in good shape and that I enjoyed it –

Am inclosing a couple of articles which appeared the other nite on the sport page of the *World Telegram* – thought Ted might get a kick out of them if he hadn't seen them before –

Am still desperately wrestling with the three B's (books, bodies and boredom) – my health is quite satisfactory and hope you all are the same –

L.

Bud.

Bud wrote Emily another note on January 28, 1939:

Dear Em –
Sorry to keep you waiting on these but I've been quite busy – tell
the family I did quite well on my Pathology exam –
I'll write sometime soon –
Love Bud

On February 19, 1939, Bud wrote to Emily:

Dear Em –
Sorry to hear you've been ill and hope all goes well by now – I
may be home in a few weeks for spring vacation – hope so,
anyway –

I seem to be making out fairly well at school – nothing
sensational but they haven't complained about anything all year
[his second year of four years of medical school] so I'm keeping
my fingers crossed –

If there's anything I can get you here let me know 'n if I can
I'll be tickled to help you out –

Pardon the brevity but this is my big study night and I shall
have much to do –
Love to Ted and the baby –
Bud.

Upon returning to New York City from Kansas City for spring
vacation, Bud wrote to Emily on April 12, 1939, the following:

Dear Em –
Am much indebted to you for your delightful letter – I really
was more than a little worried over what I might have done as
regards the antics you mention before my departure. I'm quite
sure you're taking advantage of the cloud that had gathered

around me at that time to allow your imagination to run away with you –

I talked to Norman today and he said Marjorie had written you so I guess that is all cleared up. I'm sorry to have waited so long but I tried several times during the day to call him and he was never in –

All goes well enough with me – the work isn't terribly hard but there's an awful lot of it – I find myself whipped when evening comes around –

Saw *The Gentle People* this afternoon and enjoyed it very much – it's very well done – Franchot Tone [actor] plays a part that is absolutely the farthest thing in the world from the way we have grown used to him in the movies – does a good job, too – I thought Sylvia Sydney [actress] only mediocre but Sam Jaffe [actor] was splendid.

By the way I have it on good authority that the Cardinals are just about "in" so better tell Ted – what's more the Dodgers are going to be the big surprise this year if they hold together –

And so to the books –

Much love to you all

Bud.

Bud sent a note to Emily on May 1, 1939, while listening to Leah Ray on his radio. For the return address, he wrote "A. Sophian" instead of Bud Sophian.

Dear Em –

Just a note as it's rather late and I'm tired –

Thanks for the good wishes – the celebration [his birthday was on April 28] at this end of the line didn't take place, as it seems I'm quite busy –

Leah Ray just went back on the air – I talked to her Mother a few weeks ago while she was here –

Am inclosing the documents which I have properly endorsed, I hope – About the baseball situation I'm reaching way down and ranking the Cards and the Red Sox – one never knows –

Love to everyone

Bud.

On July 1, 1939, Bud was vacationing in the family's summer place at Lake Walloon in Michigan. Emily was in Kansas City. Bud wrote to her:

Dear Em –

Have meant to write for some time but that's the old story –

We arrived in fairly good shape about noon or one o'clock after a leisurely trip up from Muskegon. I drove very slowly with my customary caution – the place looks fine – all clean and pretty – it's a little chilly today, however –

I was awfully sorry to hear that you haven't been too well – hope all is right by now – as a matter of fact my body too has been torn with pain the last week or so – somehow or other some cold bugs sneaked in and raised the devil – However, I am nearly well – Mother isn't feeling very well so the doctors, your father and brother, put her to bed –

You will be amused to hear that our very good friends the Alexanders are here – I saw them in town –

We have decided to close in part of the porch (next to the dining porch) – it seems that there will be quite an overflow here – I have invited my fiancé up here so that you might have an opportunity of seeing her – seriously. I have invited a girl up, tho – a real southerner from Mississippi with whom I spent considerable time while in Madison [Wisconsin; medical school externship?] – She's not at all pretty and definitely gawky – can't quite figure out what I see in her except that she's really very nice – I can't even figure out whether I'm very fond of her or not. She's plain as can be but lots of fun – sounds bad doesn't it – don't think so though –

I had lots of fun in Madison – did some work too –

About now I'm extremely hungry and so goodbye – give my love to Ted and the wee one –

Lots of love

Bud.

In the fall of 1939, Bud began his third year of medical school, which consisted of clinical clerkships in the hospital. On September 22, 1939, he wrote to Emily from yet a new address at 225 East 68th Street, New York City, as follows:

Dear Em –

It suddenly dawned on me that one of those 28's [Emily and Bud were both born on the twenty-eighth of the month; Emily in September and Bud in April] is pretty near at hand – I know that if I wait till the opportune moment I shall forget the event completely so shall send you birthday greetings while I am still sane –

They've pulled a horrible trick on us, revised the 3rd year schedule and we are now taking 15 separate courses – it's really pretty awful – 8 hours of lecture daily with an impossible amount of outside reading –

Happy birthday to you and many more of them – regards to Ted and the wee one –

Love

Bud.

On December 5, 1939, Bud again wrote to Emily. He wrote his name in the return address as "A. S. Jr." [Abraham Sophian, Jr.]:

Dear Em –

Just a note as I'm awfully pressed for time. Hope all goes well with you and Ted and the baby – I've been pretty busy all fall, although I sometimes wonder how much I'm learning and how much I actually know –

I'd sure appreciate it if you'd get me a ticket for that New Year's day game in Miami – Mother told me to write you for it if I planned to go – I'll pay you for it – I may not get to go but in all probability I will –

Merry Xmas to you all –

Love

Bud

Months passed. On March 23, 1940, Bud sent the following long letter to Emily:

Dear Em –

While still dazed I am replying to your very recently received letter –

As a matter of fact I've been trying to get around to writing for some time but a strange inertia has had me all wrapped up for some time – I've been on obstetrical and pediatric service these past two months and can't say that I'm particularly interested in either of them – consequently I've been in a bit of a slump out of which I am just succeeding in emerging.

Your sports resume was a masterpiece of confusion – while you demonstrate commendable enthusiasm I can't quite say that your coverage threatens any of the more mediocre sports writers of the day. Incidentally I've heard from the coast that this U.S.C. [University of Southern California] outfit is awfully good so if Kansas [University of Kansas] manages to beat them I shall be ever so surprised. While on the subject of sports I've just about made my picks for the baseball season –

134

have the Yanks to repeat in a pretty close race with the Red Sox with the big surprise being the Athletics finishing in or very close to the first division – the National League should find Cincinnati in third place with both the Cardinals and Dodgers ahead of them – New York and Chicago to fight it out for fourth – However, right now the only sure thing is the cellar in each league which will probably have to be excavated to accommodate the new lows the Browns and Phillies will inevitably reach.

I called your friend Daphne Rolph and learned (through a most confusing accent) that she is still nursing but is also going to some school or other up at Columbia. Her address is 501 W. 113th St, N.Y.C. – When I get through an awful mess of exams next week I'm going to ask her out to dinner if she'll go out with me and if I have any money – incidentally that damn stuff is certainly hard to hang onto –

As regards Ted's bet with Bland I think you have the right idea – very little short of a miracle or a court summons would find Bland paging up if the slightest suggestion of a technicality presents itself. Incidentally I hope you are able to read my writing which is getting progressively more impossible.

Certainly I know Pat Murray – I forget whether it was Bryant [Elementary School in Kansas City, Missouri, Bud's first school] or Pembroke [Bud's second school] – He's a nice fellow as I remember him – your description of him was very fine –

My life has been a very dull one – been working very hard and doing no drinking whatsoever except about every 3–4 weeks when I take a Saturday night off and have a time – Marjorie called me up a month or so ago and I went down to her place to discover that she was stinking and wanted me to make drinks at a cocktail party – the party never materialized but I stayed around and had a few too many – Norman came up later and became intoxicated in pretty short order.

About three weeks ago I went to a party with a friend of mine to discover on arrival that it was a birthday party given by Arlen Judge Topping at "21" – It was an awful lot of fun – after it was over I went to a skating party at the skating rink in Rockefeller Plaza given by a friend of mine from Andover [Phillips Academy], Tex Thompson – it was for Betty Grable [actress] and the rest of the cast of *DuBarry Was a Lady* – Tex is running around with Grable these days – it too was lots of fun – but those two outings give a pretty complete coverage of my parties since Xmas.

And now I'm off to the corner Greek's for another of his tasty dinners – give my best to Ted and Dennis –

Much love

Bud.

By June 5, 1940, Bud had completed his third year of medical school. On that date, he wrote to Emily:

Dear Em –

Sorry to hear you haven't been well – hope all goes well now.

I'm all through now and tremendously relieved – last week was the worst strain I've ever been under – the exams weren't particularly hard but there were so darn many of them and they were all awfully long – I got my clearance papers yesterday which were plenty welcome – nothing but a complete collapse can throw me out now –

I've got a job now over at the Cancer Institute which is pretty interesting but takes up all my time – it's particularly bad just now since it's so damn hot.

I've only seen 3 ball games all spring – saw the Yanks play Cleveland and the Browns and the Giants play the Dodgers – Cleveland looks pretty good but I don't think any one is going to beat the Yanks. Those damn Dodgers are the saddest collection of bums I've ever seen but they're certainly winning ball games – They're hustling like hell and are getting lots of breaks – they may hold on and finish well up there but my hunch is that they'll be lucky to finish fourth – I'm still at a loss to figure out those Cardinals – I think they're suffering from acute Blades disease [Ray Blades was the Cardinals' manager from 1939–1940].

Haven't seen Marjorie or Norman in some time – may get a chance to see them in the next few weeks –

I'm planning on seeing [Bob] Feller pitch Friday if I can get away from the hospital in time –

Give my best to every one –

Much love

Bud.

During Bud's third year of medical school (1939–1940), Adolph Hitler sent German troops into Poland, and France declared war on Germany (September 1, 1939). On May 10, 1940, Germany launched an offensive characterized as "lightning war," or *blitzkrieg* against the Low Countries (Belgium, Holland, and parts of northern France). Hitler grasped the tactical possibilities of using paratrooper and glider-born infantry. His Wermacht (Germany's armed forces) invaded France using German paratroopers with great success. Germany's one hundred and thirty-six divisions defeated the one hundred and thirty-seven divisions of four nations and repelled the British Expeditionary Force back across the English Channel from the beaches of Dunkirk (Battle of Dunkirk, May 24 to June 4, 1940).

On June 14, 1940, the troops of the Third Reich marched into Paris. On June 22, 1940, France's leader Marshal Philippe Pétain (1856–1951) signed an armistice with Germany. Then, as Bud toiled in his fourth and final year of medical school, the French government led by Petain removed to Vichy from which it instituted an authoritarian regime.

On October 30, 1940, the Vichy government recommended collaboration with the German occupier, which meant cooperating with the Germans in raids to identify and imprison all French Jews and other "undesirables" who were living in the French zone occupied by Germany (French Occupied Zone). The French government deported these unfortunate people from France on trains to concentration camps "in the east" where many of them perished. Few, if any, Jews were living in France when Bud dropped from his plane into Normandy on D-day.

As Germany was overrunning France, the US Congress was passing a federal conscription law that required Bud Sophian, Ted O'Leary, and fourteen million other American men "between the age of 21 and 35 years, inclusive, irrespective of physical condition, dependents, or other matters" to register for the draft at their local draft boards on October 16, 1940.[55] The United States did not officially enter the war until the bombing of Pearl Harbor on December 7, 1941, more than a year later. Nevertheless, US President Franklin D. Roosevelt (1882–1945) explained to Americans on draft registration day on October 16, 1940, that:

> [C]almly, without fear and without hysteria, but with clear determination, we are building guns and planes and tanks and ships—and all the other tools which modern defense requires. We are mobilizing our citizenship, for we are calling our men and women and property and money to join in making our defense effective. Today's registration for training and service is the keystone in the arch of national defense.[55]

Three months after Bud and Ted registered for the military draft, Emily gave birth to her second son on January 23, 1941. She and Ted named him Theodore Morgan O'Leary, Jr. Bud was on the homestretch of medical school when on February 4, 1941, he wrote to Emily:

Dear Em –
Meant to write you sooner but I've been pretty busy –

I'm very proud of the top producer of the Sophian family and I'm ever so glad that you and young Ted are both fine –

Nothing much new happening back here – I manage to stay pretty busy most of the time – my spare time I've been putting in looking for a girl friend – I'm still looking – believe it or no I'm almost all through drinking – my stomach's gone pretty bad on me and so with the exception of over Xmas I haven't had anything but beer in an awfully long time –

Been reading quite a bit lately – read *Not Peace but a Sword* [Vincent Sheean, 1939, describes Hitler's earliest concentration camp buildup for incarceration of Jews and other "undesirables"], *Inside Asia* [John Gunther, 1939], *For Whom the Bells Toll* [Ernest Hemingway, 1940], *My Name is Aram* [William Saroyan, 1940] and *Sapphira and the Slave Girl* [Willa Cather, 1939] – pretty good for me, don't you think –

Barring something pretty awful I'll get commenced on June 11 [1941] and plan to come home as soon as I sober up – then I take state board exams [in Kansas] and I'm off for a two year term in Cleveland [at Mount Sinai Hospital] – after that I'm liable to go to work –

Am very anxious to see your new home – the folks tell me it's quite something – [green-shuttered Tudor-style house in Fairway, Kansas] –

Hope you didn't take the shellacking Stanford gave Nebraska too hard – just another example of West Coast superiority – Herbie Hoover [former President Herbert Hoover] and I listened to the game with satisfaction –

Drop me a note when you get a chance – give my best to Ted and Dennis –

Much love

Bud –

I talked to Norman the other day – I plan to go down there for dinner some nite soon.

The next time Bud wrote to his sister (March 15, 1941), he had moved again, this time to 219 East 68th Street, New York City:

Dear Em –

Hoping you'll pardon my curiosity but I would certainly appreciate your writing real soon and letting me in on what I did and didn't do the other nite – I remember quite well up to trying to convince Diana she should have a baby but beyond that I fear I remember very little – please let me know if I did anything bad so I may apologize if necessary and also just how mad the family is –

I'm quite recovered now and hard at work but I had a pretty rough time day before yesterday – Don't quite know who put the lights out for me but I think you contributed with that scotch at the Hagels, now that I think back – or maybe I'm just way out of training – just at present I'm so reformed I won't even drink beer –

Love
Bud.

Two days after sending the letter above, Bud dropped a bombshell in a letter to Emily dated March 17, 1941—he had found someone he wanted to marry.

Dear Em.

Just have a minute so this will be very brief – hold on to your hat – believe it or not I've got a girl with whom I seem to be in love – she's really rather nice and I'm sure you'd like her (quite a bit different from Natalie or my Mississippi friend) – as a matter of fact I'm thinking very seriously of marrying her – it's nothing too imminent but here's what I want you to do – first say absolutely nothing to the family about this letter – I know I can trust you – secondly, in a

140

roundabout way try to find out how the family would react to my marrying a gentile [a non-Jew] – whether they'd mind personally or whether they'd think me very foolish – she's a catholic [Roman Catholic] but doesn't care anything about it – please don't tell the family as nothing may come out of it and there's nothing to get excited about. I'll let you know before I do anything – please drop me a line about this when you get a chance –

I'm sending this [the letter] to the *Star* [*Kansas City Star* where Ted O'Leary worked] 'cause I don't know your home address [Emily and Ted had moved into their new home in Fairway, Kansas] –

Wish you'd come east for my graduation – it'd only be a few days and we'd have a lot of fun –

Give my love to your family –

Love

Bud.

Two weeks later on March 31, 1941, Bud wrote Emily and Ted the following:

Dear Em and Ted –

Thanks an awful lot for your letters – I appreciated them more than I can say – I wrote Mother last Sunday [March 24, 1941] and told her I was going to get married – she wrote me right back saying that Dad had developed high blood pressure and was practically going to retire – that they were selling the house, the farm etc., and that in view of all this I should not get married and add further expense – all of this makes me feel like a dog but I'm going to get married anyway – Keckie [nickname of his fiancée] is going to keep right on working so we'll have very little added expense – we're getting married April 26th [1941] at the Little Church around the Corner [Episcopal Church at One East 29th Street, New York City] –

Please use your influence with the family and try to make them realize that I wouldn't do anything to hurt either of them for the world and that this isn't a sudden decision by a long shot – I'm in terrible rush –
Much love to all the family
Bud.

On April 7, 1941, Keckie wrote a letter to Estelle Sophian (the letter is addressed to "Mrs. A. Sophian Sr."; Bud was using the name A. Sophian Jr.). The return address on the letter was 320 East 70th Street, New York City: Keckie said:

My dear Mrs. Sophian: –
This matter of becoming acquainted thru letters is most unsatisfactory but I do hope to meet you shortly and really know you.

Bud, I'm sure, has told you all about our plans and reported to me that your reaction was much the same as my family's. But please don't judge us to harshly because we aren't waiting a longer period of time.

We went to my home in Philadelphia yesterday and stayed over night. Mother and Daddy were quite pleased and have recovered from their initial shock – it really was a short notice. Mother, of course felt I should be married from home with all the attending splendor but we felt a quiet ceremony here in New York would be more satisfactory. We chose the church mutual friends were married in early in December, The Church of the Ascension [Episcopal] at Fifth Avenue and tenth street. It seems to attach a little more importance and solemnity to the event to have it take place in a church rather than before a Justice of the Peace [Emily and Ted were married by a Justice of the Peace, Leah Ray and Mr. Werblin were married by a municipal court justice]. And the date was decided by the fact that your anniversary is the twenty-sixth of this month also [Abraham and Estelle were married on April 26, 1911].

Mother would appreciate it if you would send a list, or at least a tentative estimate of the announcements you would like mailed in order that she may attend to them as soon as possible. We are inviting only our closest friends, about twenty I think, almost have invitations made up.

We realize that the medical profession [referring to Bud's father] doesn't allow for unplanned vacations, nevertheless we are hoping against hope that you both will be able to be with us.

Believe me, we are not entering into this as hastily as it may appear, and if I were not able to support myself I would never have considered undertaking these next two years together [during Bud's anticipated two-year hospital residency]. Again, I am anticipating knowing you and hope that you find me an adequate daughter-in-law and wife.

Sincerely

Dorothy Murphy Keck.

The next day, April 8, 1941, Bud dashed off another letter to Emily and Ted, care of the *Kansas City Star* in which he wrote:

Dear Em and Ted –

This is just going to be about 10 words since it's very late and I'm dead tired – I've been meaning to write and thank you for everything but just haven't had time –

I'm sure the family has kept you up on the progress of our revolution – I hope they understand and will come to the wedding – I know you realize that the only reason I haven't said anything to you about coming is because of your previous statement that you couldn't possibly get away.

Much love

Bud

P.S. How did the handball tournament come out [Ted played handball]? I like the Reds in the National and the Yanks in the American – don't see how the latter can miss –

Another month had passed when Bud lobbed another note to Emily on May 5, 1941, as follows:

Dear Em –

Just a note as I'm awfully pressed for time –

Please for God's sake talk the family out of this idea of theirs of having a joint ceremony [rabbi and priest] – if they insist it will mean that the whole thing is off [Dorothy Keck would terminate the engagement] – the whole idea is not very sensible at best as the only people who will be offended by the present plans will be offended no matter who marries us just because I'm marrying a gentile –

Please try your best to help us out – I don't think that they're being at all fair now – it just looks like they don't want me to marry Keckie and are trying to make obstacles for us –

I'll write you in greater length later –

Loads of love

Bud

On May 27, 1941, Emily received a very long Special Delivery letter from Miss Keck, as follows:

My dear Emily: —

Your letter was very sweet and I realize my response is long overdue but you must realize how many things there are for me to do these days. Every spare moment is spent writing thank-you notes. I cleared last week's up tonight and tomorrow night my two roommates are giving another shower in my honor and I'll start all over again. Of course, that is supposed to be a secret but I'll be surprised in the proper fashion when the time comes.

I returned the blanket [for Emily's new baby Ted, Jr.] Monday and the manager said she would look up the purchase and determine the price and let me know the details. They haven't the same article in stock at present thus the delay. I do wish I could have chosen a suit right then. They had all the knitted wear reduced and there was a simply adorable angora suit valued at fifteen dollars and selling for seven. It was a one year size but I told Bud it was sweet and by the time you get it the baby will have grown that much.

Mother and Daddy had a cocktail party in our honor last Sunday and we had a marvelous time. Everyone was there — some of our friends from New York, all my step-relations and millions of people I had never met before and will probably never see again. Of course, all of my actual relatives live in New England so it was impossible for them to be there. A few are coming for the wedding and that is more than I expected.

Our plans are going quite smoothly now. Everything is taken out of my hands and mother is going simply mad buying clothes, making lists and writing me enumerable letters, full of impossible questions. The whole affair has assumed enormous proportions which is just what I wished to avoid but it only happens once and Daddy wants everything to be right. He really is good to me.

Bud has told me that you plan to come in with your mother for the wedding and I would be terribly pleased, and Bud would be too, if you would be in the wedding party, Matron of honor in other words. It will be very small, my younger sister is to be a bridesmaid and is simply agog. I have chosen rather plain and quite inexpensive dresses and flowers for their hair. If you feel you would like to and I do wish you would I'll send a dress out to you and you can have it fitted or altered to your taste. I have no idea how large you are but the dress can be obtained in sizes from twelve to eighteen. My dress is to be ivory embroidered organdy, also very plain.

All the arrangements are made at the chapel [the venue had been changed to Washington Memorial Chapel, Valley Forge, Pennsylvania (Episcopal) and the date changed to June 28, 1941] and it would require special legal arrangements to have a rabbi assist so I do hope your Dad [Dr. Abraham Sophian] is not adamant about the matter. You probably realize that my being married in a Protestant Church [Episcopal] alienates me from my affiliations [Roman Catholic] but I can't feel that is so awfully important under the circumstances. At any rate, we are adopting the attitude that the less said about the religious angle the better and anything is better as far as I'm concerned than the legal ceremony [Justice of the Peace or rabbi plus a priest] suggested.

Perhaps you could tell me what type of activity and weather to come prepared for [to Kansas City for a visit prior to the wedding]. I have always spent my summers in Maine or on the Jersey coast and the last time I was west I was much too young to recall. All the aid anyone will give me is that it is quite warm, but then so is New York. Bud is better or no help along these lines. He tells me you ride [a horse] and I hope we will be able to do lots of that together when I come to Kansas City permanently.

Now I'm doing just as my mother does and asking lots of questions, but it would help me to travel a little lighter if I

146

know what to expect. I am anxious to meet you all, your boys sound elegant. I think of you quite often because I do pediatric nursing almost exclusively and my current charge is a four-year-old boy.

Thank you again for writing and I shall be anticipating my trip to your home.

Affectionately yours

Dotty Keck.

Who was Dorothy Murphy Keck? She was born in Portland, Maine, on February 13, 1918, as Dorothea Annie Murphy (the name recorded on her birth certificate). She later adopted and used the name Dorothy Anne Murphy.

Dorothy's mother was Genevieve Madden Murphy, who was born on August 15, 1894, in New York City. Genevieve's parents were immigrants from England. Dorothy's biological father was Thomas Ambrose Murphy, who was born on January 2, 1889, in Portland, Maine. When Dorothy was two years old, her father stated his occupation as "garage man." Dorothy and her parents lived in a rental property at 68 Congress Street adjacent to Thomas's father Edward W. Murphy.

Edward W. Murphy was born in Canada in 1859. He and his brother Thomas J. Murphy (as distinguished from Thomas Ambrose Murphy, Dorothy's father) owned a drug store where they sold Murphy's Balsam, Murphy's Root and Herb Bitters, and Murphy's Famous Fly Paper. Dorothy's father later worked as a traveling salesman for the family-run drugstore. Edward W. Murphy served in the Maine legislature as a state representative from Portland (1911–1912) and as a state senator (1913–1914, 1915–1916).

Thomas Ambrose Murphy died in 1926 when Dorothy was eight years old. Thirty-three-year-old Genevieve then married thirty-two-year-old Eugene Sylvester Keck, Jr. (his first marriage) one year later in 1927. Shortly after the remarriage of her mother, Dorothy assumed the last name of her stepfather and became known as Dorothy Murphy

Keck. However, her stepfather never carried out formal adoption proceedings.

Eugene Sylvester Keck, Jr. was born on April 26, 1895, in Philadelphia to Eugene Keck, Sr., who was a carpenter. Dorothy's stepfather was working as an insurance representative in the auto industry in 1930. He and Genevieve had one biological daughter together whom they named Virginia ("Ginger") Keck.

In 1930, Eugene S. Keck, Jr. owned a home at 555 Abbottsford Avenue, Philadelphia, about five miles north of Independence Hall in Philadelphia and one half of a mile from the Wayne Junction train station and a steel mill. His younger brother John G. Keck, who lived next door at 557 Abbottsford Avenue, owned a real estate business. By 1942, the Eugene Keck family had moved to a larger home at 714 Roberts Avenue, Drexel Hill, Pennsylvania, about nine miles southwest of their first address.

Dorothy Murphy Keck earned a three-year nursing diploma from the New York Hospital School of Nursing in 1940, according to her obituary on November 25, 1990 (newspaper name withheld). The educational requirement for admission to the New York Hospital School of Nursing was four years of high school at the time that Dorothy applied.[56]

The engagement announcement for Dorothy Keck and Bud Sophian published in the *Chester Times* (Pennsylvania) on May 26, 1941, one month before the wedding, read:

> Mr. and Mrs. Eugene S. Keck of Drexel Hill, announce the engagement of their daughter, Miss Dorothy Murphy Keck, and Dr. Abraham Sophian, Jr., son of Dr. and Mrs. Abraham Sophian, of Kansas City, Mo. Miss Keck is a granddaughter of the late Senator Edward L. [*sic*] Murphy and Mrs. Murphy, of Portland, Me. Dr. Sophian is a graduate of Phillips Academy, Andover, Mass., Leland Stanford University, and the Cornell University Medical School.

As wedding preparations moved forward apace, President Roosevelt announced on May 27, 1941, "an unlimited national emergency confront[ing] the United States" that required "military, naval, air and civilian defenses be put on the basis of readiness to repel any and all acts or threats of aggression directed toward any part of the Western Hemisphere."[57] Twenty-six-year-old, soon-to-be-wed Dr. Abraham (Bud) Sophian, Jr., Ted O'Leary, and millions of other men who had registered for the draft in October 1940 now faced a certain draft call in July 1941.

On June 10, 1941, wedding invitations were issued from Drexel Hill, Pennsylvania. The wedding invitation read:

Mr. and Mrs. Eugene Sylvester Keck, Jr.

Request the honour of your presence

At the marriage of their daughter

Dorothy Murphy Keck

To

Dr. Abraham Sophian, Jr.

On Saturday, June twenty-eight

Nineteen hundred and forty-one

At four o'clock

Washington Memorial Chapel

Valley Forge, Pennsylvania

An enclosed card read: "Reception immediately following the ceremony—714 Roberts Avenue, Drexel Hill."

On Wednesday June 11, 1941, Abraham Sophian, Jr. proudly received his medical degree from Cornell University Medical College. His wedding to Miss Keck took place as planned two weeks and three days later on Saturday June 28, 1941, in Valley Forge, Pennsylvania. Emily and Estelle attended, but Ted and Dr. Abraham Sophian stayed home.

On June 26, 1941 (two days before the wedding), Ted wrote to Emily, care of Eugene S. Keck, Jr. at 714 Roberts Avenue, Drexel Hill, Pennsylvania, the following:

Dearest Em,

There is no news at all, since you have been gone less than twenty-four hours and nothing of any moment has happened. I hope you are feeling more cheerful about your trip and are excited rather than sad and gloomy. I am counting on your feeling better so get a feeling of pleasure whenever I think of my darling sweetie pie having a good time with H. [Harriet O'Leary, Paul O'Leary's wife; Paul was Ted's older brother)] and M. [Marjorie Bloch, Smith College friend] and actually getting to <u>New York</u> [Emily and her mother were planning to visit New York City after the wedding].

I'll write you again care of Marjorie.

Love and kisses

Theodore

Emily described the wedding in a letter to Ted that she penned in New York City on June 29, 1941 (the day after the wedding):

My Dearest Darling Sweetheart –

Excitement, panic, a dash of spirits and general confusion carried us through our stay in Philadelphia in pretty good shape. Today, though, the reaction has set in with a vengeance. I woke up on the verge of tears and felt I just couldn't go on another minute without seeing you. Had mother been willing I would have taken the train home instead of here [New York City]. I just can't stand much more of this. One good look at you would mean more to me than a jillion trips to New York with the Dodgers, Yanks, and all the whole routine here thrown in. You are a fine boy. I love you so much it doesn't make sense and it sounds vaguely immoral after six years [of marriage]. However, as Harriet and I told everyone who would or would not listen yesterday [at the wedding], there is no one in the world like the O'Leary men – especially you and Paul [O'Leary].

The wedding really was very nice. Our Dotty was a beautiful bride with a long train, a sweet smile and a bad case of the jitters. Bud looked well in his cutaway and lovable hangover. He got mixed up during the ceremony and said, "I will" much too soon but the minister was unruffled and never stopped talking.

I behaved reasonably well and looked appallingly young. My nerves were so bad, though, that when I got half way down the aisle my [word?] gave way and I would have fallen if the other bridesmaid hadn't held me up.

I got mad too during the ceremony. When the minister said, "Do you take this woman etc." and ended up with "in the name of the Father, the Son, and the Holy Ghost" and Bud repeated it, I felt like woopsing. It's just as well Dad wasn't there.

When it was all over we shook hands with people outside the chapel then went back to Keck's for the reception where we shook hands some more and drank a lot of spiked punch, ate a bridal dinner, drank some sparkling burgundy, then more punch. Mother created quite a sensation in her white dress and live gardenia hat. I was tremendously proud of her. Tell Dad that his wife stole the show because it's true – she did! Everyone kept saying what a shame it was that you and Dad couldn't be there and I felt worse and worse about it until I reached a stage when, as you anticipated, I wanted to call you up. Fortunately, since you had strictly forbidden it, my nerves failed me so I had to resort to Western Union which isn't nearly as satisfactory.

Marge and I took Harriet to the [train] station at ten. Then we had some food and went to bed. We were both tired but my Mother went on a party with the Keck's, the Mattiello's and that loathsome Franklin Murphy, until the wee hours of the morning.

Ginger Keck [Virginia, Dorothy's half sister] and her young cousin, incidentally, sent the bride and groom off in fine fashion with a big sign and tin cans on the back of the car. The children were delighted about it but Dotty and Bud looked a little panicked.

Mother and I left Philadelphia early this afternoon and just got to New York. Marge is driving back with her Mother later, probably around five. We're staying in quite a fancy suite [at the Navarro, 112 Central Park South] practically next door to the Bloch's and I immediately went over and got my letter from you from the doorman. It did me a tremendous amount of good – you do write such beautiful letters! – and that's why this is relatively cheerful. Had there been no word from you I would have been sunk.

In a little while we're going to have dinner with Bud and Dorothy, then probably go to theater. They're leaving around eight for Cleveland [where Bud planned to start his two-year hospital residency at Mount Sinai Hospital on or around July 1, 1942].

Tomorrow we shop – I'll try to get everything for you – and tomorrow night we're more or less involved with the Mattiello's who want us to eat with them. We're going to try to get out of it and go to theater instead. We'd like to see *Arsenic and Old Lace* tonight and *Pal Joey* tomorrow … Em

Physicians as a group were not exempt from military conscription as the United States prepared to enter the Second World War. Bud received a deferment from the army to complete a one-year internship at Mount Sinai Hospital in Cleveland, Ohio. The army ordinarily did not call out a physically qualified doctor until after he had completed a one-year internship following successful graduation from an approved school of medicine. From the army's standpoint, the one year of post-medical-school training qualified a physician for army medical service as a general practitioner. Physicians eligible for appointments in the Medical Corps Reserve automatically received commissions in the Officers Reserve Corps for duty as medical officers. They did not train as enlisted men.[58]

The Young Ladies' Hebrew Association founded Mount Sinai Hospital in Cleveland in 1892. It became a teaching hospital in the 1940s and permanently shut down in February 2000. In March 2001, Case Western Reserve University purchased its vacant buildings.[59] Information about its long service remains sketchy, as its records have become unavailable since its closure.

Little information is available about Bud's professional and personal life during the year he spent at Mount Sinai Hospital in Cleveland (1941–1942). One document that has survived indicates he received a license (No. 12564), issued on January 6, 1942, after examination by the Ohio State Medical Board, to practice medicine and surgery in that state, which reads as follows:

> This certifies that Abraham Sophian, Jr. of the County of Cuyahoga, State of Ohio having presented to the Ohio State Medical Board satisfactory evidence that he received the degree of M.D. from Cornell University located in the City of New York State of New York on the 11th day of June A.D. 1941 is hereby authorized to practice Medicine and Surgery in the State of Ohio in accordance with and subject to the provisions of "An Act to Regulate the Practice of Medicine in the State of Ohio" – Given under the hands and seal of the Ohio State Medical Board at the City of Columbus this sixth day of January A.D. 1942.

A second surviving document shows that Bud received a license (No. 21935) to practice medicine and surgery issued on April 17, 1942, by the State Board of Health of Missouri. It reads as follows:

> This certifies that The State Board of Health of Missouri has examined the Diploma issued by Cornell University Medical College; also license issued by State Board of Medical Examiners of the State of Ohio to Dr. Abraham Sophian, Jr. Proposed residence Kansas City Missouri, and has found him

to possess the requisite qualifications, and does hereby issue to him this license to practice medicine and surgery, in accordance with the provisions of the "Act to Regulate the Practice of Medicine, Surgery and Midwifery, and to prohibit treating the sick and afflicted without a license and to provide penalties of the violation thereof." Approved March 12, 1901, as amended; being now Articles 1 and 2. Chapter 53, Revised Statutes of Missouri, 1929. Given under the hands and Seal of The State Board of Health of Missouri, this 17th day of April in the year A.D. 1942.

The state of Missouri granted Bud a license through a reciprocity agreement between the Medical Examiners of Ohio State Medical Board and the Medical Examiners of the State Board of Health of Missouri. In other words, Missouri officials honored the findings of the Ohio officials who had issued a license to Dr. Bud Sophian three months earlier.

The next existing letter written by Bud to Emily after his marriage to Keckie carries the date December 28, 1942, about six months after his induction into the US Army and exactly eighteen months after his wedding.

Postcard of Cornell University Medical Center,
Manhattan, New York, 1940. *Sophian Archives.*

Bud Sophian, Cornell University Medical College, ca. 1940.
Sophian Archives.

Class of 1941, Cornell University Medical College.
Bud Sophian ("A. Sophian, Jr.) is in the second row from the bottom,
and is the second person from the right. *Sophian Archives.*

Dorothy Murphy Keck Sophian's wedding photo, June 28, 1941, Valley Forge, Pennsylvania. *Sophian Archives.*

85:—MOUNT SINAI HOSPITAL, CLEVELAND, OHIO.

Postcard of Mount Sinai Medical Center, Cleveland, Ohio.
Sophian Archives.

Chapter Six: Surgeon and Paratrooper Training, July 1942–December 1943

The Medical Department of the US Army began to train physicians to care for the country's servicemen in 1940–1941.[58] Senior army staff planners in 1940 estimated a need for 9,100 military physicians to care for the then 1,400,000 men in uniform. The regular army contributed 1,200 physicians, the National Guard 1,100 physicians, and the Medical Reserve Corps 1,500 physicians, which left a considerable gap of approximately 5,300 physicians. Dr. Bud Sophian and a large number of other young medical officers who had graduated from medical school in 1941, and who had spent one year in internships (1941–1942), formed a portion of these "gap" physicians. These young physicians generally lacked previous military experience.[58]

On August 17, 1942, Dr. Bud Sophian entered active military service as a first lieutenant in the 31st Medical Regiment of the US Army at Camp Barkeley near Abilene, Texas. Dorothy accompanied him to Abilene. The US Army first constituted the 31st Medical Regiment on October 1, 1933, but did not officially activate it until July 15, 1942 at Camp Barkeley; thus, Bud was assigned to the regiment about one month after its official activation. Fourteen months later in September 1943, the army reorganized and redesignated the 31st Medical Regiment as the 421st Collecting Company, which deployed to Europe in 1944 and participated in both the Rhineland and Central

Europe Campaigns.[60] However, Bud already had separated from the 31st Medical Regiment in the summer of 1943 to volunteer for the medical company attached to the US Army's 507th Parachute Infantry Regiment. As was the custom, he followed the command of the 507th Parachute Infantry Regiment from then on.

Major General Paul R. Hawley, the genial but strong-willed chief surgeon of the European Theater of Operation, established training objectives and standards of proficiency for the Second World War ground force medical units, while army and base section commanders supervised the conduct of instruction. Military medical historians Cosmas and Cowdrey explained:

> General Hawley laid down both military and professional training requirements. On the military side, medical units were to make sure that their people mastered basic service customs [e.g., saluting] and wore the correct uniform. Both male and female personnel were to engage in close-order drill, calisthenics, and cross-country marching. They were to learn to read maps, use compasses, and interpret aerial photographs, as well as how to protect their patients and themselves under air and gas attack. Hospitals and collecting and clearing companies were to practice setting up, taking down, and moving their equipment. The chief surgeon [Hawley] directed that professional instruction of doctors and nurses concentrate on practical elements of war medicine and surgery. He opposed efforts to train people in specialties for which they had not been qualified before entering the Army, although he provided extensive refresher courses for doctors already proficient in various fields. Enlisted medics were to be well versed in basic anatomy and physiology, medical nomenclature, first aid, and ward management. Hawley also wanted them to be able to speak and write clear

English so as to make themselves understood to patients and doctors alike.[61]

On December 28, 1942, Bud Sophian wrote to Emily and Ted, who was a navy lieutenant stationed in Kansas City.

Dear Em and Ted –
Been meaning to write these several months but it's the same old story – no time to do anything – I've been working like hell ever since I got here and there isn't a sign of a letup – We have a Prussian [probably referring to Colonel Rudolph Bloom, MD] for a commanding officer and there's no pleasing him – Lord only knows what's going to happen from here out – I haven't any idea except that I'd like to get out of here and get somewhere where we can do something –

Had a letter from Don Edwards yesterday – he's an ensign in the navy stationed temporarily in San Francisco – he told me about a lot of our classmates who are almost all in the navy and end up somewhere in the Pacific – a number of them are in the [navy] air corps [recall the setting of *The Holy Terror* in 1937] – more than a few have been killed – one, a fraternity brother of mine who was a captain in the artillery on Bataan [province of the Philippines] is reported to be leading a group hiding out in the hills of the islands –

Thanks a lot for the spoon – it's very pretty – Hope to see you all soon – how did you like the National League's pennant race? – Give my love to every one – Happy New Year!
Love
Bud.

Two months after Bud wrote the above letter, the *Abilene Reporter News* (Abilene, Texas) ran a story on February 25, 1943, that mentioned Dorothy Sophian (Mrs. A. Sophian, Jr.), as follows:

Quiz Contest Held by 31st Officers' Wives

A quiz contest, called Stumping the Experts, was the highlight of a program arranged for a meeting of the 31st Medical Regiment officers' wives at the Second street USO club Wednesday afternoon. Nineteen members of the group were present.

Conducting the program was Mrs. Rudolph Bloom, wife of Colonel Bloom, commanding officer for the 31st Medical regiment. Mrs. Bloom has just returned from spending three months in the East – New York City, Philadelphia, Washington, D.C., Miami, Fla., New Orleans and San Antonio.

Winning the quiz contest were Mrs. George S. Allen, Mrs. Durwood J. Smith and Mrs. Charles S. Whitaker. Mrs. Allen was recognized as a historian, Mrs. Smith as a personnel psychologist branching into nutrition, and Mrs. Whitaker as an "angel of mercy," an expert on the old adages.

Hosting the officers' wives meeting were Mrs. A. Sophian Jr., Mrs. William Z. Eaton, Mrs. Thomas P. Wenzel and Mrs. H. Bangeri.

Dorothy became pregnant in February 1943.

A paratrooper medical officer with the rank of captain most likely appeared at one of Dr. Bud Sophian's military medicine classes at Camp Barkeley to inform him, other medical officers, and enlisted medics that the parachute troops were looking for volunteers. The recruitment by the US Army of physicians and medics to join the burgeoning paratrooper regiments was moving into high gear at the time, recalled one medical officer who joined the US Army's 508th Parachute Infantry Regiment.[62] The paratrooper captain invited all interested officers and enlisted medics to meet that night, where he explained the concept of parachute troops, shared jump paraphernalia, and showed a training film. The medical officer who joined the 508th Parachute Infantry Regiment noted, "About four hundred medics showed up that evening.

After the talk and viewing of the equipment, about three hundred were left. After the film, only twelve were present. Of these twelve, after physical exams," four were chosen to volunteer.[62]

Bud Sophian applied to the US Army's parachute training program ("jump school") at Fort Benning, Georgia, and the US Army accepted him for reasons difficult to understand today. He was married, his wife was pregnant, and both of these conditions theoretically should have invalidated his application.

Why did Bud choose to become a paratrooper on top of being a medical officer? First, as Bud noted in his December 28, 1942, letter to his sister, he wanted to "get out of" Camp Barkeley and "get somewhere where we can do something." Bud's sentiment was not unusual among young soldiers and sailors during the long and stressful American military build-up to the Normandy invasion on D-day, June 6, 1944.

Second, paratroopers comprised an elite combat force whose requirements for athleticism, physical conditioning, and a courageous temperament would have appealed to Bud (recall his riding two horses in the circus ring at camp in Maine). One observer described the extraordinary type of person required to become an effective parachute infantryman:

> For most men, merely jumping from an airplane with a parachute required unusual courage or daredeviltry. To jump from an airplane directly into enemy-held territory with none of the usual military backup such as tanks or artillery covering fire, no organized command headquarters or well-laid communications, no well-defined "front line" with flank protection and possible egress to the rear and no transportation whatsoever, required courage and resourcefulness of an extraordinarily high degree. To be sure, such men could be found in all armies, but if too many were siphoned off to staff elitist paratrooper units, that might dangerously sap the leadership and readiness of the units from which they were drawn.[63]

Another observer noted:

[I]t is impossible to appreciate the caliber of the fighting done by airborne troops without knowing the caliber of the leadership they were given by their battalion, company and platoon leaders. It is taken for granted in airborne troops that each trooper is a potential leader himself. Every trooper does carry a baton in his knapsack. But more than this, he needs and expects exemplary personal leadership from his immediate superiors.[63]

Third, some men joined the paratroopers because pay was higher to offset the increased risk of harm, including death, associated with serving in the paratrooper force. Bud was on his own financially after he married Dorothy. To what extent increased monthly pay may have appealed to Dorothy and Bud is unknown.

Bud was also a patriot. Values instilled at Phillips Academy and by his religion to help his country in its time of need influenced his decision to fight on the ground against the fascist regimes that had overrun much of Europe.

Lastly, Bud was an optimist. As a Jew, he knew he faced an increased risk of harm and even death if captured. At the same time, Bud believed that he would survive the battle and the war, and if he did not, his life was worth sacrificing to rid the world of tyrants such as Hitler and Mussolini.

The US and British militaries were latecomers among the Western powers to embrace infantry parachuting. The German military was first to implement the idea after observing Soviet Red Army paratrooping maneuvers in 1935. Historian Clay Blair observed:

Russian airborne warfare demonstrations made a strong impact on Hitler and the German General Staff. Hitler ordered Hermann Goring's *Luftwaffe* to organize airborne forces. The task was delegated to a *Luftwaffe* colonel, Kurt Student, who had been a decorated pilot in World War I and afterward a glider enthusiast. He formed and trained three types of German airborne forces: paratroopers, glider-borne infantry and air-transportable infantry.

When Hitler launched World War II, Student's airborne forces were in the vanguard. German paratroops first jumped into Norway to help seize that country. Employed in the May 1940 attacks on the Netherlands, paratroopers were particularly effective in seizing bridges over the Maas and Waal rivers in front of the advancing *blitzkrieg* previously noted. Similarly, in Belgium, a small force of paratroopers and glider-borne infantry was utilized to capture Fort Eben Emael, a key fortress on the King Albert Canal. Later in the year, when Hitler was poised to invade the British Isles, the British, believing German paratroopers and glider-borne infantry might spearhead the attack, were compelled to divert enormous energy and resources to a defense against this possible threat.[63]

The Germans assigned their paratroopers to the *Luftwaffe* (Germany's air force) rather than to the army infantry as did the United States. German paratroopers were the "strongest of the various types of infantry," wrote Dwight D. Eisenhower (1890–1969) in 1948. He continued:

These were carefully selected, well-trained and -equipped crack infantry divisions ... Because they had an authorized strength of 16,000 officers and men and a larger allotment of machine guns than the normal infantry divisions, the parachute troops were the best fitted of the German units for stout resistance on an extended and open front.[64]

One of the young Nazi *Luftwaffe* pilots was Werner Ostendorff, who would one day command his soldiers to murder Captain Sophian and troops under his command in Graignes, France.

The US Army finally launched its formal study of air infantry in early 1939 (recall that Hollywood had already released *The Holy Terror* depicting American naval paratroopers in 1937). US Army Chief of Staff General George C. Marshall (1880–1959) tasked Major General George A. Lynch (1880–1962) with performing the seminal air infantry study. General Lynch articulated clearly in his final report that:

> Air infantry had the following four practicable uses:
> * To deposit small combat groups within enemy territory for special specific missions where the possible accomplishments of the detachment warrant the risk of possible loss of the entire detachment [i.e., a suicide mission]. These missions may include demolitions to vital communications, factories, munitions, etc.
> * To deposit small raiding parties for special reconnaissance missions to gain vital information not otherwise obtainable.
> * To deposit small combat groups, possibly as large as a battalion or regiment with artillery, to hold a key point, area, or bridge-head until the slower moving elements of the army arrive.
> * To work in conjunction with a mechanized force at a considerable distance from the main body.[65]

Major Charles Johnson, Captain Bud Sophian's commanding officer in Graignes, Normandy, internalized these applications of paratrooping and applied them in Graignes, much to the consternation of some of the officers and men under his command.

Transport aircraft shortages placed the American air infantry concept on hold until December 1939 when a few planes became available for use by the Infantry Board at Fort Benning, Georgia. Early in January 1940, General Marshall accelerated development of the parachute infantry program by appointing as its leader Colonel William C. Lee, a "homely and lanky 'southern gentleman' with a heavy drawl and courtly manners," winked Blair.[66]

Soldiers of Fort Benning's 29th Infantry Regiment formed the newly-named Parachute Test Platoon. Each soldier had volunteered, served a minimum of two years in the army infantry, weighed no more than 185 pounds, was in excellent physical condition, and was unmarried. One directive issued to volunteers read:

Because of the high degree of risk associated with parachute jumping, all those volunteering must understand that duty with the Parachute Test Platoon is strictly voluntary. It will require frequent jumps from airplanes in flight at various altitudes, which may result in serious injury or death. Therefore, *only unmarried men may volunteer*" [emphasis added].[67]

By early October 1940, Major Lee had assembled the first American parachute group called the 501st Parachute Infantry Battalion, and by mid-January 1941, the bulk of the 501st Parachute Infantry Battalion was jump qualified. On July 1, 1941, the 502nd Parachute Infantry Battalion was activated at Fort Benning with "a skeleton detachment taken from the two companies of the 501st Battalion."[68] Colonel Lee then received orders to form the 503rd Parachute Infantry Battalion by August 1941. He did this successfully, albeit with "loud protestations of having virtually no men or equipment for it." He and his staff formed yet another unit by October 1941—the army's 504th Parachute Infantry Battalion.[69] Note that the United States had not formally entered the Second World War during the formation of these parachute infantry battalions.

The carnage produced by Imperial Japan's bombing of Pearl Harbor on December 7, 1941, launched the United States into the Second World War. The United States and the United Kingdom had become close partners by the time of the Pearl Harbor attack; however, they had not agreed on a plan to defeat Germany. On December 24, 1941, Great Britain's Prime Minister Winston Churchill (1874–1965) and US President Franklin Roosevelt met secretly in Washington, DC

(Arcadia Conference), where they agreed to many items, including a "Europe First" policy, which meant that "the first four American airborne operations of the war would be aimed at the liberation of Europe."[70] Senior staff at Fort Benning reorganized existing parachute infantry battalions into larger parachute infantry regiments and formed additional parachute infantry regiments.

The product of the rapid evolution of the US Army parachute infantry program was a set of six parachute infantry regiments numbered 501, 502, 505, 506, 507, and 508. The paratroopers making up these regiments fell like confetti over Normandy in Operation Overlord—code name for the Allied invasion of Western Europe—on D-day June 6, 1944. (Note that Neptune was the operational name for the Normandy invasion.) A seventh parachute infantry regiment, the 504th, fought in Sicily and Italy against Mussolini in the months before Operation Overlord. The 507th Parachute Infantry Regiment (Bud's regiment) replaced the 504th for execution of Operation Overlord because units of the 504th were still fighting in Italy and Sicily and were exhausted or depleted of men as the ramp up to Operation Overlord accelerated. At the time of Operation Overlord (Neptune), Parachute Infantry Regiments 505, 507 (Bud's regiment), and 508 were part of the US Army's 82nd Airborne Division, while Parachute Infantry Regiments 501, 502, and 506 belonged to the US Army's 101st Airborne Division.

The US Army activated the 507th Parachute Infantry Regiment on July 20, 1942, with Colonel George V. Millett, Jr. in command. Bud Sophian was just beginning his military training at Camp Barkeley at this time. After completing about one year's training as a military medical officer (July 1942–June 1943), Bud Sophian attended jump school at Fort Benning as a physician paratrooper assigned to the medical attachment of the 507th Parachute Infantry Regiment. When Bud moved to Fort Benning in the summer of 1943, his pregnant wife returned to Drexel Hill, Pennsylvania, to live with her mother and stepfather.

In the summer of 1943, Bud and the other paratrooper trainees proved their fitness and endurance during the first week of jump school

(A stage), performing physical exercise eight to nine hours each day. The training during this week was designed to "weed out weaklings, those lacking stamina and character," commented one trainee who continued:

> The weeding out process was in pushing us physically beyond what we were capable of. The sergeants running this stage were in superb physical condition—much better condition than any of the trainees. For one week they pushed us beyond our physical capability, primarily with long runs. You could pass out from fatigue. But, if you quit, you were washed out. Only about fifty percent of the class that started "A" Stage got their jump wings.[71]

During the second week (B stage), physical training continued, as instructors added ground training and showed trainees "how the parachute worked, how to exit the plane, how to control the chute in the air, and how to hit the ground without getting hurt." One trainee noted:

> We learned that we would be wearing a main chute on our back and a reserve chute on our chest. Our main chute would be pulled open automatically when we jumped. As we went out the door, we were to begin counting "one thousand and one, one thousand and two, one thousand and three." If we reached "one thousand and three" without our main chute opening, we were to open our reserve.
>
> The main chute opened like this: All planes rigged for parachute jumping had a steel cable running down the middle of the plane just above our heads. Our main chute, which was strapped to our back, had a 12-foot long web strap (called a static line) which was tied to the top of our main chute canopy with a strong string. The other end of the static line was attached to a snap hook that we could hook over the cable and as we moved to

the door to jump, we pulled the snap hook along the cable. When we jumped, the static line would pull tight, pull the cover off the main chute, and pull the chute canopy out of the pack. When the static line was fully extended, the string that tied the top of the canopy to the static line would break, leaving the static line hooked to the cable in the plane, and leave us floating free.

The men who jumped together, and who will follow each other out the door as fast as possible, were called a "stick." We needed to get the "stick" out of the plane at the rate of about two per second. The faster we got out of the plane, the closer we would be when we hit the ground, and the quicker we'd be ready to fight as a cohesive unit. Again and again, we practiced on a wooden mock-up plane getting the stick out of the door as fast as possible.[71]

At the beginning of B stage, trainees received their paratrooper boots, which they highly valued. The men immediately donned them, stood in a tub full of water, and walked the boots dry. "This was the quickest way to break them in and adapt them to our feet. After that, we shined them every day. We had worn the boots during jump training; but until we made our fifth qualifying jump we could not wear them out of the training area," declared one proud paratrooper trainee.[72]

The third week of training (C stage) in jump school continued physical training and ground training, added instruction on how to pack a parachute, and required jumps from 250-foot towers and thirty-four-foot towers. Every trooper learned to pack a parachute. "As incentive to pay attention and learn, we would have to jump with the parachutes we had packed. Believe, me, that's a real incentive," explained a trainee. The trainees were also harnessed into a chute, pulled up to the top of the tower, and released. This activity gave trainees "the experience of landing in a parachute, which is the most dangerous part of the jump," noted a trainee. "As we came down we had to turn our back to the wind, look at the horizon (never look at the ground), bend our knees, and as we land, do a right or left tumble to take up the shock of landing. We were told that the landing shock was equivalent to jumping from the second story of a house."[72]

During the fourth week of jump school (D stage), trainees made jumps from airplanes flying in the sky. One trainee said, "All of us were scared on that first jump. I had never even been in an airplane in my life, let alone jumped out of one. But, we jumped." He continued:

Monday morning of D Stage we were marched to the packing sheds to draw the chutes that we had so carefully packed the Friday before. We were then trucked to the airfield, where the C-47s were waiting. We were formed in sticks of twelve, and climbed aboard a plane—one stick per plane, and sat down on the bucket seats along each side of the plane. The plane circled for a while, then headed for the drop zone [DZ]. The instructor-jumpmaster took us through the jump sequence we had practiced so often.

"Stand up and hook up."

"Check your equipment."

"Sound off for equipment check."

"Stand in the door."

Finally, when we were over the DZ, the jumpmaster shouted to the first man, "Go" and out he went. As each man would come to the door the jumpmaster would shout, "Go," "Go," "Go," until we all had jumped. But that was the last time we jumped as individuals. Thereafter, when the first man jumped, the rest of the stick followed him as fast as possible—which was the way we would expect to jump in combat.[72]

Paratrooper trainees made five jumps from airplanes at Fort Benning, one jump each on Monday, Tuesday, Wednesday, Thursday, and Friday. Upon completing these jumps satisfactorily, they received their jump wings. They also earned the privilege of blousing their pant legs at the top of their boots in classic paratrooper style.[72]

Indeed, parachuting was a revolutionary form of war art. Military historian Martin K. A. Morgan described it as follows:

> The airborne vertical envelopment concept itself represented a revolutionary military doctrine at the very cutting edge of technology. Vertical envelopment made it possible to drop a large autonomous combat team behind enemy lines that could disrupt enemy operations and seize otherwise inaccessible objectives deep in enemy territory. With a reputation for being composed of the best of the best, America's airborne began attracting attention as it grew. Even before Pearl Harbor, the American public and the American media sat up and took notice of what was being developed at Fort Benning.[73]

In 1943, military historian and strategist Liddell Hart described parachuting in this way:

> The "rear attack" has always been the most demoralizing form of attack. But it has also been the most difficult to bring off, so long as military operations remained two-dimensional. The advent of airborne forces has endowed this stroke with new potentialities—and thereby given an incalculable extension to the horizon of land warfare.[73]

The medical attachments in the US Army Parachute Infantry Regiments 501, 502, 505, 506, 507, and 508 that participated in Operation Overlord were the first soldiers of the US Army Medical Department to set foot in Normandy, France.

In each airborne division (82nd and 101st), medical officers and medics dropped by parachute or rode in on gliders with their organizations. Each parachute infantry regiment contained nine medical officers and sixty enlisted medics, according to Cosmas and Cowdrey.[85] Theoretically, Captain Sophian was one of nine physicians (surgeons) assigned to the 507th Parachute Infantry Regiment. Cosmas and Cowdrey continued:

> Anticipating heavy drop losses and days of isolation behind enemy lines, unit medics landed with all the extra supplies and equipment they could collect—either carried on their persons, parachuted down in special containers, or packed in glider-borne vehicles. The 101st [Airborne] Division, for example, went into Normandy with two-hundred-and-fifty litters and two-thousand-five-hundred blankets above its regular allowance, twenty-five instead of the regulation seven aerial delivery containers per regiment, and two-thousand units of [blood] plasma. The 101st's field artillery battalion brought along two complete sets of aid station equipment. Each paratrooper carried two British-made individual dressings and a copper sulphate sponge for use on phosphorus burns. Much of this equipment—and many of the people carrying it—were lost, as paratroopers and gliders plunged into the hedgerow-lined fields and marshy river bottoms of the Cotentin [Peninsula] and as men in the early morning darkness began the tense, deadly hide-and-seek game of finding comrades, assembling units, and getting on with their missions.[74]

Three battalions comprised each parachute regiment. Captain Abraham Sophian, Jr. MC (Medical Corps) was officially one of two surgeons assigned to the 3rd Battalion of the 507th Parachute Infantry Regiment (composed of 2,004 soldiers) of the 82nd Airborne Division of the First Army.[75] When the 507th Parachute Infantry Regiment was pulled out of Normandy and sent back to southern England after thirty-five days of combat, it had lost approximately four hundred paratroopers killed in action, including Captain Sophian, i.e., about 20 percent of the total number of paratroopers in the 507th.[74-75]

A battalion surgeon at his aid station during the Second World War diagnosed, stabilized, and made the decision to evacuate wounded paratroopers further to the rear of the evacuation chain. The chain began on the battle frontline and extended all the way back to hospitals in England and the United States. Second World War medic Private Keith Winston explained the medical evacuation process:

You asked me to describe the exact function of the Aid Station. First let me tell you how evacuation works: A boy gets hurt on the line. Within a minute or less a telephone message is sent back to our forward Aid Station, a distance of three-hundred to one-thousand yards from the front where a Sergeant and four litter-bearers are always on hand. They rush right up to the line with a litter. During this time, the Company in which the casualty is a member, has their Aid-man administering first-aid on the spot—usually consisting of stopping the bleeding with Sulfanilamide powder, bandaging and giving wound pills internally. By that time, another litter team is there and carries the casualty to the nearest point where a jeep can travel—anywhere from twenty-five to three thousand yards, depending on conditions. The injured boy is then rushed to the Aid Station, one to three miles behind the line. Here the physician removes the first-aid bandage, makes a proper diagnosis and applies a more permanent bandage, administers blood plasma if needed, and in severe cases, gives morphine; makes the patient comfortable, warm, gives coffee, etc. Whereupon he's rushed back to a point known as Clearing Company, pretty far in the rear—this time by a comfortable ambulance which stands ready for action at the Aid Station's door. Now—here, if the wound requires it, he's given emergency operation or attention. This place is well-staffed and well-equipped. Then the casualty is taken by ambulance to an Evacuation hospital further back where first-class attention is administered. If the case is one whereby the wound or casualty is so severe and he won't get better very soon, he's shipped back even further to a General Hospital, and eventually back to the States. Reason for the continual moves? One of room. As the patient warrants a further move back, he leaves space for another boy, and needed room is of the essence. The Aid Station has no beds. Its job is the most important—to evacuate the wounded boy from place of incident to the rear, after essential treatment is administered to save his life. The well-equipped rear station [is where] the[y] bandage him with the skill that is possible only in a quiet hospital.[76]

The evacuation process described above was ill-suited to the circumstances in which paratrooper medical officers and medics found themselves in Normandy on D-day. Airborne medical personnel were as badly scattered in the night drop on June 6, 1944, as everyone else. Fifty percent of the medical officers in the 82nd Airborne Division (Bud's division) were "unaccounted for during the first seventy-two hours of combat; in one of the 101st battalions, which landed in swamps, only two members of a sixteen-man medical detachment initially rallied with the unit," stated Cosmas and Cowdrey.[74] This reality caused military planners to reassess the deployment of physician paratroopers behind enemy lines in the earliest drops. Experience taught that enlisted men trained to be medics could do much of the work at the battalion level previously assigned to surgeons such as Captain Sophian.

Before Captain Sophian joined the 507th Parachute Infantry Regiment in Fort Benning, it had conducted maneuvers across the Chattahoochee River in the Alabama Training Area near Uchee Creek.[77] On October 30, 1942, nine officers of the 507th trained for a water landing—a low number given the reality of the surprise water landing faced by many paratroopers, including Bud Sophian, on June 6, 1944. The 507th Parachute Infantry Regiment continued to train until March

1943, when it travelled to Barksdale Field near Shreveport, Louisiana, for twelve days of maneuvers with the Third Army, which it decisively defeated.

One paratrooper with the 507th Parachute Infantry Regiment remembered that in Shreveport, Louisiana, he began to realize that:

> We were a "maverick," or better yet, a bastard regiment (not assigned to a division). The 505th Regiment had filled out the 82nd Division. I can't explain how disappointed we were. We were battle-ready and now found we were headed for Nebraska to start more training. It caused a lot of troopers to go AWOL [absent without leave]. The stockade was full due to fights and other behavior problems. It seemed at the time our regiment was falling apart. On March 21, 1943, we traveled by rail to Alliance Air Base, near Alliance, Nebraska. The regiment was stationed there from March 23 until November 20, 1943. While we were there, we jumped for air shows, rodeos, blood donation campaigns etc. On July 3, 1943, 250 troopers were picked to jump in Denver, Colorado, for a blood donation campaign.[78]

Captain Sophian was with the 507th Parachute Infantry Regiment at Alliance Air Base, Nebraska. The US Army established the army air base at Alliance as a joint training center for paratroopers and troop carrier groups composed of the airmen who flew the planes that would transport Bud Sophian and thirteen-thousand other American paratroopers and glider infantry troops to Normandy on D-day.[79] For example, the 507th Parachute Infantry Regiment was teamed up with the 403rd and 434th Troop Carrier Groups to conduct joint training operations at Fort Alliance.

The troop carrier group pilots in Alliance flew Douglas C-47 aircraft produced by the Douglas Aircraft Company based in Long Beach, California. The rugged Douglas C-47 (also known as *Skytrain* and *Dakota*) was a military transport aircraft developed from the twin-engine Douglas DC-3 airliner (DC stands for "Douglas Commercial") that entered service in 1931. A cargo door and strengthened floor distinguished the Douglas C-47 from the civilian DC-3. Blair wrote:

> The maximum payload of a C-47 was a mere six thousand pounds. Manned by a pilot, copilot, navigator and crew chief, the C-47 could carry only eighteen paratroopers or regular infantry with equipment. The paratroopers had to leap from a single side door in the left rear fuselage. To transport or drop one regular battalion of infantry required about fifty C-47s; a regiment would fill about a hundred fifty [C-47s]. Very large-scale operations would require hundreds or even thousands of aircraft. Even if such numbers of aircraft could be produced and made available for the purpose, it was clear that airborne operations would never be other than very expensive.[80]

While stationed at Alliance, the paratroopers of the 507th trained and performed demonstration jumps before tens of thousands of spectators in Alliance, Omaha, and Denver.[81] In September 1943, the regiment enjoyed a bivouac at Stockdale Lake in Custer State Park in Black Hills, South Dakota, underwent final review by senior officers on October 23, 1943, and then began to deploy overseas. On November 23, 1943, the 507th Parachute Infantry Regiment arrived via train at Camp Shanks near Orangeburg, New York. Dorothy Sophian gave birth in November 1943 after Bud had deployed to Europe.

At Camp Shanks, the 507th Parachute Infantry Regiment remained unassigned to the US Army 82nd or 101st Airborne Divisions, which were created in late July 1942. The two airborne divisions were formed in the following way. The 82nd Infantry Division became the 82nd Motorized Division. Soon thereafter, the 82nd Motorized Division became the 82nd Airborne Division. The 82nd Airborne Division then provided the cadre of officers and men to form a second airborne division—the 101st Airborne Division.[82] Six months before D-day, the

507th and 508th Parachute Infantry Regiments were known simply as the "2nd Parachute Brigade."[83]

Camp Shanks (1942–1946) was the site of one of the largest US Army staging areas and embarkation points in the United States during World War II. The only other staging areas on the eastern seaboard of the United States were Fort Hamilton in Brooklyn, New York, and Camp Kilmer in New Brunswick, New Jersey.[84] More than 1,300,000 men and women passed through Camp Shanks en route to the European Theater of War. The camp was two and a half miles long by one mile wide and spread over some two thousand acres. It was accessible to the Piermont and New York Piers and had a total bunk capacity of almost fifty thousand troops.[85]

The paratroopers staying at Camp Shanks were ordered to maintain strict secrecy about their training and intended use to avoid detection by German intelligence. Morgan wrote:

> The Camp Shanks staging area was subject to tight security. Because of the enormous volume of troops being funneled through the facility, it was feared that details would leak [to the Germans] pertaining to the names and types of units being prepared to go overseas there. To minimize the risk, every effort was made at the camp to conceal what units were there and where they were going. In the case of the 507th, the Army did not want to give the impression that an airborne parachute element was going overseas. The men of the regiment were therefore required to remove their jump wings and the cap insignia that identified them as paratroopers. They were also prohibited from blousing their trousers into their jump boots—something else that could identify them as airborne men at a glance.[84]

While in Camp Shanks, every paratrooper was inspected to identify and resolve problems with uniforms, weapons, or equipment. Two weeks later, the two thousand paratroopers of the 507th Parachute

Infantry Regiment marched about four miles from Camp Shanks to Piermont Pier on the west bank of the Hudson River and boarded a ferry that carried them in a southerly direction towards the Verrazano Narrows. Their destination was Fort Hamilton on the Brooklyn side of the Verrazano Narrows, which they reached on December 3, 1943, according to Morgan. For the first time, many paratroopers were viewing the mid-twentieth-century Manhattan skyline that included the then-tallest building in the world: the Empire State Building (completed in 1931). Bud Sophian was already quite familiar with the city after having spent four years in medical school there.

On December 5, 1943, the 507th Paratrooper Regiment Infantry left the United States through the New York Port of Embarkation and boarded the twelve-year-old British ship *Strathnaver*. The air circulation in the lower decks and the food on the ship were of poor quality. The officers, including Bud Sophian, enjoyed tolerable conditions because their quarters were located on the upper decks. Stories abound about the difficult Atlantic crossing by the 507th Parachute Infantry Regiment on the *Strathnaver*.[86] The ship encountered a storm on the sixth day. It had to zigzag to move past the dangerous southern end of the Republic of Ireland, where German U-boats skulked beneath the surface of the water (recall the *Lusitania* disaster). Finally, ship physicians decided to establish a quarantine after a patient in sickbay was diagnosed with meningitis. This pronouncement could have meant fourteen more days aboard the ship.

However, the quarantine was lifted upon the ship's arrival in Liverpool, England, on December 16, 1943, and 507th Parachute Infantry Regiment paratroopers bolted off *Strathnaver*, relieved to have survived the ship's food, the ship's air, the wicked North Atlantic storm, the possible case of meningitis, and the possibility of death by trauma or drowning courtesy of German U-Boat torpedoes.

Bud Sophian holding his nephew Theodore Morgan O'Leary, Jr., at his sister's home in Fairway, Kansas, summer 1943. *Sophian Archives.*

Captain Bud Sophian in his US Army 507th Parachute Infantry
Regiment uniform, at his parents' home in Mission Hills,
Kansas, 1944. *Sophian Archives.*

Captain Bud Sophian in his US Army 507th Parachute Infantry Regiment uniform, at his parents' home in Mission Hills, Kansas, 1944. *Sophian Archives.*

Chapter Seven: Marshalling for D-day: Northern Ireland and the English Midlands, December 1943–June 1944

Extensive preparations for the assault on Normandy began in November 1943 as the 507th Parachute Infantry Regiment was making its way to Camp Shanks. Major General James M. Gavin, commander of the 505th Parachute Infantry Regiment of the 82nd Airborne Division, explained:

> Most of the required troop-carrier aircraft were still in the United States and one of the airborne divisions [101st] was in Italy. But studies and planning for their commitment in Normandy were begun at COSSAC (Chief of Staff, Supreme Allied Command] in Norfolk House in London in the fall of that year [1943] ... US airborne troops were represented by the senior US airborne commander and the then commanding general of the 101st Airborne Division, Major General William C. Lee. Later, after the arrival of the 82nd Airborne Division in England, its commander, Major General Matthew B. Ridgway, was designated as commander of the US airborne control and advisory group.[87]

The 507th Parachute Infantry Regiment could not proceed from the *Strathnaver* directly to its pre-D-day marshalling destination area in England, because the assigned area was not ready. General Lewis Brereton's Ninth Air Force supposedly caused the delay because the "embryonic" IX Troop Carrier Command was astonishingly disorganized, sputtered Blair.[88] Captain Sophian and the 507th Parachute Infantry Regiment paratroopers instead boarded trains in Liverpool, England, and chugged and whistled north to Greenock, Scotland. There they transferred to the fourteen-year-old transport ship USS *Susan B. Anthony* bound for Belfast, Northern Ireland.[89]

After arrival in Belfast, the 507th Parachute Infantry Regiment boarded another train that wound it through dark dank winter scenery to the mostly shuttered summer resort town of Portrush.[89] Portrush is near Giant's Causeway, a geologic outcropping of some forty thousand interlocking red basalt columnar prisms that resulted from a volcanic eruption some fifty million years ago. Portrush is also home to the Royal Portrush Golf Club, which was founded in 1888. The 507th Parachute Infantry Regiment arrived in Portrush, Northern Ireland, shortly after Christmas 1943.

On January 13, 1944, American General Dwight D. Eisenhower left the United States to undertake his role as the newly designated supreme commander of the Allied Expeditionary Force, the organization of the mightiest fighting force that the two Western Allies (United Kingdom and the United States) could muster. One senior commander, Chief Marshal Sir Trafford Leigh-Mallory, carried the title of air commander in chief. "He had much fighting experience, particularly in the Battle of Britain, but had not theretofore been in charge of air operations requiring close cooperation with ground troops," wrote Eisenhower.[90] They would later disagree about the planned airborne attack in the Cotentin Peninsula.

General Eisenhower moved quickly to make important decisions relating to the Normandy invasion after he arrived in London on January 14, 1944. For example, members of the 507th Parachute

Infantry Regiment learned in Ireland that they finally had been assigned to an airborne division (the 82nd). The 507th replaced the 504th Parachute Infantry Regiment in the 82nd Airborne Division because most of the 504th Parachute Infantry Regiment paratroopers were still fighting in Italy, as noted earlier. By the time paratroopers of the 504th Parachute Infantry Regiment returned from Italy, the 507th was part of the 82nd Airborne Division preparing for Operation Overlord. "In the end, a large number of 504th men were attached to the 507th for the upcoming invasion, especially in the regiment's three Pathfinder teams," noted Morgan.[89] Pathfinders were parachute infantrymen who dropped before anyone else to set up and operate navigation aids on the ground to guide the main airborne body of C-47s to their drop zones.

One of the most difficult decisions immediately facing General Eisenhower in London involved the planned airborne attack in the Cotentin Peninsula. He explained:

> The assault against the east coast of that peninsula, to take place on a beach called Utah, was included in the attack plan because of my conviction, concurred in by [US Army General Omar] Bradley, that without it the early capture of Cherbourg [on the tip of Cotentin Peninsula] would be difficult if not almost impossible. Unless we could soon seize Cherbourg, the enemy's opportunity for hemming us in on a narrow beachhead might be so well exploited as to lead to the defeat of the operations. Rapid and complete success on Utah Beach was, we believed, prerequisite to real success in the whole campaign.
>
> The only available beach on the Cotentin Peninsula was, however, a miserable one. Just back of it was a wide lagoon, passable only on a few narrow causeways that led from the beaches to the interior of the peninsula. If the exits of these causeways should be held by the enemy our landing troops

would be caught in a trap and eventually slaughtered by artillery and other fire to which they would be able to make little reply.

To prevent this, we planned to drop two divisions of American paratroopers [82nd and 101st] inland from this beach, with their primary mission to seize and hold the exits of the vital causeways. The ground was highly unsuited to airborne operations. Hedgerows in the so-called "bocage" country are high, strong, and numerous. The coast lines that the vulnerable transport planes and gliders would have to cross were studded with anti-aircraft. In addition, there were units of mobile enemy troops in the area and these, aside from mounting anti-aircraft fire, would attempt to operate against our paratroopers and glider troops before they could organize themselves for action.[90]

Eisenhower thought the matter of dropping two divisions of paratroopers behind enemy lines was settled, as Generals Bradley and Matthew Ridgway, the senior American airborne general, had resolutely agreed as to its necessity and feasibility. "At an early date it was approved for inclusion in plans and I supposed the matter settled, but it was to come up again in dramatic fashion, just before D-day," lamented Eisenhower.[90]

As General Eisenhower was managing the various components of Operation Overlord, Bud and Emily suddenly renewed an active correspondence. They communicated via the V-Mail (Victory Mail) system, a process developed in England whereby the postal service microfilmed specially designed letter sheets onto rolls of film. The military sent the rolls of film instead of the actual letter sheets. In this way, available cargo space could hold many more letters per transport trip from the Europe to the United States and vice versa. For example, a single mail sack containing rolls of film replaced the thirty-seven mail bags that would be required to carry 150,000 one-page letters. The single sack of rolls of film weighed forty-five pounds in contrast to the one-and-a quarter-ton weight of the thirty-seven mail bags of one-page letters. Postal services on both sides of the Atlantic Ocean sent the rolls of film to specific destinations for developing at a receiving station near the addressee. Finally, the postal service reproduced individual facsimiles of the letter sheets, which it magnified to about one-quarter the original size, and delivered the miniature mail to the addressee.[91]

Superior officers reviewed all the mail of enlisted men and censored any "sensitive" material, such as clues as to location, military strength, and upcoming military engagements that would interest the enemy if intercepted. Officers censored their own mail; thus, Bud as Captain Sophian functioned as his own censor. His signature is visible in the censor's circle in the upper left hand corner of each V-Mail he sent to Emily.

Bud and Emily exchanged around ten V-mails between January and June 1944. Nine of the V-mails Bud wrote to Emily and one of the V-mails Emily wrote to Bud (the final one) have survived. The postal service returned to Emily her final V-mail to Bud (which she had sent soon after D-day), because it could not locate Bud.

Bud wrote one V-Mail to Emily on January 20, 1944, but its postmark date was February 3, 1944, thus indicating the length of time required to move a letter from sender to receiver through the V-Mail system. Bud's January 20, 1944, letter read, as follows:

Dear Em –
Received your letter a few days [ago] and enjoyed it very much – what's all this about Ted's leaving [the *Kansas City Star*] – no one has written me anything about it – your reunion with Francis sounds very touching – hope it lasts – very little of interest over here – it's always dark in the daytime it's cloudy and raining and at nite we have the blackout – chief excitement is drinking of which we have partaken little lately due mainly to the difficulty of supply – I'm feeling fine and am really in excellent physical condition – my mental development receives its only stimulation from field manuals and *War & Peace* [Russian novel by Leo Tolstoy] – I'm pretty near through the latter which I consider

my major accomplishment of the war to date – give my love to every one – see you in a year or so – Much love Bud.

(Ted O'Leary did leave his job as a reporter at the *Kansas City Star*, which he had held for about ten years from 1934 to 1944.)

Bud mentioned Keckie in the letter he wrote to Emily on February 13, 1944 (postmarked February 23, 1944):

Dear Em –

Enjoyed your letter very much – before I forget I must answer your question about letters being the things that keep us alive – it's not quite that bad but we really do look forward to the mail every day – most every one is homesick to some degree and mail helps out quite a bit – Keckie tells me you and Ted are thinking of raising dachshunds – sounds fascinating – We're all getting pretty tired of this business over here – all is well but we want to get started with the business across the channel – we've trained for so blooming long that it's really a tremendous effort to get interested in anything – just at present the vogue seems to be long marches which are murder on these hard roads – we went 25 odd miles the other nite and every one's feet looked like raw meat – My stomach started kicking up a few weeks ago so I had to stop drinking – This Irish whiskey we get is just plain fire – give my love to everyone – probably see you in a year or so – Dennis [Emily's oldest son, age six years] will undoubtedly be more [word?] by that time. Loads of love Bud

To help pass the time in Portrush, members of the 507th Parachute Infantry Regiment played various organized sports. For example, the 507th and the 508th regimental basketball teams, the Spiders and Red Devils, respectively, played in a championship basketball tournament held in the American Red Cross gymnasium in Belfast.

Captain Sophian undoubtedly spotted the famous Royal Portrush Golf Club course, which local authorities subsequently made available for a tournament open only to American servicemen. An article in the sports section of the *Stars and Stripes* (the independent newspaper of the US military) dated February 15, 1944, noted Bud's golfing prowess:

Touring the windswept Royal Portrush course in 78, Captain A. Sophian, Jr., of Kansas City, Missouri, yesterday shot his way to the lead in the Ulster Golf tournament open only to American servicemen. The Captain thus became the first contestant to break 80 in the qualifying test, which will determine sixteen entries for the matchplay competition, scheduled to start next week. Two Ohioans, Corporal Bernard Emmerson, of Norwood, and Private First Class Robert Plummer, of Sharonville, trailed Captain Sophian with 81 and 83, respectively. Private W. Randall, of Los Angeles, fired an 84, two strokes better than Sergeant J. Hume, Jr., of Detroit. Two other scores were posted yesterday. Second Lieutenant W.C. Aubel, of Syracuse, N.Y., had 90, and Private First Class E.L. Haws, of Lakeland, Ohio, 108.

On February 22, 1944, Bud sent another letter to Emily (postmarked March 4, 1944) that praised her writing:

Dear Em –
Your burst of literary energy fair overwhelms me – I can't get over this regular flow of letters from such a long dormant source – it's truly delightful and enjoyable – I went off the wagon last Saturday after almost three weeks of thirst – I had accumulated a pretty good stock in that time so I threw a party – it was really a beauty – this local Irish whiskey is different from anything I ever saw – it has a delayed action and when it takes hold it really doses a violent job – this Thursday night the Colonel is throwing a party for the officers at one of the local auditoria –

seems he has drawn our whiskey ration for several months – it promises to be a good one – I'm feeling fine – all of us are homesick and spend most of our idle time talking about home but I'm afraid it will be a long time yet – Give my love to Ted and the kids – Much love Bud.

In mid-February 1944, the 82nd Airborne Division finally received orders to move to the English Midlands to its pre-D-day marshalling area in the Leicester-Nottingham area. Its marshalling area was near the troop carrier command headquarters and the 52nd Troop Carrier Wing, which Major General Paul L. Williams and Brigadier General Harold L. Clark, commanded, respectively.[92]

Major General Paul L. Williams (1894–1968) headed the US Army Air Force IX Troop Carrier Command during World War II and was responsible for the airlift of the paratroopers, gliders, and infantry in North Africa, Sicily, Italy, Normandy, southern France, Holland, and Germany. Brigadier General Harold L. Clark (1893–1973) had weathered withering criticism of his 52nd Troop Carrier Wing, whose pilots chronically underperformed in the precise formation flying and pinpoint navigation required for effective parachute and glider tow operations, particularly at night.[92]

On February 14, 1944, Brigadier General Matthew Bunker Ridgway (1895–1993), commander of the 82nd Airborne Division, opened his division command post at Braunstone Park in Leicester and ordered movement of the units of the 82nd Airborne Division to their new location in England. This movement was complicated and took a month to complete.[93] Paratroopers lived in Nissen huts, which had been erected in advance of their arrival.

US Army Chief of Staff General George C. Marshall had appointed Matthew Ridgway commander of the newly activated 82nd Infantry Division in August 1942, according to records at Arlington National Cemetery. When the 82nd Airborne Infantry Division became one of the US Army's first two airborne divisions, Ridgway remained in command

and earned his paratrooper wings. In North Africa in the spring of 1943, he planned the army's first major night airborne operation, part of the invasion of Sicily. The Sicily invasion, which began on July 10, 1943, led to rapid conquest of the island, but with severe losses of the lives of Allied paratroopers dropped from planes and troops flown in on gliders. The army also lost more than a dozen transport planes. Acutely aware of these grave losses, General Eisenhower and his senior staff concluded that the Allies nevertheless must use the same night drop and landing approach for the invasion of Normandy.

Bud wrote the following letter to Emily on March 8, 1944 (postmarked March 20, 1944), telling her about his recent ecstasy in eating eggs:

Dear Em –
Just finished eating 5 eggs and feel wonderful – we've been on a problem for the past couple of days and I managed to acquire the eggs from various henhouses along the way. I think I could have eaten a dozen more if I had them – Enjoyed your letter – was not positively surprised to hear that Marjorie [Bloch] had gotten married again [Fields] – from what I've been able to gather she hasn't anything very pleasant to look forward to with her scleroderma – if I were she I'd grab just whatever I could as long as I had the opportunity – Struck me as funny that you say you have nothing to write about – our topics of correspondence are so blooming limited that it's pathetic – not that we don't do quite a few interesting things but to speak of them is strongly verboten [forbidden] – all of which is rather amusing since there's so darn many IRA [Irish Republican Army] people around here that anything we do must be known – however they must draw the line somewhere, I guess – Liquor is scarce as hell so I've been drinking very little of late – Feel fine but get more anxious all the time to get on with the thing – Love to every one – Bud.

On March 20, 1944, Bud wrote to Emily from his new base of operations in England and reflected on his happiness that their years of silence (since his marriage) had ended. He also mentioned his child with Dorothy:

Dear Em – Somewhere in England
This correspondence that has sprung up between us is nothing short of remarkable – after all those years of silence it needed a war to start this outflow of literary genius – your dissertation on meeting people in the street belongs with some of Charles Lamb's spies [English writer, author of *Tales from Shakespeare*] or perhaps with those of Robert Benchley [American writer and humorist] –

Nothing much new with me – as you probably know we're "somewhere in England" – it's a nice country I guess – haven't had a chance to get around but the weather at least is better than Ireland – whiskey is unobtainable, however – we just keep getting readier and readier for what ever it is we're going to do – I for one am anxious to get on with this darn thing –

You certainly seem to be having your trouble with those hellions of yours – wish I could sit in on one of those dinner sessions – Keep an eye on that young [child] of mine – Give my love to everyone – Bud

In mid-March 1944, the 82nd Airborne Division began the intensive airborne training that it had been unable to do in Northern Ireland because of the paucity of available airplanes, the restricted number of daylight hours, and the poor weather. However, as it turned out, the weather in the English Midlands in mid-March 1944 was only slightly if at all better than the weather in Northern Ireland, as the short daylight hours continued to restrict operations. Once again, commanders were forced to confine most divisional training to ground operations launched from simulated drop zones (paratroopers) and landing zones (gliders). By April 1944, airborne training had increased but "time and time again, in big and little exercises ... wind and low visibility, particularly at night ... scattered troop formations, twisted them off course or spoiled their drops." One battalion commander bitterly complained about the troop carrier pilots who "had scattered us all over—dropped us in deep forests and everything else."[93]

Bud wrote to Emily on April 8, 1944 (postmarked April 20, 1944), reiterating his enthusiasm for the parachute infantry, as follows:

Dear Em –

Sorry to hear of your multiple troubles – what with the boys getting more than their share [of] childhood ills and Ted having teeth trouble, your turning up with your disorder seems like making too much of a bad thing – hope all is straightened out by now. This is Saturday nite and a very small percent of our people are allowed to go into town but I didn't go – nothing really to do there what with everyplace being so crowded and closing so early – there's no whiskey to be had – as a matter of fact this is the first Saturday nite since we've been in England that we haven't been on a problem – I'm still very enthusiastic about this branch of the service and the closer we come to action the more satisfied I am – I'm feeling very fit although our time for physical hardening as such is practically nil these days – however, forced marches of 15 or so miles are not at all uncommon – Congratulate Ted for me on his handball victories – he certainly did a good job – Weather here has finally turned nice after several weeks of the kind of foggy soup we've always read about – we're on double summer time which would be the same as war time plus daylight saving so it's light until 9 or 10 o'clock. Love to every one Bud.

In late April 1944, foul English weather turned a full 82nd Airborne

Division-size (more than six thousand paratroopers) rehearsal of Operation Overlord into a fiasco, declared Blair. James M. Gavin, commander of the 505th Parachute Infantry Regiment, noted:

> The takeoff was normal, we got most of the division into the air and then found that we could not get it down. Fog and bad weather closed in on us, the drop zones could not be located, and close troop carrier formations could not be flown. A few drops were made but most of the troops had to be airlanded at airdromes scattered all over England."[93]

Another observer wrote:

> The weather was unfavorable, the regiment staged at the airport for more than a week waiting for an opportunity to take off. When the planes did finally take off the weather was still unfavorable. After a fifteen-minute flight, word was received from the air bases to return. However, heavy clouds prevented the visual signals from the lead planes from being seen in most cases. Over the DZ confusion reigned as planes approached from all angles at different altitudes. Most had become lost from their formation and had found the DZ on their own. Here ... was a premonition of what was to happen later in Normandy.[94]

On April 30, 1944, Bud expressed his new feelings of appreciation for the United States since living in the British Isles in the following letter to Emily:

Dear Em –
Was terribly sorry to hear about your latest illness – also about Morgan's and Dennis's repeated trouble – hope you'll get a little respite now for a change – nothing at all new around

here – we lead a pretty dull existence although we've had more chance to get off evenings the past 10 days since we arrived in England – every place is so very crowded that it's hardly worth the fight – no real nightclubs – just a lot of pubs which close at 10 but which individually run out of liquor by 7:30 or 8:00 – the last show of the movie starts at 5:45 which is too early for us to make – so we usually stay around camp and play fastball or cards – Wish Ted luck for me in his Chicago tournament – I envy him the trip to Chicago but then I'm afraid I envy any one who has the opportunity to go anywhere in the States – I've really gotten so that I appreciate that country of ours – Much love Bud.

The weather turned favorable when the 101st Airborne Division undertook its full Overlord dress rehearsal on May 10 and 11, 1944. The exercise was code named Eagle and was modeled after the earlier 82nd Airborne Division Overlord simulation. Blair noted that by mid-May 1944, General Eisenhower and his senior staff had moved forward the time of the 82nd Airborne Division's D-day drop to coincide with that of the 101st Division's drop. Furthermore, the 82nd Airborne Division pilots flying the C-47s badly needed practice. Thus, Exercise Eagle was expanded to include pilots and token paratroopers from the 82nd Airborne Division.

In this rehearsal, the 50th and 53rd Wings dropped the 101st Airborne Division's three parachute infantry regiments (501, 502 and 506; more than six thousand men) from four hundred and thirty-two aircraft and towed in fifty-five gliders. Brigadier General Harold L. Clark's 52nd Wing mounted three hundred and sixty-nine aircraft and dropped two 82nd Airborne Division paratroopers per plane for a total of about six hundred and thirty-eight 82nd Airborne Division paratroopers.[93]

Some senior staff of the 101st Airborne Division judged Exercise Eagle a great success. For example, the official historian reported, "In the 101st ... an astonishing seventy-five percent of the parachutists landed on or close to the proper DZs" and "forty-four of the fifty-five gliders, landing at dawn, found the proper LZ [landing zone] and made 'good' touchdowns." However, the true situation was not so rosy—twenty-eight planes got lost and returned to base, and eight other planes mistakenly dropped about one hundred and thirty parachutists into the town of Ramsbury, nine miles from the DZ. In addition, four gliders aborted and seven landed on the wrong LZs.[93]

Blair decried the historian's upbeat assessment, noting that Brigadier General Clark's 52nd Wing and the six hundred and thirty-eight paratroopers from the 82nd Airborne Division did *not* perform well, which did not bode well for D-day. Blair wrote:

> The pilots of the green [meaning not tested in combat] 315th [Troop Carrier] Group got fouled up and did not drop at all. Only sixteen of forty-five planes of the green 442nd [Troop Carrier] Group found the DZ; the rest tried again by the light of dawn only to drop ten miles off target. Nine planes of the veteran 314th [Troop Carrier] Group also gave up and came home; another nine from the group dropped far off target. The rest of 314th [Troop Carrier] Group and most of the planes of the veteran 313th, 316th, and 61st [Troop Carrier] Groups made fair-to-good drops. In sum, 226 of the 638 paratroopers affiliated with the 82nd Airborne Division who participated in Eagle—almost one-third—either did not jump or jumped far from the DZ.[93]

Historian Gerald M. Devlin also criticized Exercise Eagle:

> The ... Airborne Division[s'] preinvasion training culminated in Exercise Eagle, a full-dress rehearsal of the Normandy drop ... The maneuver was to be as close to the real thing as possible. Departure airfields were, in almost every case, the same ones from which the division would eventually depart for Normandy.

All combat loads and jump equipment carried by the troops were the exact same ones they would carry on D-day, right down to the last bullet and grenade.

Preceded by their pathfinders, troops ... began taking off one hour before midnight on May 11 [1944] for a one-hour flight to their DZs. As would be the case on D-day, only the lead plane of each serial was equipped with a radar device that could home in on the signal being sent by pathfinders already on the DZs. Also in the lead planes was an Aldis lamp which, at the proper time, would be inserted into the rooftop plexiglass astrodome and turned on. Upon seeing the brightly flashing Aldis lamp, all pilots behind the lead ship were to turn on their interior green jump-signal lights, sending the jumpers out into the night.

Exercise Eagle went well until there was a serious misunderstanding between the pilot and radio operator of the lead plane carrying Company H of the 502nd Parachute Infantry Regiment. While still several miles out from his DZ, the pilot, speaking over the plane's intercom, told the radio operator to check the Aldis lamp. The radio operator understood the pilot to say, "Turn on the Aldis lamp." And so he did. For the next several minutes paratroopers rained down on top of the quiet English village of Ramsbury, nine miles short of the DZ. Twenty-eight other planes of another serial failed to find their DZs in the darkness and returned with full loads [of paratroopers] to their departure airfields.

Despite these mistakes, by 3:30 in the morning, the bulk of the ... troops and hardware had been assembled. Just before daylight a number of gliders loaded with troops and heavy weapons landed in the maneuver area without incident. With these reinforcements the parachute units launched a series of attacks at dawn, capturing all assigned objectives before noon.

Though termed a complete tactical success, Exercise Eagle produced a large number of jump casualties. No fewer than 436 paratroopers were treated at aid stations for broken bones, sprained ankles, and other assorted jump injuries. [94]

Paratrooper Thomas M. Rice (501st Parachute Infantry Regiment, 101st Airborne Division) described his experience during Exercise Eagle as follows:

> The jump started at 2400 [midnight] on May 11, 1944 and three hours later seventy-five percent of the personnel and ninety percent of the jettisoned equipment bundles were gathered. Numerous tactical pilot errors occurred again, of the same nature of the two previous exercises. Twenty-eight planes brought back 528 parachutists to their departure airports. Four hundred men were treated for broken bones, sprained ankles, and other jump injuries. Company C had three injuries. Sergeant A. Kromholtz came down between power lines and cut his throat. He dangled above the ground and couldn't extricate himself from his harness, without help, which was slow in coming.[95]

The biggest problem with Exercise Eagle, according to Blair and other observers, was that it induced "a mood of heady optimism throughout the ranks of troop-carrier and airborne forces." For example, Major General Paul L. Williams, commander of the troop carrier groups that serviced the 82nd and 101st Airborne Divisions, predicted that 90–100 percent of airborne forces would be delivered to proper drop zones and landing zones on D-day. Blair observed, "The weather during Eagle had been so 'halcyon' that the previous training fiascos caused by bad weather seemed to have been forgotten, ignored or pushed into the background." The result was that the D-day operational orders failed to include "full and specific precautions against bad weather," a lapse that was to "prove costly indeed," he intoned. A historian for the troop carrier groups noted that the optimism expressed by Major General Williams and others was premature and would lead to grave and tragic error in the actual combat operations.[96]

Meanwhile, alert Allied intelligence officers noted that the German enemy was expanding its defensive preparations in Normandy. The Allied intelligence officers obtained their intelligence from "decoded German radio intercepts, photoreconnaissance and reports from the French underground and other sources. The decoded radio intercepts, in particular, were invaluable. They revealed in utmost detail the German chain of command, troop dispositions and strategy."[96]

The Germans expected an imminent Allied invasion on the Western Front but disagreed on where it would occur. The most common belief was that the Allies would invade Europe at Pas-de-Calais, France—the shortest distance across the English Channel between England and the European continent. Hitler, however, had a "sudden and uncanny intuition that the landings would actually take place in Normandy." Thus, in spring 1944, he ordered his bickering top commanders, Field Marshal Gerd von Rundstedt (1875–1953) and under him tank force commander Erwin Rommel (1891–1944), to "greatly strengthen the so-called Atlantic Wall, which stretched more or less from Cherbourg to Calais." Cherbourg is located at the tip of the Cotentin Peninsula (also known as Cherbourg Peninsula) that juts out from Normandy into the English Channel. The name of the area cordoned off by the Atlantic Wall was *Festung Europa*—Fortress Europe. The Atlantic Wall was largely "imaginary" but "beloved of the German Propaganda Ministry," observed military historian Christopher Chant.[97] One clever American paratrooper snickered, "Hitler made one mistake when he built his Fortress Europe—'he forgot to put a roof on it.' It was through the nonexistent roof that Allied airborne troops would make their uninvited entrance into the fortress."[98]

General Dwight D. Eisenhower, the Supreme Commander of the Allied Expeditionary Force in the European Theatre of War during the Second World War, speaks with Lieutenant Wallace C. Strobel, a paratrooper in the 101st Airborne Division, at Greenham Common Airfield on the evening of June 5, 1944. *Courtesy of the National World War II Museum (formerly the National D-day Museum).*

A paratrooper "stick" somewhere in England, just before they
boarded their airplanes to invade the continent of Europe
on June 6, 1944. Moore, 111-SC-194399.
Courtesy of National Archives and Records Administration.

T-4 Joseph F. Gorene of 3rd Battalion/506th Parachute Infantry
Regiment of the 101st Airborne Division as he boards a C-47 at
Exeter on his way to Normandy on the night of June 5-6, 1944.
Courtesy of the National Archives and Records Administration.

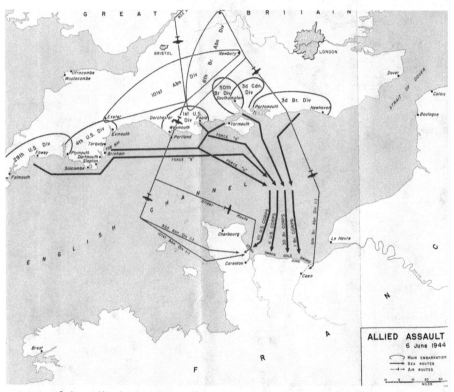

Map of the Allied assault on the continent of Europe on June 6, 1944.
Courtesy of United States Army Colonel Roy S. Marokus (obtained
during his visit to Graignes War Memorial in late 2008).

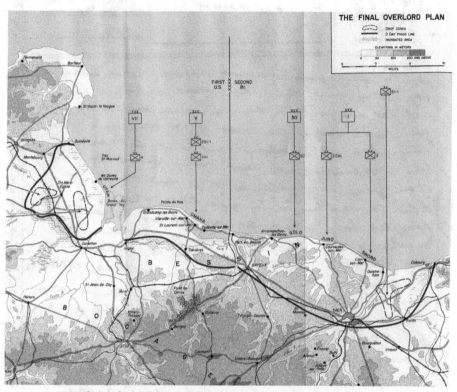

Map of the final Overlord military map for the Allied assault on the continent of Europe on June 6, 1944. *Courtesy of United States Army Colonel Roy S. Marokus* (obtained during his visit to Graignes War Memorial in late 2008).

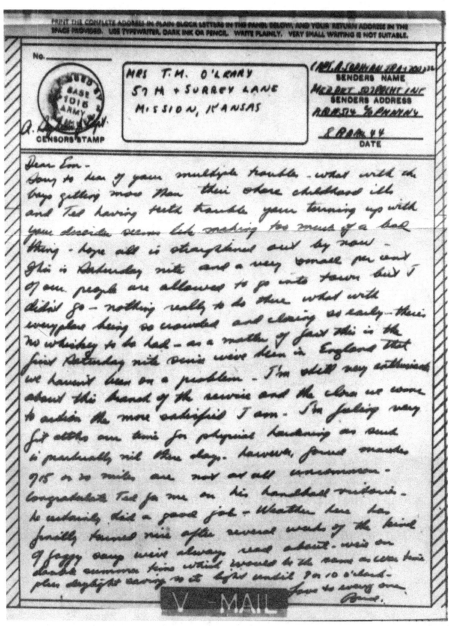

V-Mail from Captain Bud Sophian to his sister Emily Sophian
O'Leary, dated April 8, 1944. *Sophian Archives.*

Chapter Eight: Errant D-day Drop, June 6, 1944

On May 26, 1944, Major General Ridgway and his senior staff at 82nd Airborne Division headquarters in the English Midlands finished all plans and preparations for Operation Overlord. They then learned that Germany's 91st *Luftland* division had arrived in Normandy and set up a headquarters with powerful artillery in Saint-Sauveur-le-Vicomte near the center of the Cotentin Peninsula. This alarming development forced Allied commanders to scotch Plan A and develop Plan B. "Had the 82nd Airborne actually carried out this 'Plan A' the entire division would have dropped on top of the divisional headquarters of the 91st *Luftland* [infantry] Division," observed Morgan dryly. In other words, Plan A showed the 82nd Airborne Division dropping near or on top of Saint-Sauveur-le-Vicomte.[99]

Plan B directed the 82nd Airborne Division to land about ten miles east of Saint-Sauveur-le-Vicomte, near Sainte-Mère-Église. This meant that the 82nd Airborne Division now had to fly ten additional miles through anti-aircraft fire from German anti-aircraft artillery that was concentrated in the Saint-Sauveur-le-Vicomte area.

The 82nd Airborne Division planned to use three drop zones for its paratroopers and one landing zone for its glider infantry in Normandy. The 2,004 members of the 507th Parachute Infantry Regiment were supposed to drop in DZ "T" near the west bank of the Merderet River.

According to Plan B, the mission of the 507th was to establish defensive positions in DZ "T" and prepare to attack westward in order to seal off the Cotentin Peninsula from Germans retreating from Cherbourg and from German divisions rushing to Cherbourg from the interior of France to support the stressed German line.

On May 25, 1944 (postmarked June 4, 1944), Captain Abraham Sophian, Jr., Medical Corps, penned his last V-Mail to his sister Emily Sophian O'Leary. It read:

Dear Em –

Been meaning to write for some time but just haven't gotten around to it – I was very upset to hear about your most recent illness – hope it's all cleared up now – in Keckie and Mother's letters today they both said that Dennis and Morgan looked better than ever – let's hope they stay that way for a long time – You must have had a lot of fun with Paul [O'Leary, Ted's older brother] and Hattie [Paul's wife] – wish I could have gotten in on it – our recreation has been very much restricted by training in [one] form or another – just at present I'm brushing up on my German – it's amazing how much you forget a language when you don't use it for a long time – Spent a few days in the hospital last week with a bellyache but I'm feeling fine now – my biggest worry at the moment is the fact that I've lost the top off my fountain pen so you can see things can't be too bad – liquor is still the great unsolved problem although we do manage to get the key to it once and so often – Congratulate Ted for me on his showing in the Nationals – give my love to every one – Much love Bud.

Acceleration to D-day began a few days after Bud wrote the letter above to Emily. On May 28, 1944, the 507th Parachute Infantry Regiment's three battalions and Regimental Headquarters Company were ordered to congregate at an ancient stone manor in the village of

Tollerton just south of Nottingham. White arm bands marked with a red cross distinguished medical company paratroopers from the other paratroopers. All of the paratroopers except for the three sticks of pathfinders boarded civilian buses that growled about twenty-five miles to the northeast to reach Fulbeck Airfield and Barkston-Heath Airfield near Grantham in Lincolnshire.[100]

The 507th Regimental Headquarters and 1st Battalion, consisting of forty-five sticks, went to Fulbeck Airfield, and the 2nd and 3rd Battalions (Captain Sophian was attached to the 3rd Battalion), consisting of seventy-two sticks, went to Barkston-Heath Airfield. The three pathfinder sticks went to North Witham Airfield.[101] The five other 82nd Airborne Division mustering airfields were further south by as much as thirty miles at Folkingham, Saltby, North Witham, Cottesmore, and Spanhoe.[102]

The airfields were "sealed" (meaning they were surrounded by barbed wire and guards) to reduce the possibility that the German enemy would learn of the imminent airborne invasion of Normandy. The tactic worked. The men slept on thousands of cots in the hangars and showered in canvas stalls awaiting the order to move out.

On May 30, 1944, (British) Air Chief Marshal Leigh-Mallory suddenly approached General Eisenhower to question the wisdom of launching the imminent airborne operation in the Cotentin Peninsula. Eisenhower recalled the episode:

[Air Chief Marshal Leigh-Mallory] came to me to protest once more against what he termed the "futile slaughter" of two fine divisions [American 82nd and 101st Airborne Divisions]. He believed that the combination of unsuitable landing grounds and anticipated resistance was too great a hazard to overcome. This dangerous combination was not present in the area on the left where the British airborne division would be dropped and casualties there were not expected to be abnormally severe, but he estimated that among the American outfits we would suffer some seventy per cent losses in glider strength and at least fifty per cent in paratroop strength before the airborne troops could land. Consequently the division would have no remaining tactical power and the attack would not only result in the sacrifice of many thousand men but would be helpless to effect the outcome of the general assault. Leigh-Mallory was, of course, earnestly sincere. He was noted for personal courage and was merely giving me, as was his duty, his frank convictions.[90]

What did General Eisenhower do? He recalled:

It would be difficult to conceive of a more soul-racking problem. If my technical expert [Leigh-Mallory] was correct, then the planned operation was worse than stubborn folly, because even at the enormous cost predicted we could not gain the principal object of the drop. Moreover, if he was right, it appeared that the attack on Utah Beach was probably hopeless, and this meant that the whole operation suddenly acquired a degree of risk, even foolhardiness, that presaged a gigantic failure, possibly Allied defeat in Europe.

To protect him in case his advice was disregarded, I instructed the air commander to put his recommendations in a letter and informed him he would have my answer within a few hours. I took the problem to no one else. Professional advice and counsel could do no more.

I went to my tent alone and sat down to think. Over and over I reviewed each step, somewhat in the sequence set down here, but more thoroughly and exhaustively. I realized, of course, that if I deliberately disregarded the advice of my technical expert on the subject, and his predictions should prove accurate, then I would carry to my grave the unbearable burden of a conscience justly accusing me of the stupid, blind sacrifice of thousands of the flower of our youth. Outweighing any personal burden, however, was the possibility that if he were right the effect of the disaster would be far more than local: it would be likely to spread to the entire force.

Nevertheless, my review of the matter finally narrowed the critical points to these:

If I should cancel the airborne operation, then I had either to cancel the attack on Utah Beach or I would condemn the assaulting forces there to even greater probability of disaster than was predicted for the airborne divisions.

If I should cancel the Utah attack I would so badly disarrange elaborate plans as to diminish chances for success elsewhere and to make later maintenances perhaps impossible. Moreover, in long and calm consideration of the whole great scheme we had agreed that the Utah attack was an essential factor in prospects for success. To abandon it really meant to abandon a plan in which I had held implicit confidence for more than two years.

Finally, Leigh-Malloy's estimate was just an estimate, nothing more, and our experience in Sicily and Italy did not, by any means, support his degree of pessimism. Bradley, with Ridgway and other airborne commanders, had always supported me and the staff in the matter, and I was encouraged to persist in the belief that Leigh-Mallory was wrong!

I telephoned him that the attack would go as planned and that I would confirm this at once in writing. When later, the attack was successful he was the first to call me to voice his delight and to express his regret that he had found it necessary to add to my personal burdens during the final tense days before D-day.[90]

The day after the Leigh-Malloy incident (May 31, 1944), senior military officers briefed the congregated paratroopers about Operation Overlord, so the latter finally knew for sure *where* they were going and that they *were* going. The men of the 507th Parachute Infantry

Regiment were "promised that the regiment would be brought back to England after only about seven days of combat." Cruel circumstances prolonged the 507th Parachute Infantry Regiment Normandy stay to thirty-five days of intense combat and carnage.[100]

After solving the imbroglio presented to him by Leigh-Mallory, General Eisenhower, as Supreme Commander of the Allied Expeditionary Force in Europe, set D-day for June 5, 1944. However, a howling North Atlantic storm raged over England and the Continent early on June 4, 1944, forcing him to postpone Operation Overlord for twenty-four hours. "He was told [by senior staff] that, under the present conditions [the night of June 4–5], eighty percent of the paratroopers would be killed and wounded and ninety percent of the gliders would be casualties before they reached the ground."[103]

On the night of June 5–6, 1944, General Eisenhower ordered the invasion to go forward. Seventy-two C-47s flown by the veteran 61st Troop Carrier Group at Barkston-Heath airfield waited patiently as 1,230 paratroopers of the 2nd and 3rd Battalions of the 507th Parachute Infantry Regiment boarded their planes, stick by stick, one stick per C-47, an average of eighteen paratroopers per stick. At Fulbeck Airfield, forty-five C-47s of the green 442nd Troop Carrier Group filled up with the 770 paratroopers from the 507th Regimental Headquarters and 1st Battalion.[103] When the three pathfinder sticks were added to the total, 120 C-47s carried around two thousand paratroopers of the 507th Parachute Infantry Regiment to meet their individual fates in Normandy.

Captain Sophian's stick was composed of sixteen paratroopers. He jumped second, right after Captain Richard H. Chapman. Private Jesus Casas (medical company) jumped fifth and Private First Class Frank P. Costa jumped ninth. The aircraft was Chalk #47 out of the seventy-two planes in Serial 25. The aircraft's tail number was 42-92773. The aircrew was from the 53rd Troop Carrier Squadron and consisted of First Lieutenant Ted E. Simon (pilot), First Lieutenant Edwin K. Tester (co-pilot), First Lieutenant David H. Hill (navigator), T/Sgt. Fred A.E.

Wilson (crew chief), and S/Sgt. Wayne M. Sutphin (radio operator). The aircraft also carried six bundles attached to blue parachutes. One bundle contained wire (213 pounds) and another bundle, batteries (230 pounds). Two other bundles carried medical supplies (150 pounds and 153 pounds). The last two bundles carried mines (251 pounds per bag).[101]

Devlin described the plan developed by the air corps for transporting American paratroopers from their airbases to their drop zones in Normandy as follows:

After forming above their individual departure airfields in massive V of V formations, all air units were to fly southward through an imaginary aerial funnel that emptied out into the English Channel at checkpoint Flatbush—the English city of Portland. From Flatbush, all units were to fly southward through a ten-mile wide corridor at an altitude of five hundred feet until they reached checkpoint Hoboken. There a British submarine would signal them to turn left toward the Cotentin Peninsula. After passing over the sub, all planes were to climb to one thousand five hundred feet to avoid enemy shore batteries, keep that altitude until they passed over the coast of France, and then drop back down to five hundred feet for the final run into their DZs. All pilots had orders to stick to their designated courses no matter what happened. This order was given because even the slightest deviation from the proper azimuth would result in paratroopers being dropped miles away from their DZs, severely jeopardizing their chances for success on the ground. Those pilots who were unable to find their DZs were to proceed to DZ D, in the southern most part of the airhead, and drop their troops there. No paratroopers were to be returned to England.[104]

Blair called the Operation Overlord aerial pathway from England to the Cotentin Peninsula the "back door" route. Cotentin Peninsula is oriented on a north–south axis. Airborne elements of the Allied invasion approached the peninsula from its west side (the "back door"), and seaborne elements approached the peninsula from its east side.

Devlin continued:

Starting some one and a half hours before midnight on the fifth of June [1944], the whole of central and southern England began to reverberate with the pounding roar of aircraft engines. One thousand eighty-six paratroop airplanes were warming up for takeoff. At 11:00 P.M. sharp, six serials of three planes each, all loaded with pathfinders, thundered down the runways. Behind the pathfinders, and right on schedule, the first elements of the main body of paratroopers began taking off at 12:21 A.M. [June 6, 1944]. For the next two hours hundreds of C-47s climbed into the dark sky from nine different airfields to tag onto the tail of the great sky train ... Overlord was off to a magnificent start.

Flying fast and low, the pathfinder airplanes knifed undetected across the cloud-covered west coast of the Cotentin Peninsula. Eight minutes after his plane had been over land, Captain Frank L. Lillyman, leader of the 101st Airborne's pathfinders, leaped out into the darkness to become the first Allied paratrooper to set foot in occupied France. The time was 12:15 A.M., Tuesday, the sixth of June [1944].[104]

Following close on the heels of the pathfinders were between twelve thousand and thirteen thousand paratroopers of the combined US Army 101st and 82nd Airborne Divisions.

Blair was an expert on the history of the experience of the 82nd Airborne Division, whose lead C-47s began taking off about thirty minutes behind the lead C-47s of the 101st Airborne Division. He explained that the 82nd Airborne Division forces of about 6,400 men from the 505th, 507th, and 508th Parachute Infantry Regiments were flown by six air groups of the 52nd Wing (Troop Carrier Groups 661, 313, 314, 315, 316, and the temporarily attached 442) in about three hundred and seventy-seven aircraft. The "great aerial armada formed up smartly over England" and proceeded toward the Cotentin Peninsula on the same complicated "back door" route as the pathfinders and the 101st Airborne.[105]

The 505th Parachute Infantry Regiment led the way—2,100 men in one hundred and twenty planes of the 315 and 316 Troop Carrier Groups. The flights were uneventful until the C-47s reached the western coast of the Cotentin Peninsula where they encountered unexpected turbulence and clouds. General Ridgway was on one of these C-47s with the 505th Parachute Infantry Regiment, making his fifth lifetime parachute jump. He recalled:

Wing to wing, the big planes snuggled close in their tight formation, we crossed to the coast of France. I was sitting straight across the aisle from the doorless exit. Even at fifteen hundred feet I could tell the Channel was rough, for we passed over a small patrol craft—one of the check points for our navigators— and the light it displayed for us was bobbing like a cork in a millrace. No lights showed on the land, but in the pale glow of a rising moon, I could clearly see each farm and field below. And I remember thinking how peaceful the land looked, each house and hedgerow, path and little stream bathed in the silver of the moonlight. And I felt that if it were not for the noise of the engines we could hear the farm dogs baying, and the sound of the barnyard roosters crowing for midnight.

A few minutes inland we suddenly went into cloud, thick and turbulent. I had been looking out the doorway, watching with a profound sense of satisfaction the close-ordered flight of that great sky caravan that stretched as far as the eye could see. All at once they were blotted out. Not a wing light showed. The plane began to yaw and plunge, and in my mind's eye I could see other pilots, fighting to hold course, knowing how great was the danger of collision in the air.[105]

Many planes climbed above the clouds to about 1,500 feet and stayed there. One paratrooper recalled, "The pilot I had was extremely reluctant to come down to the correct jumping altitude. We came in at 1,400 feet and our speed was excessive." When the planes abruptly broke out of the clouds, many were flying too high and fast, with too little time to readjust altitude and speed.[105]

Colonel James M. Gavin (505th Parachute Infantry Regiment) described his experience:

And then our planes entered into clouds, dense clouds. The clouds were so thick I could not see the wing tips from the door and my first reaction was to think that we were in a smoke cloud put up by the German defenders. But we kept on riding through the clouds, and soon I had the feeling that we, in the ship in which I was riding and those nearby, were entirely on our own.

But every jumpmaster of every ship had memorized his time of flight from landfall to various check points within the Normandy countryside. I knew that we in the ship of which I was a passenger had to jump at about seven and a half minutes after passing above the French coast, if we were to hit our drop zone.

And as I remember now (a most important item), the east coast [beachheads] of France would come just about twelve minutes later. After that, if we jumped we would jump into the ocean. As a matter of airborne record some troopers did.

But we in my plane continued on into the fog. And about seven minutes after we had crossed the [west] coast the clouds began to clear. As they did, I could see a great deal of heavy flak coming up off to the right of our flight ... We were down to about six hundred feet when the green light went on. I waited about three seconds to get a last look at the terrain before I took

216

the stick out. The time was about eight minutes after we had crossed the coast.[87]

The 508th Parachute Infantry Regiment followed the 505th. The 508th was made up of about 2,200 paratroopers carried in one hundred and thirty-two C-47s flown by the 313 and 314 Troop Carrier Groups, according to Blair. When the 508th aircraft entered the dense cloud layers over the western edge of the Cotentin Peninsula, the formations came apart as they encountered intense flak from German artillery on the ground. The flak was nonstop as the Germans realized the Allied airborne invasion of Western Europe was in progress.

The drop of the 508th was a shambles, despaired Blair. It was "so badly dispersed that the men were seldom able to organize into platoons and companies, let along battalions." Some men were dumped into the English Channel, beyond Utah Beach, and one full company landed almost completely intact eight miles east of the DZ on Utah Beach and had a ringside seat for the invasion.[105]

The 507th Parachute Infantry Regiment—Captain Sophian's regiment—was the last American parachute infantry regiment to fly into the aerial battle zone at the western edge of the Cotentin Peninsula. Some two thousand men in one hundred and seventeen aircraft flown by the veteran 61st Troop Carrier Group and the green 442nd Troop Carrier Group were supposed to drop at DZ "T" west of the Merderet River about half a mile north of Amfreville. This drop was also a shambles, declared Blair. "The veteran 61 Group held together fairly well in the cloud layers, but the green 442nd broke up, dispersed, and was badly harassed by flak. When the planes came out of the clouds, they were flying too high and fast. Only two or three sticks hit the DZ. Many pilots overshot the DZ by a thousand to two thousand yards and dropped their sticks into the Merderet marshes, where some were drowned … One man refused to jump."[105]

The 507th Parachute Infantry Regiment's third battalion commander (Captain Sophian's commander) was William A. Kuhn. He bailed out of his plane at high speed, later reporting that "he had never had such a 'hard' parachute opening." The shock dislocated his collarbone (clavicle), and he was evacuated to England to recover.[105]

Colonel Gavin of the 505th declared optimistically (his stick hit its drop zone), "Except for approximately fifty plane loads [some nine hundred paratroopers, including Captain Sophian], the parachute force of the 82nd Airborne Division was landed in an area about five by seven miles, with its center of impact roughly at La Fiere."[87]

The 507th Parachute Regiment Infantry experienced the worst drop of Operation Overlord. Morgan explained:

> While it is generally understood that the 82nd and 101st Airborne drops were badly scattered during the Normandy operation, it is not well known that the 507th was spread out over a greater area than any of the other parachute infantry regiments making the jump. While a few 507th troopers landed on the DZ, others landed in 101st drop zones. Elements of the 2nd Battalion landed far north of where they were supposed to—some came down near the village of Le Ham while one unfortunate stick of eighteen troopers landed north of Valognes just a few miles south of Cherbourg [held by the Germans]. Some troopers came down well to the east of the drop zone between Sainte-Marie-du-Mont and Hebert. A few men even ended up on the beach itself. Finally, ten sticks from 3rd Battalion [one of these ten sticks included Captain Sophian] landed twenty-five miles south of the DZ near the village of Graignes. In all, it is estimated that the regiment was spread-out over sixty square miles. Strangely, there was a positive element to this scattering. With such broad dispersion of landings, the German commanders on the scene were reporting that a much larger area was being attacked than was actually intended that night and they therefore concluded that a much larger force had been inserted in the Cotentin than actually had. With the magnitude of the airborne operation

still an unknown quantity, the enemy reaction was slow and uncertain. This bought time that the men of the 507th would need—time that would prove to be of decisive importance in the battles of the coming days.[106]

German anti-aircraft gunners were hyper-alert by the time the 82nd Airborne Division paratroopers poured over the western edge of Cotentin Peninsula. The latter faced "a heavy curtain of fire" that looked like an "impressive 4th of July." One paratrooper with the 82nd Airborne Division recalled that he "noticed an impressive fireworks display" and "admired the show until [he] realized what [the flashes of red, yellow, blue and white] were: anti-aircraft shells ... No amount of training could have prepared any of the men in those C-47s for what they were flying into," Morgan declared.[107]

The C-47s themselves were vulnerable to German artillery flak coming from the ground, and some paratroopers sustained serious injuries before they even jumped. For example, Captain Loyal K. Bogart, B Company commander of the 501st Parachute Infantry Regiment, 101st Airborne Division, was hit by flak inside his plane before he jumped. Nevertheless, he jumped with his stick, which was errantly dropped near Graignes. Upon landing, he broke his leg and asked his men to leave him behind. They refused and carried him to Graignes, where Captain Sophian put him to bed in the command post that Major Johnson had established in the Graignes boys' school, not far from the Graignes church.[108] Captain Bogart was given the job of monitoring the radio for messages. He was killed in his bed by mortar fire at the end of the Battle of Graignes.[109]

Pilots flying the C-47s on D-day had a rough night. Besides the inclement weather on the western side of the Cotentin Peninsula and the curtain of flak, other problems plagued them. For example, Morgan noted:

Under normal loading circumstances, the aircraft were capable of maintaining stable flight at the relatively slow forward air speed of ninety miles per hour. However, the gross overloading of aircraft that occurred on D-day increased the stall speed of the C-47s to the point that ninety miles per hour was so dangerously slow that aircraft could potentially stall and then drop out of the sky. To compensate for the higher stall speed, Troop Carrier pilots were forced to drop their paratroopers at a forward air speed approximately twenty to thirty miles per hour faster than the ninety miles per hour speed of training jumps. Thus the Troop Carrier C-47s were dropping their paratroopers at speeds of 110, 120 [miles per hour] or even faster.[109]

In addition, only about two of every five troop carrier group C-47s had a navigator aboard on D-day (Captain Sophian's C-47 did have a navigator aboard on D-day), an arrangement that had worked well during exercises held in broad daylight under ideal conditions. But this arrangement did not work well in the dark and disorienting conditions of Operation Overlord. Further challenging their accuracy in reaching drop zones, troop carrier group pilots were under orders to maintain strict radio silence, which eliminated their ability to adapt and adjust their plans "to mitigate or overcome the problems encountered during the approach to the drop zones. The C-47s were not only prohibited from communicating with their bases back in southern England, but they were also prohibited from communicating from plane to plane when that may very well have helped the situation tremendously."[109]

Finally, the winds on D-day were twenty to thirty knots and generated sudden patches of turbulence that buffeted the C-47s and knocked many of them off course. The airspeed and altitude of the C-47s allowed pilots a very narrow window of opportunity to line up on their drop zones before they dropped their sticks of paratroopers.[109] Pilots were under orders to return no paratroopers to England. Two and a half percent of the American C-47s that flew to Normandy on the night of June 5–6, 1944, were lost in combat, according to Morgan.[110]

Some observers accused troop carrier group pilots for irresponsibly scattering paratroopers all over the Cotentin Peninsula. Sergeant Thomas J. Blakely of the 505th Parachute Infantry Regiment Infantry disagreed with this assessment:

> Those guys flying those planes had all they could handle. They had an airplane that had eighteen guys in the back, and six equipment bundles. They were in formation, they were going in and out of clouds, they were getting shot at, they had no idea where they were, the Pathfinders hadn't worked, so they had no way of knowing what was going on and where they were. They were scared of running into each other because everybody was dodging. They had their hands full. So I can understand why they got to some place and said get 'em out, because they were going to be back over the channel before long. I never did hold it against any of those pilots.[111]

Sergeant Blakely's 505th Parachute infantry Regiment was the only regiment of the 82nd Airborne Division whose pilots found their drop zone.

Blair disagreed with Blakely, opining that:

> The poor American drops were due, principally, to lack of vigorous training in the American troop-carrier command. The buildup of IX Troop Carrier Command aircraft and glider forces had been too slow and casual. Bad weather, short daylight hours and other factors had impeded training in March and April [1944], but even so, the airborne forces believed it had never been pursued with a real sense of urgency. In the mission itself, provisions should have been made for possible bad weather; at best an advance "weather plane" to test the skies and radio back

an encoded report to Troop Carrier Headquarters. At least there should have been a provision for the pathfinders or lead serials to break radio silence in order to warn those planes coming behind. To allow some nine hundred planes, manned by undertrained crews (twenty percent of them completely green) and all too few navigators to fly completely unwarned into bad weather suggest incompetence and stupidity. The resulting loss in life, injuries and wounds and the utter disorganization created within the 82nd and 101st division was nothing short of scandalous.[112]

Blair continued his analysis:

There had also been too many problems in locating the DZs. Not enough American planes had been equipped with Gee [British radio navigation system forerunner of LORAN, an American navigation system] and other electronic navigation devices, and the few crews that had such gear were not sufficiently trained in its use. The result was that many pilots, disoriented and dispersed by the turbulent clouds, were never able to regain their bearings. Without Rebecca electronics [portable homing beacon system, airborne receiver] to receive Eureka signals [portable homing beacon system, ground transmitter] from the pathfinders, too many American planes were left to find the DZs "by guess and by God." In addition, the DZ marker lights and panels put in operation by the pathfinders proved to be inadequate.[112]

Chapter Nine: Church of Graignes, June 6–11, 1944

The tiny French farming village of Graignes is located near the neck of the Cotentin Peninsula. Its location was so far south of Operation Overlord on D-day that it was not recorded on the official Operation Overlord military map. In other words, the map ended slightly below (south of) Carentan at the neck of Cotentin Peninsula; Graignes was about five miles further southeast of Carentan, across low swampy land at or below sea level.

Graignes during World War II consisted of about two hundred widely dispersed farmhouses and several businesses, such as the café and grocery store owned and operated by Madame Germaine Boursier. Graignes also was home to a twelfth-century Norman church with a belfry that overlooked miles of flat, flooded terrain at the time of the Normandy invasion.

The Germans had not occupied Graignes prior to Operation Overlord despite its strategic location in part because they were struggling to find enough soldiers simultaneously to defend their eastern and western fronts. Thus, the citizens of Graignes were stunned on the morning of June 6, 1944, when wet, bedraggled, and disoriented paratroopers with their faces painted black (to become less visible to the enemy) knocked on the doors of their café, church, and many farmhouses. The church priest wrote in his diary the following about Operation Overlord, as he saw it unfolding from Graignes during the early morning hours of June 6, 1944:

The night of June 5 [–6, 1944] was a terrible one. From the town, especially from the belfry of the church, one could perceive in the distance, in the direction of Sainte-Marie-du-Mont [around ten miles to the north] reddish lights and artillery fire. The air was filled with airplanes that striped the night sky by the thousands. The German artillery units in Carentan [around five miles to the northwest] fired without stopping. Planes were dropping bombs [no bombs were dropped; perhaps he was seeing some unfortunate C-47 aircraft crashing to earth] and the distant explosions shook the earth. Others were leading gliders and dropping parachutists over the region … Around 2:20 a.m., a wave of aircraft approached Graignes at a very low altitude and dropped close to two hundred parachutists into the swamps of the community and neighboring areas. Soon they were heading for Graignes.[113]

Captain Sophian survived his night jump without injuries and in the dark night located four other officers of the 507th Parachute Infantry Regiment. These officers were Major Charles D. Johnson, Captain Richard H. Chapman, and First Lieutenants Elmer F. Hoffman and Earcle R. Reed. General Ridgway explained how paratroopers were trained to find one another once they reached the ground:

The first men out of plane note its general heading in relation to the ground. When they hit and shuck out of their harness, they start moving along the track of the plane. The last men out back-track along the path the plane has followed. Somewhere toward the middle they come together. But this takes time. Under the best of conditions the men in one battalion will be strung out along a path one thousand yards long [more than a half mile] and three hundred yards wide. Along their route enemy gunners may block their way until they [the gunners] can be killed. In Normandy the assembling was further complicated by the fact that the fields were compartments, separated each from the other by the high thick hedges. The first objective, of course, is to get a battalion together, for the battalion is the basic fighting unit.[114]

Captain Sophian and the four other officers made for Graignes' Norman church, which they espied silhouetted on high ground in the distance, and finally reached the town about noon on June 6, 1944. Captain Leroy D. Brummitt (3rd Battalion S-3 [an S-3 during wartime is the lead member of a commander's staff who is responsible for training and operations]) had reached Graignes about two hours earlier with some two dozen men.[114] Major Johnson was the most senior officer present and, as a major, had previous experience in company-level command. He took command of the Graignes paratroopers and assigned Captain Brummitt as his second in command.

The ability to speak French of Captain Sophian and Sergeant Benton J. Broussard, a bilingual francophone Cajun from Acadia Parish, Louisiana, facilitated communication between the French villagers and the American paratrooper infantrymen.[115] Both men gave up their lives in Graignes.

Major Johnson and Captain Brummitt disagreed about the best way to manage their perilous situation in Graignes. Major Johnson advocated digging in and defending Graignes while harassing German communications, German resupply to Carentan, and German retreat from Carentan toward the interior of France. He believed the small American paratrooper battalion-sized force could defend its territory long enough to link up with friendly forces moving inland from the Normandy beachheads. Captain Brummitt advocated a forced night march through flooded swamps to German-held Carentan to search for and link up with American paratroopers who were attempting to capture the town. The area between Graignes and Carentan was mostly under water, and the inundation extended for miles north and northwest of Graignes, i.e., in the general direction of Carentan. "This flooded area, though interspersed with some islands of dry ground contained only a few elevated trails, and these generally meandered back into the swamp," wrote Naughton.[116] Major Johnson "curtly" rejected Captain Brummitt's plan, according to Brummitt.

The plans of Major Johnson and Captain Brummitt each had pros and cons, according to an analysis offered by military historian G. H. Bennett:

> Major Johnson had resolved that even though they were miles from American lines, the forces at Graignes could play a valuable role in harassing the enemy rear and in conducting ambushes. This was despite the suggestions of Captain Brummitt, who on June 6 [1944] came up with a plan for a night march across the swamps to rejoin American lines around Carentan. Brummitt knew the vulnerability of their position and above all the need to attain battalion objectives. Major Johnson surmised that by holding Graignes, they could still play a valuable role in attacking enemy forces retreating from the beach and in threatening the enemy's lines of communication to the interior. The roads that connected Carentan to the interior would contain retreating enemy units broken by the American units coming off the beaches, as well as fresh units from the interior [of France] who would have to contain the Allied bridgeheads ... Landing at Graignes was an accident, but in Johnson's eyes, it could be turned into a major opportunity."[117]

Major Johnson's analysis of the Graignes situation was consistent with the original study by Major General George Lynch in 1939 that listed the practicable uses of an American parachute infantry program. These four uses were to deposit small combat groups within enemy territory for special specific missions where the possible accomplishments of the detachment warrant the risk of possible loss of the entire detachment (suicide mission); to deposit small raiding parties for special reconnaissance missions to gain vital information not otherwise obtainable; to deposit small combat groups, possibly as large as a battalion or regiment with artillery to hold a key point, area, or bridge-head until the slower moving elements of the army arrive; and to work in conjunction with a mechanized force at a considerable distance from the main body. Major Johnson believed his troops were ideally positioned to carry out the four practicable uses of paratroopers in a combat situation.

During the afternoon of June 6, 1944, additional 507th 3rd Battalion paratroopers of the 82nd Airborne Division and more than a dozen errantly dropped men from the 101st Airborne Division found their way to Graignes. Captain Loyal Bogart, mentioned earlier, was with the latter group. Still more paratroopers arrived during the night hours of June 6, 1944. By late Wednesday, June 7, 1944, Major Johnson counted one hundred and seventy enlisted men and twelve officers (a total of one hundred and eighty-two soldiers) from the two airborne divisions, a lost US Army glider pilot, two French gendarmes with fourteen escaped Basque detainees, and two 29th Infantry Division soldiers.[119]

Major Johnson's decision to defend Graignes "entailed an on-the-spot reorganization of ... specialist personnel into provisional infantry fire teams reinforced by machine gun and mortar platoons," noted Captain Brummitt in his after-action report. Historian Morgan described the situation:

The Americans immediately began preparing defensive positions, and the village became a hive of activity. Soldiers started digging-in around the town's perimeter, cutting fields of fire, installing communications and otherwise making ready to receive a counterattack. The mortar platoon dug-in around the cemetery [which surrounded the Norman church] and sent a detachment to occupy the church belfry as an observation post. From that vantage point, the observer enjoyed an unobstructed view of the network of roadways and trails leading to the village form the west and southwest. The view would make it possible to adjust fire on any enemy force attempting to approach the village from any direction.[120]

The American paratroopers at Graignes were so far from the rest of the Operation Overlord paratroopers that radio communications equipment was useless. However, Major Johnson succeeded in contacting the 82nd Airborne Division headquarters by using a carrier pigeon. He attached a note to the bird, which read: "Am in position at Graignes coordinate four one five eight zero zero with practically all of hardware blue three four behind enemy lines no contact with friendly forces am remaining in position impossible to get to regiment signed Johnson Major."[121] The pigeon took flight.

The carrier pigeon died en route to wherever it was going. Someone found the dead bird and the note and delivered the latter to Lieutenant Colonel Walter F. Winton, the G-2 of the 82nd Airborne Division headquarters in Normandy. He broadcasted the following message to American units in the region: "No communication with 3d BN [Battalion] 507th CNF. Request unit in whose zone of action this BN is located be notified. Request every possible assistance including air support and resupply by air be rendered this BN and that they be reached with medical assistance as soon as possible."[121]

However, the American paratroopers at Graignes were in no-man's land, meaning no American unit had been assigned Graignes as its zone of action. Thus, no unit could or would come to the aid of the stranded American paratroopers at Graignes until it was too late.

Acting Mayor Alphonse Voydie organized and led the citizens of Graignes, who worked closely with the Americans to secure the village against enemy attack. To avoid arousing German attention, farmers nonchalantly combed the marshes for ammunition bundles and other supplies dropped from C-47s aircraft. These scavenging parties were so successful that the paratroopers soon had an abundance of ammunition and several automatic weapons. "First Lieutenant Reed declared, 'We never did recover the full complement of 'heavy weapons' but we certainly had more ammunition than we thought we could ever fire.'"[122] Other villagers, organized and led by Madame Boursier, fed the paratroopers two meals each day. The Americans meanwhile prepared defensive positions to make ready to receive an enemy attack.

Norman church in Graignes, France, prior to its shelling by German SS troops on June 11, 1944. *Courtesy of the National Archives World War II Museum (formerly the National D-day Museum).*

Chapter Ten: Battle of Graignes, June 6–11, 1944

The German enemy already in the area of the Cotentin Peninsula generally failed to notice for one or two days the collection of 507th and 501st Parachute Infantry Regiment paratroopers dug in at Graignes. The reason was that German battalions were fully occupied trying to hold Carentan against the onslaught of the 101st Airborne Division's 501st, 502nd, and 506th Parachute Infantry Regiments.[118] These three American parachute infantry regiments had successfully consolidated by June 9, 1944, despite being badly scattered during Operation Overlord, losing men, and suffering casualties in taking Saint Côme-du-Mont two and a half miles to the north of Carentan. The three parachute infantry regiments of the 101st Airborne Division now focused their energy on taking Carentan from two German battalions that had escaped from Saint Côme-du-Mont on June 8, 1944.

However, there were more German military divisions waiting in the interior of France. One of them received orders to move to the Cotentin Peninsula to reinforce German troops in Carentan and to close the breach in Fortress Europe at the Normandy beachfronts. Field Marshal Erwin Rommel on June 7, 1944, ordered the 17th SS Panzer Grenadier Division *Gotz von Berlichingen* on a forced march from Thouars to Carentan, a distance of about one hundred and sixty-five miles. The 17th SS Panzer Grenadier Division would wreak devastation on the American paratroopers defending Graignes.

The 17th SS Panzer Grenadier Division was a relatively new German division named after an imperial knight and mercenary named Goetz von Berlichingen (c. 1480–1562) who wore an iron arm prosthesis after losing his right arm when a cannon forced his own sword against his arm. A panzer grenadier division was composed of two motorized infantry regiments of two battalions each, a motorized artillery regiment, and six battalions of supporting troops, with an authorized strength of approximately fourteen thousand officers and men.[123] Hitler ordered formation of this new panzer grenadier division on October 3, 1943. It began forming in December 1943, as the 507th Parachute Infantry Regiment was making its perilous way across the Atlantic Ocean in the *Strathnaver* to Liverpool, England.

Most of the thirty-eight SS divisions in existence in 1945 contained some foreign (i.e., not native German) personnel and nineteen of them consisted largely of foreign personnel, noted historian Stein.[123] The 17th SS Panzer Grenadier Division was one of the nineteen divisions that contained a sizable number of *Volksdeutsche*, or ethnic Germans of Eastern Europe.[134] "According to a document issued by the German government in 1938, *Volksdeutsche* were those who were not citizens of the German Reich but who were German in language and culture." By mid-1944 (when Captain Sophian was killed), "more than 150,000 ethnic Germans were serving in the Waffen SS." These recruits came from Romania, home to the region of Transylvania and semi-fictional character Count Dracula, and "to a lesser extent, the whole of the Balkans region," and "warfare in the Balkans was traditionally brutal," explained Stein.[124]

The acronym "SS" stands for *Schutzstaffel*, which means "protective shield" or "protective squad" in the German language. The SS was a paramilitary organization within the Nazi party that provided Hitler's bodyguard, security forces, including the Gestapo, concentration camp guards, and a corps of combat troops called the Waffen SS. Stein wrote,

> One characteristic that the three great totalitarian systems of the twentieth century—Communism, Fascism, and National

Socialism—had in common was the development of a paramilitary party militia alongside the regular state security organs; the armed forces and police. Originally the instrument of terror and repression, whose function was to ensure the primacy of the dictator, the party militia characteristically grew a new appendage in the face of war. Thus the elite GPU and NKVD division of the Soviet Union during Stalin's rule, the Italian divisions composed of members of Mussolini's Fascist Militia (MVSN), and the armed SS formations of Hitler's Third Reich were all similar manifestations of the modern totalitarian party-state. The Waffen SS emerged during World War II as the largest, most highly developed, and most efficient of the militarized party armies.[124]

Waffen SS troops wore an all-black uniform and a skull and cross-bones emblem on their hats. They were known for their criminality in carrying out a still unknown number of military atrocities during the Second World War, including the murder of Captain Sophian and others in Graignes. As early as 1938, Waffen SS head Heinrich Himmler (1900–1945) began to recruit foreigners of "Germanic" blood for the armed SS. At that time, he was "simply indulging a personal passion. Just as King Frederick William of Prussia (1688–1740) sent his recruiting officers throughout Europe to hunt for exceptionally tall soldiers for his Potsdam Guards, so Himmler sought recruits from all the Germanic countries for a racial show regiment."[124] When Hitler needed more soldiers to fend off increasingly effective assaults on his eastern and western fronts, his commanders conscripted and drastically reduced the training time for *Volksdeutsche*, as described elsewhere by Stein.[124]

Werner Ostendorff (1903–1945) commanded the 17th SS Panzer Grenadier Division from October 30, 1943 to June 15, 1944. Born in Konigsberg in 1903, he joined the army in 1925 and was transferred to the *Luftwaffe*. He qualified as a *Luftwaffe* pilot in 1934 and most certainly interacted with the elite paratroopers held in high regard by Hitler beginning in 1937. Ostendorff served on the frontlines as an observer with the Panzer Division *Kempf* during Hitler's savage overrun of Poland in 1939. *Kempf*—renamed *Das Reich*—became the first SS division on October 10, 1939, and Ostendorff became a Nazi Party SS commander.[125]

Waffen SS Commander Ostendorff was known to lead battles from the front even more so than was typical for SS commanders. For example, in 1941 he drove in person into a dangerous battle situation to obtain first-hand information. Another time he reconnoitered the enemy himself.[125] Indeed, he was so far forward when he reached Carentan on June 15, 1944, after crushing Graignes, that he sustained life-threatening injuries that required his immediate evacuation to Germany for treatment.[125–127]

On June 8, 1944, the 17th SS Panzer Grenadier Division was moving northward from Thouars toward Carentan, as a German field artillery battalion was retreating southward from Carentan. The retreating Germans had aggregated in a field kitchen close to the neighboring village of Montmartin-en-Graignes (northeast of Graignes and southeast of Carentan), according to Bennett. Captain Sophian and Acting Graignes Mayor Voydie observed their activity. Mr. Voydie recalled:

> The American commander, [Major] Johnson, sent seven of his men to wipe them out, for there could be no question of taking so many men prisoner. I said to Captain Sophian that it was very bold to send seven men to wipe out two hundred. He replied, "M. Le Maire [Mr. Mayor], you must realize that one of my men is worth sixty German gunners." But they arrived too late, the Germans had disappeared.[128]

Captain Sophian's comment reflects the high level of morale in the battalion-sized unit in Graignes on that Friday. General Eisenhower stressed the importance of morale during battle as follows:

> As always, the matter of the Army's morale attracted the

attention of all senior commanders ... Diffidence or modesty must never blind the commander to his duty of showing himself to his men, of speaking to them, of mingling with them to the extent of physical limitations. It pays big dividends in terms of morale, and morale, given rough equality in other things, is supreme on the battlefield.[129]

On Saturday morning, June 10, 1944, Major Johnson ordered communications specialist First Lieutenant Francis "Frank" E. Naughton and the unit's demolition squad, with support, to destroy the bridge at Le Port des Planques. The bridge spanned the Vire-Taute Canal and was on the road between Graignes and Carentan, about three-fourths of a mile north of Graignes. Major Johnson ordered destruction of the bridge to deny "Germans the use of a road that would facilitate their withdrawal from Carentan." He did not want retreating German soldiers to have egress to safety in the interior of France, and he did not want them backing into his troops at Graignes. The American paratrooper demolition squad successfully bombed the bridge, killing some German soldiers who had unknowingly approached the bridge. Details of this maneuver are available elsewhere.[130]

On Saturday afternoon, June 10, 1944, Commander Ostendorff's 17th Waffen SS Panzer Grenadier Division reached the ancient walled city of Saint-Lô in the center of the neck of the Cotentin Peninsula ten miles southeast of Graignes. The division had covered some one hundred and fifty miles in three days. The Germans set up a command post in Saint-Lô, which they maintained vigorously until forcefully expelled around July 11, 1944, by the rapidly advancing Allies.[131] Major Johnson's troops and Graignes citizens were unlucky in war in laying directly in the path of the 17th SS Panzer Grenadier Division driving from Saint-Lô to Carentan. The Germans in Saint-Lô immediately sent a reconnaissance party in the direction of Graignes.

American paratroopers monitoring the perimeter of Graignes identified and ambushed the approaching German mechanized patrol, killing at least one German soldier.[132] The Americans found intelligence papers on the German that indicated he belonged to an advance guard of an *armored division* (i.e., the 17th SS Panzer Grenadier Division). The American paratroopers lacked the weaponry necessary to repel an attack by an armored division. They hoped that Allied reinforcements from the beachheads would arrive imminently to reinforce their Graignes ranks against the approaching Panzer division.

Sunday, June 11, 1944, was to become the day of reckoning for the American paratroopers and citizens of Graignes. A link up with Allied troops from the beachheads had not occurred, but the defensive perimeter around Graignes was so quiet on Sunday morning that Major Johnson gave sixty-four-year-old Father Albert Leblastier the go-ahead to officiate at a ten o'clock mass in the Norman church. Both Graignes villagers and some paratroopers attended the mass. Captain Sophian and Privates Jesus Casas and Joseph Stachowiak (enlisted medics)— were also in the church as usual caring for wounded paratroopers.

Meanwhile, two American paratroopers were sent to bury the German soldier with the intelligence papers they had killed the day before "but were met by fire that drove them back and seemed unusually heavy."[133] Captain Brummitt investigated the situation and found German soldiers approaching in force from the south of Graignes. Madames Pereete and Bazire also saw the force approaching Graignes and ran into the church shouting, "The Germans are coming!" Father Leblastier was only ten minutes into the liturgy.[133]

American paratroopers inside the church ran to their guns to close the southern perimeter of Graignes, while village parishioners were asked to remain inside the church. Captain Sophian provided reassurance to the upset citizens who were fully aware of the nature of a German reprisal. Father Leblastier started reading nonstop from *The Appearances at Fatima*.[145] Some parishioners slipped out of the church and ran home anyway. However, twelve-year-old Raymond Lareculay was content to use the time sequestered in the church to study for an upcoming religious studies examination.[134]

The Germans struck the southern defense perimeter of Graignes at about noon on Sunday, June 11, 1944. The first attack lasted only thirty minutes. It was disorganized and ineffective, according to witnesses, which suggested to observers that the advancing German division initially under-appreciated the strength of the American forces at Graignes. The American paratroopers inflicted heavy casualties on the German SS troops while sustaining only a few themselves, which buoyed their spirits. American paratrooper casualties were taken to the church where Captain Sophian and the medics cared for them. The American paratroopers at Graignes fought with light machine guns, mortars, hand grenades, carbines, and a few rifles.[135]

Two hours later, Major Johnson ordered all citizens still in the church to move quietly along the hedgerows to their homes. He had learned of the deployment of twelve truckloads of German infantry in the fields around the village of Le Mesnil-Angot located less than one mile south of Graignes. Major Johnson now possessed full situational awareness, meaning he understood the size of the enemy and what it was preparing to do, and that he needed to prepare Graignes citizens and his troops for the worst.

Thirty minutes later (around two-thirty in the afternoon on Sunday June 11, 1944), even more German troops arrived at Le Mesnil-Angot. They positioned artillery one-third mile south of Le Mesnil-Angot in the village of Thieuville. Indeed, Le Mesnil-Angot may have become the German's command post for the Battle of Graignes.[136] Waffen SS Commander Ostendorff may in fact have been in the command post in Le Mesnil-Angot, as he was known for leading from the front in battle. German artillery gunners from their vantage point in Thieuville had a direct line of sight for much of Graignes, including its vulnerable Norman church belfry.

Fighting resumed in earnest. The American paratroopers believed their fighting was effective because they could see German trucks moving from "collecting point to collecting point" to pick up piles of dead or wounded soldiers.[137] However, American casualties also began to mount. "As the aid station filled to overflowing, women and teen-age girls serving as nurses were assisting Captain Sophian ... and his [two] medics in coping with the demands of the wounded with pitifully few medical supplies," wrote Fox.[137]

The intensity of the fighting increased throughout the afternoon. The final German assault occurred at twilight on Sunday June 11, 1944. Heavy mortar and a German antitank gun now supported a regiment-size German attacking force (around two thousand men).[138-139] Fox explained what happened next:

> The Germans had installed a couple of Eighty-eights [artillery] on the heights of a farm at Thieuville belonging to M. Octave, the assistant mayor. From there the Germans aimed at the village (Graignes) and opened fire, peppering the boys' school, the church and the square reaching even the wounded soldiers in the church. In the belfry (tower) an observation post had been set up and an early salvo destroyed it killing [First Lieutenant] Elmer Farnham and an assistant. [First] Lieutenant "Pip" Reed, who had been in the belfry with Farnham just prior to the enemy's incoming round, remembered, "I went up to the belfry to coax Farnham and another observer to abandon their position because of imminent enemy artillery fire. We could see through our binoculars two enemy 75 mm (more than likely 88's) guns digging in. Farnham wanted to stay and I left the belfry and returned to my machine guns. Farnham directed his mortars in an unsuccessful attempt to disable the enemy artillery pieces before they could fire; he couldn't and they did." Succeeding salvos systematically reduced other buildings and prepared positions to shambles. During this bombardment, Major Charles Johnson, the Graignes force leader, was killed along with [First] Lieutenant Lowell C. Maxwell.[140]

First Lieutenant Maxwell had become very ill, and Major Johnson was at his bedside when a shell tore into the command post in the boys' school instantly killing both officers. Captain Leroy "Dave" Brummitt became the battalion's commanding officer.

At around eleven o'clock at night on June 11, 1944, two young girls at their family's farm in Le Pont Saint-Pierre, about two and a half miles from Graignes, witnessed a dispiriting sight: "We saw the red flares signaling for help go up from the church. Since the Americans were out of ammunition, they could no longer hold off the enemy."[141] Captain Sophian and the other men in the church were signaling their desperate situation by launching flares that turned the night sky red.

Chapter Eleven: Abandoning Graignes, June 11–12, 1944

As red flares cut open the night sky, Commanding Officer Captain Brummitt ordered the able-bodied paratroopers to head for safety in the marshes. Private Harvey Richig recalled, "We had to evacuate our positions when our ranks were decimated and ammunition expended. We were told by our officers to disassemble our crew-served weapons, pair off and try to make it to Carentan or Sainte-Mère-Église as best we could."[142] Captain Brummitt abandoned Graignes because ammunition was low and to stay there meant imprisonment or death or both. He more or less implemented the general plan he had devised five days earlier.

Heading for safety in the marshes proved to be a "difficult experience" for the fleeing officers and enlisted men. For example, First Lieutenant Frank Naughton, according to historian Morgan, led approximately twenty paratroopers who spent all night wandering through the marshes until they were "absolutely exhausted [Naughton's words]. It was three feet of water and every hundred yards or so, six or eight feet of water because of the drainage ditches. It was a grueling experience with these soldiers. We'd lost a couple nights' sleep anyway and were on meager rations and we were out of ammunition for all practical purposes."[143]

The Rigault family was part of the French underground and provided safe haven in its barn for many desperate paratroopers who climbed back out of the marshes looking for shelter and food. The family found some paratroopers roaming aimlessly in the outskirts of Graignes awaiting link up with Normandy beachhead forces, which never came. Naughton and his group spent several hours in the Rigault barn on Monday June 12, 1944. Morgan wrote:

> Just after noon, they were joined by a group of approximately sixty troopers being led by Captain Brummitt, who had been wandering in the marshes all night, too. Captain Brummitt was anxious to get the force out of the area and join the rest of the [507th] regiment [such as those members who had dropped successfully to the assigned DZ "T"]. The combined group [Naughton and Brummitt] remained at the Rigault farm until dusk [the evening of Monday June 12, 1944], at which time French volunteers took them north in boats across the marshes.[143]

At dawn on June 13, 1944, the band of Americans climbed out of the boats and continued their dangerous journey on foot, finally arriving safely in Carentan that evening.[143] Captain Brummitt's group first made contact with a reconnaissance patrol from US Army 2nd Armored Division at six o'clock in the evening, according to Fox. Then:

> Around midnight, Captain Brummitt along with First Lieutenant George C. Murn and twelve 101st Airborne men reported into 101st Division headquarters [which held Carentan]. Here Brummitt gave all available information he had concerning Germans in the area. He then called [by phone] 82nd Airborne Headquarters [in Sainte-Mère-Église] which directed him to report in. In the meantime, the Five-O-Seven men were rested and fed before being trucked to Ste.-Mere-Eglise. Captain Brummitt reported to Division (82nd) Headquarters at 3:00 p.m., June 14, 1944, with a total strength of seventy enlisted men and five officers.[144]

Fox noted that eight officers representing the 82nd and 101st Airborne Divisions left Graignes after midnight on Monday June 12, 1944, and safely reached American lines. They were, according to Fox, Commanding Officer Captain Leroy D. Brummitt, Captain Richard H. Chapman, First Lieutenant Willard E. Chambers, First Lieutenant George C. Murn, First Lieutenant Francis E. Naughton, First Lieutenant Earcle R. Reed, First Lieutenant H. Edward Wagner, and Second Lieutenant William A. Comstock.[145]

Captain Brummitt's order to abandon Graignes did not reach many paratroopers who were widely dispersed in foxholes and hedgerows. They made their own decisions about what to do as German soldiers swarmed over Graignes. Private Edward (Eddie) T. Page was in a foxhole with Private First Class Frank P. Costa, according to Costa's son, who wrote down his father's memories of the horrific night. Private Page did not want to abandon Graignes and told Costa that they "ought to stay and fight to the last man." Costa and a third man responded by giving "a surprised look at each other." What happened next?

> The[y] turned to Eddie and said, "What for?" They were unimpressed with Eddie's reasoning based on the fact that they were paratroopers. So they hid for two days in the hedgerow. [Costa] was getting light-headed from a lack of food. Eddie wanted to stay and wait for relief, if it would ever come. [Costa] and Charlie decided to try to make their way back to friendly lines. Eventually, they convinced Eddie to come along. On a road they met a farmer and held him at gun point. [See the appendix.]

The farmer took the three men to the Rigault family's barn on Tuesday, June 13, 1944, where ten other paratroopers had found safety in the hayloft since the departure of Captain Brummitt's group the day before. Eventually a second set (the set after the Brummitt group) of twenty-one Americans occupied the hayloft of the Rigault barn, determined to wait for the Allied breakthrough from the beaches. They believed that the the paratroopers previously evacuated by the Rigault family would send help to retrieve the eighty enlisted men and one officer (Captain Sophian) who remained trapped in or near Graignes. Morgan declared:

> As long as they believed that such a possibility existed, there was no need for the Americans to risk venturing from their hiding place in the barn. The fact that the 101st Airborne captured Carentan on the 12th [of June] hinted that such a break through might happen, so everyone waited and hoped for the best. Disappointingly, Tuesday the 13th [of June] brought no news of an advance from Carentan. When the situation remained unchanged on Wednesday the 14th as well, it began to sink in that the 101st was simply consolidating its position around Carentan and that a breakthrough might be days, if not weeks away.[146]

On Wednesday night June 14, 1944, Gustave Rigault arranged for a boatman to take the second set of paratroopers in his barn through the marshes to dry land near Carentan. They climbed out of the boat to enter a heavily defended perimeter in a combat zone. "When an American sentry challenged them, they knew they were home. They were taken into Carentan where they told their story. Before sunrise, they were on trucks bound for Ste.-Mere-Eglise [headquarters of the 82nd Airborne Division]."[146]

Did Captain Sophian receive Captain Brummitt's order to flee Graignes? The question is moot. Morgan eloquently summarized the situation that confronted Captain Sophian at the time Captain Brummitt left Graignes: "Captain Sophian was at the aid station and was in no position to evacuate." As battalion surgeon:

> He was the ranking physician [officer] present and he was

treating a number of non-ambulatory wounded men. Since there was no possibility of carrying the wounded out through the marshes, Sophian realized that it was inevitable that they would all fall into German hands. Thus, he was faced with the most important decision of his life: the choice between duty and self … Without hesitating, he chose to stay behind to care for his wounded comrades—he chose duty. He was not ordered to do it; he did it of his own free will. It was a decision that would cost him his life.[146]

Captains Brummitt and Sophian likely hoped for the textbook case for American paratroopers stranded in Graignes—that is, treatment by the German enemy according to the principles of the Geneva Convention of 1929. Their training probably led them to believe that the worst scenario was imprisonment in a concentration camp. But time proved that there was an even worse scenario: summary execution by *Volksdeutsche*.

Several hours after Graignes fell to the Germans around midnight June 12, 1944, Carentan fell to the Americans. The two events were related. The American paratroopers at Graignes had harassed, inflicted serious casualties on, forced use of ammunition, and delayed the 17th SS Panzer Grenadier Division in its forward movement toward Carentan. This courageous stand by the battalion of American paratroopers led by Major Charles D. Johnson in Graignes helped to guarantee an American (101st Airborne Division) victory in Carentan. Historian Phil Nordyke described the battalion's achievement, as follows:

The gallant stand by those few 507th paratroopers contributed substantially to the success of the Normandy campaign, by delaying and inflicting heavy casualties upon the 17th SS Panzer Grenadier Division. Captain [he was actually a first lieutenant] Frank Naughton, with Headquarters Company, 3rd Battalion, 507th, summed up their achievement this way: "For five days, the Americans were able to outwit, out maneuver, and out fight a German force that desperately needed the road network that Graignes overlooked, whether to evacuate Carentan or reinforce it."[147]

Bennett concurred with Nordyke:

The defense of Graignes played a significant, but largely forgotten, part in securing the Allied beachhead. It had restricted the enemy's freedom of maneuver in the days after June 6. Most importantly, Graignes prevented the speedy advance of the Gotz von Berlichingen Division at a time when the fate of Carentan hung in the balance.[148]

Axis powers military historian Antonio J. Munoz noted that by July 23, 1944, American forces had decimated the fighting strength of the 17th SS Panzer Grenadier Division. The German Seventh Army reported for that date:

1. Battalions: two weak, five exhausted, and one replacement battalion.
2. Artillery: five light batteries.
3. Armor: ten PAK-75 mm anti-tank guns mounted on turretless chassis, ten *Sturmgeschutz IVs* (assault guns carrying the 75-mm gun).
4. Motorization: thirty percent.
5. Battle Rating: "4."

The German battle ratings were as follows:

- Rating 1: Capable of full attack.
- Rating 2: Capable of limited attack.
- Rating 3: Capable of full defense.
- Rating 4: Capable of limited defense.[149]

On June 15, 1944, the 17th SS Panzer Grenadier Division reported 18,354 men (584 officers, 3,566 non-commissioned officers, and 14,204 men). Two weeks later on June 30, 1944, the total strength had been drastically reduced by more than one-half to 8,530 men (226 officers, 1,765 non-commissioned officers, and 6,539 men).[128] The American paratrooper battalion in Graignes had initiated this death-spiral of a German division's fighting power in Normandy.

Chapter Twelve: Massacre at Graignes, June 12, 1944

American paratroopers hiding in their foxholes and floundering soaking wet in the marshes around Graignes watched as German soldiers swarmed the village early Monday morning, June 12, 1944. Many German soldiers "were observed to be wearing black uniforms, giving substance to an early report that at least a part of the attacking force was composed of SS troops."[147]

Responding to the extreme situation in which he now found himself, Captain Sophian walked from the interior of the crumbling church structure to its entrance and waved a white flag, according to information provided by US Army personnel to Captain Sophian's kin in early April 1945. This practice signified to the enemy his status as a surrendering unarmed medic caring for wounded men and his appeal for humane treatment by the enemy in accordance with the Geneva Convention rights of unarmed medical personnel and patients during battle. Captain Sophian hoped the Germans would take him, Privates Casas and Stachowiak, and the seventeen injured paratroopers as prisoners of war and, at worst, send them to a concentration camp.

The German troops instead forced Captain Sophian, Privates Casas and Stachowiak, and the ambulatory wounded men against the wall in the courtyard of the church and prepared to execute them, according to eyewitnesses. However, the SS troops abruptly stopped, probably because Graignes citizens observing the situation would report the atrocity.

The SS troops instead divided the American paratrooper prisoners into two groups and marched each group away from the church and prying eyes, according to witnesses. The smaller group of five paratroopers were directed to the edge of a shallow pond behind Madame Boursier's café where the "SS murderers bayoneted the helpless, wounded men and threw them into the water one on top of the other. Some of them were not even dead when they were pushed in. There were later found there all huddled together," reported French witnesses.[150] A bayonet is a sharp knife that fits over the end or underneath the muzzle of a rifle barrel, effectively turning the gun into a spear. At some point during the early morning hours, SS troops also likely executed three critically-injured, non-ambulatory paratroopers still in the church. Acting Mayor Voydie said he found their bodies at dawn.

It is difficult to reconstruct with certainty what happened to the larger group of American prisoners that SS troops marched away from Graignes in the direction of Le Mesnil-Angot. Bennett speculated that the 17th SS Panzer Grenadiers may have interrogated the prisoners in Le Mesnil-Angot.[162] The Geneva Convention of 1929 required that a prisoner give his name, rank, and serial number and no further information of any kind. Examples of other types of information often sought by the enemy was the strength of the prisoner's unit, location of other units, training received, signals and radio equipment used, everything about the ground forces of the US Army, and information about food supply, politics, morale among civilians, and the armed forces in the United States and Great Britain.[152]

What happened after the possible interrogation postulated by Bennett? Many officers of the Waffen SS Panzer divisions were known for their egregious disregard of the Geneva Convention of 1929. Some of them ordered and sometimes personally observed military atrocities. For example, twenty captured Canadian soldiers from the North Nova Scotia Highlanders and 27th Canadian Armoured Regiment, the

Sherbrooke Fusilier Regiment, were executed by members of the SS Panzer Division *Hitler Jugend* on June 7, 1944 (D-day plus one day), inside the Ardenne Abbey near Caen, France.[153]

Another Nazi SS atrocity occurred shortly after the D-day drop when seven American paratroopers, also with the 507th Parachute Infantry Regiment, surrendered after a brief firefight with German soldiers near Hemevez, Normandy (seven miles northwest of Sainte-Mère-Église). After disarming the Americans, German soldiers executed each one with a single rifle shot to the back of the head, which had been hooded. The German soldiers hurried off, leaving burial of the slaughtered Americans to French civilians. Members of a company of the US Quartermaster Graves Registration Service recovered the Hemevez bodies in late June 1944.[154]

Mayor Jean Poullain of Le Mesnil-Angot told US Army personnel in June 1947 that on June 12, 1944, German soldiers took "nine American parachutist prisoners ... to a field and kill[ed] them." He continued, "A few days later I saw these bodies in a hole."[155] Mayor Poullain's testimony suggests that SS troops killed the group of paratroopers at Le Mesnil-Angot in the early morning of June 12, 1944, in the same manner as described for the soldiers at Hemevez.

After executing the American prisoners in the early morning hours of June 12, 1944, SS troops continued their ugly reprisal in Graignes by murdering Fathers Leblastier and Charles Lebarbanchon inside their beloved Norman church. Their bodies were found by the sacristan's wife Mother Marguerite who brought milk to the rectory each morning. When she arrived to deliver the milk during the Monday morning of June 12, 1944,

> She was met by two German soldiers at the gate to the courtyard who said to her, "Madame, the priest has gone, priest finished." Quite surprised she threw a quick glance at the rectory door which was still open. In the courtyard she saw two small puddles of blood and not far from them a pair of glasses and a

key ring belonging to the pastor. All this seemed rather strange and suspicious to the woman. She entered and finally found both priests in the apartments close to the walls covered over with sticks. The men of God had been killed. Abbe Leblastier had been pumped with bullets, while Charles Lebarbanchon, O.F.M., a Franciscan from the house of Bernay, seemed only to have received one bullet through the back of the neck. Their bodies had been dragged.[156]

The German soldiers also murdered elderly rectory housekeepers Eugenie DuJardin and Madeleine Pezeril. Morgan wrote, "Overwhelmed with fear, the two ladies had been cowering in their beds ever since the beginning of the final assault. The Germans shot both women in their beds."[157]

Meanwhile other German soldiers rounded up and held captive forty-four Graignes villagers. They interrogated the villagers as suspected American collaborators, but they did not execute them, as this act would have raised questions in the outside world. In addition, the gruesome day had witnessed sufficient bloodletting, according to one German officer who had the power to stop the carnage. The earlier executions of American paratroopers, priests, and rectory housekeepers probably saved the lives of many Graignes residents. The Germans sent the captive villagers south to nearby Le Haut Vernay to remove the hundreds of German soldiers slain or wounded during the Battle of Graignes.

However, the SS troops were not done with their retribution. When dawn broke on Monday, June 12, 1944, German soldiers ransacked every house in Graignes, overturning furniture, rifling through belongings, and plundering valuables. They then set the town on fire. Morgan wrote,

On Tuesday the 13th [June 13, 1944], the Germans attempted to destroy the evidence of the atrocity [murdering the priests and housekeepers]. They poured gasoline over the bodies of Father Leblastier, Father Lebarbencon, Eugenie DuJardin and

Madeleine Pezeril and set them on fire. The ensuing blaze burned out of control, destroying sixty-six homes, the boys' school, Madame Boursier's café and the Norman church. Another 159 homes and other buildings were damaged either as a result of that fire or the fighting...Only two houses survived unscathed.[157]

The final figures for American deaths and survivals, according to the data obtained by Fox, are as follows: Of the initial one hundred and eighty-two American paratroopers who congregated in Graignes on D-day, June 6, 1944, thirty-one lost their lives (17 percent). Of these thirty-one dead Americans, six were officers (19 percent) and twenty-five (81 percent) were enlisted men. The six officers who lost their lives, according to Fox, were:

- Major Charles D. Johnson (commanding officer)
- Captain Loyal K. Bogart
- Captain Abraham (Bud) Sophian, Jr.
- First Lieutenant Elmer F. Farnham
- First Lieutenant Elmer F. Hoffman, and
- First Lieutenant Lowell C. Maxwell.[158]

The remaining one hundred and fifty-one men (83 percent) left Graignes to safely reach American lines. Of these American paratrooper survivors of the Battle of Graignes, eight (5 percent) were officers and one hundred and forty-three (95 percent) were enlisted men. The eight officers who survived their Graignes ordeal were, according to Fox:

- Captain Leroy D. Brummitt (successor commanding officer)
- Captain Richard H. Chapman
- First Lieutenant Willard E. Chambers
- First Lieutenant George C. Murn
- First Lieutenant Francis E. Naughton

- First Lieutenant Earcle R. Reed
- First Lieutenant H. Edward Wagner and
- Second Lieutenant William A. Comstock.[158]

Captain Brummitt and the other seven officers accompanied seventy enlisted men to safety. The other seventy-three enlisted men must have made it to safety on their own, their stories lost to the ages or possibly buried in family scrapbooks. Thirty-two Graignes citizens perished during the Battle of Graignes.[158]

Chapter Thirteen: Captain Sophian's
Long Trip Home, 1944–1949

Eight days after the execution of Captain Sophian, his sister (Emily Sophian O'Leary), who was unaware of his awful fate, sent a single-spaced, typed V-Mail to him. The postal service returned the letter to her on September 10, 1944, because Bud's whereabouts were unknown. Her letter read as follows:

Bud Darling –

This is a supreme gesture of sorts because my hands are still crippled, but you are so much in my thoughts I can't stand not writing any longer. There has been no news of you since the invasion and it is gradually becoming impossible to think of anything but how you are and where you are and wish like hell that a letter dated after the sixth [June 6, 1944, D-day] would arrive. Mother and Dad are putting up a remarkable front but we'll all sleep better when word from you reaches us.

   At this point my maid is on vacation, and Marjorie is still with us. She cancelled her reservation for the third time Sunday night, a couple of hours before her train was due to leave and now is beginning to be afraid that she may have stalled herself here for the duration. Ted assured her that he could get her out of here whenever she wished to go but the word from the railroads is that the first available space is the eighteenth of July [1944]. We think it's pretty funny but every now and then, she gets a conscience and says she ought to be home and does not share our amusement.

It could be, of course, that our sense of humor is distorted. The night she got here we welcomed her in typical O'Leary fashion and just when we were at our blindest our neighbors, the Lathrops, dropped in. One of our adorable dogs bit the seat/butt of Mrs. L. and she has said since that she didn't mind losing her bottom nearly as much as did the fact that Ted and I slapped our thighs and nearly went into convulsions over it. I guess it's little tricks of that nature that have endeared us so to all who know us. We have now definitely decided that we are the most unpopular pair in town. We never miss an opportunity to distinguish ourselves—the Guettel wedding, for instance. I will say, though, that as far as that occasion was concerned, our behavior was not much worse than that of everyone else. Even our father [Dr. Abraham Sophian] was feeling no pain. We got a drunken photographer from the *Star* to take our pictures so that you will be able to see for yourself, if he ever makes up the prints that he promised even ten days ago. I personally think that he has long since drowned in his developing solution during an attack of drunkenness from drinking but my spies on the *Star* report that there is still hope that the pictures will be forthcoming.

Both the children continue to have health for the time being and Ted is looking reasonably well too considering the fact that he has been existing in a practically constant state of hangover since Marjorie's arrival. As for me, I'm battered but still around. My hands are still swollen and sore but the rest of me has improved to some extent. Dad [Dr. Abraham Sophian] is now filling me full of snake venom which will probably cure my ails at some future date but which will undoubtedly leave me even more poisonous than before—and that, I'm afraid, will be something to conjure with!

Be as careful as you can. I find that we miss you appallingly much and love you even more and it will be very nice to see you again. Em

Allied troops liberated Graignes on or around July 11, 1944.[159] Acting Mayor Voydie said he returned to Graignes on July 20, 1944, whence he learned that the bodies of the American paratroopers he had placed in the field for burial had been removed by American authorities sometime between July 13 and 20, 1944.[158] Mrs. Lareculay recalled that "in April 1945 officers came on investigation, and went [to] the place where the bodies were burnt, and [said] they recognized human bones." Mr. Voydie, however, disputed her claim.[155]

Recall that on June 12, 1944, Mayor Jean Poullain of Le Mesnil-Angot said he had witnessed nine American parachutist prisoners taken by German soldiers to a nearby field in Le Mesnil-Angot, where they were killed and that a few days later he saw bodies in a hole. He furthermore told American authorities, "The Germans ordered us [Le Mesnil-Angot residents] to evacuate on June 30, 1944. We came back on August 4 [1944]. During that time [June 30–August 4, 1944] the nine parachutist bodies were removed by American authority, but I could not say where they were taken to."[155]

Graignes schoolteacher Miss Renee Meunier told US Army personnel in June 1947 that the bodies of the American paratroopers in the pit in Le Mesnil-Angot were removed by American authorities sometime in July 1944 and buried at the US Military Cemetery of Blosville.[155]

What and where was the US Military Cemetery of Blosville? The US Military Cemetery of Blosville was a temporary cemetery located about three miles south of Sainte-Mère-Église. Squad leader of the 603rd Quartermaster Graves Registration Company Sergeant Elbert E. Legg established this cemetery on D-day after landing in a glider. "By the time the Saint-Lô breakout took place and Allied forces moved east into central France, this cemetery contained over six thousand [temporary] Allied graves," reported Sergeant Legg.[160]

In the weeks before D-day, Sergeant Legg noted that the 82nd Airborne Division did not know how graves registration services would work in a battle setting such as Normandy. In training, Legg said that he was taught "combat units would evacuate their dead to a regimental, or in some cases, division collecting point. From there the supporting graves registration units would evacuate and process the dead and establish area cemeteries, as opposed to unit cemeteries."[161]

The Graves Registration Service of the US Army cares for deceased military personnel interred outside the continental United States. Its main functions during the Second World War were:

- Selection of a site for a temporary cemetery, although its acquisition and plotting would normally be performed by the Corps of Engineers.
- Location and control for preservation of temporary cemeteries, including the proper marking and official recording of all graves, until permanent burial [could] be accomplished, or remains [could] be returned to the next of kin.
- Proper burial of all dead in accordance with existing regulations, reducing the number of isolated or single graves to a minimum.
- Receipt, collection, and disposition of all personal effects found on the dead.
- Registration of all graves in order to enable proper identification of the dead and relocation of isolated graves, cemeteries, and graves within cemeteries. This includes the preparation of sketches, maps, and data to show the location of graves and cemeteries, with particular reference to permanent landmarks.
- General supervision and control of all personnel assigned to the Graves Registration Service.[161]

Before D-day no one in Sergeant Legg's platoon was parachute-qualified, so he assumed that "everyone would journey to France as part of the seaborne 82nd Airborne Division logistical trains. The schedule called for the Graves Registration Service unit and its vehicles to arrive on the beach about D+3" (D-day plus three days, i.e., around Friday, June 9, 1944). Legg realized "this would be too long for mass casualties to go unprocessed on the battlefield. Estimates of battle dead for establishing the beachhead ran as high as ten thousand American soldiers."[160]

Sergeant Legg asked his platoon leader to ask the 82nd Airborne Division senior staff for permission to accompany a glider on D-day as a graves registration representative. The 82nd Airborne Division staff "was delighted to have a graves registration representative accompany the glider elements."[160] On D-day, Legg took a seat in a glider, flew across the English Channel, came in over a hedge of trees about eighty feet high, and lived through a "hard pancake-type landing" that caused the front strut to come "through the wooden floor of the glider [ripping] through the floor and [coming] to rest near ground level on ... vehicle rigging gear." No one in the glider was hurt. The glider had landed about three miles south of Sainte-Mère-Église.

Sergeant Legg continued:

After a quick check of the surrounding area, I selected a large field southwest of and adjacent to Les Forges Crossroads as the first work site. Four [dead] paratroopers already lay in the corner by the Crossroads. Five gliders were in the hedgerows that surrounded the field [probably containing bodies]. As I examined the site, two jeeps with trailers loaded with bodies drove in, and were directed to the corner of the field where the other bodies lay. The drivers made it clear they were delivering but not unloading. I sized up the situation and decided the time had come for me to be, and to act like, the graves registration representative that I was. For the first time in my life I touched a dead man. I grabbed the leg of one of the bodies and rolled it off onto the ground. As I struggled, the drivers gave in and assisted me with the remainder of the bodies. There were now fourteen dead lying in a row and more loaded vehicles were driving into the field.[160]

Sergeant Legg laid out a cemetery in the field by going to one corner and sticking his heel in the ground. This indentation marked the upper left corner of the first grave. He found an empty K-ration carton and split it into wooden stakes, paced off the graves in rows of twenty, and marked each one with a stake. He said, "I had no transit, tape measure, shovels, picks or any other equipment needed to establish a properly laid out cemetery." He also lacked burial bags (the US Army used mattress covers as burial bags), grave registration forms, and personal effects bags. The bodies recently delivered to the nascent cemetery were still lined up in a row. That night (June 6–7, 1944) he found an abandoned foxhole, curled up in it, and fell asleep.

A column of Frenchmen arrived the next day to dig the graves. Legg stated:

> Once everyone had his assignment and was digging, I began the job of processing bodies. There were plenty of parachutes in the field, so nylon parachute panels served as personal effects bags and body bags. Each body was searched and all personal effects were secured, but no inventory was taken. A ruled table served as Graves Registration Form No. 1.[160]

A Graves Registration Form No. 1 lists the place of burial, the name of the cemetery, the exact geographical location, and the name of the chaplain (or other officer) conducting burial rites. This form ordinarily was completed and forwarded in several copies through army channels. A personal effects bag contains the items removed from the soldier, such as identification tags, toiletry kit, and wallet. The personal effects inventory, which Sergeant Legg was unable to complete, is a list of the personal effects removed from the deceased and signed by the person responsible for removing the effects. The inventory ordinarily is included in every personal effects bag.[161]

Sergeant Legg attached an identification tag to each body and another to the stake that served as a grave marker. He kept the personal effects and Graves Registration Form No. 1 together and wrapped them in a parachute that served as a filing cabinet during the first days of the invasion. American paratroopers started bringing Sergeant Legg map coordinates and other information about the location of bodies and crashed gliders and planes that needed to be cleared. Legg kept a log of information and a map marked with body locations that he would later pass on to other graves registration personnel when they finally arrived. Each deceased paratrooper was buried with his jump boots on, much to the dismay of the French laborers who wanted the finely made boots for themselves.

By D-day plus three, Sergeant Legg had hundreds of bodies aboveground requiring burial. Half of them were German bodies, which were buried in an area separate from the fallen Americans. Finally, on D-day plus seven, a portion of his unit arrived and took over operation of the cemetery. "They found that much of the work had to be done over, including relocation of all bodies." About 350 Americans and one hundred Germans were underground by this time, and the backlog of American dead was less than one hundred. Sergeant Legg then sent out collecting teams to recover some of the bodies at locations marked on his map. The fighting units of the 82nd Airborne Division began to evacuate their battle dead directly to the cemetery.[160]

Allied forces that liberated Graignes learned from local residents about the mass grave near Le Mesnil-Angot. Between July 13 and July 20, 1944, members of the Quartermaster Graves Registration Company apparently retrieved and moved the remains of the American paratroopers in the pit, possibly to the US Military Cemetery of Blosville (around eleven and one half miles north of Le Mesnil-Angot), as suggested by the Graignes schoolteacher.

However, Captain Sophian's body was *not* in the mass grave observed by Mayor Poullain. Rather, Captain Sophian's body was found in an isolated grave "[o]ne kilometer from Graignes on route to Tribehou, Coord. 395–745," according to the *Report of Investigation of Isolated Grave or Unburied Remains,* which Second Lieutenant Sam S. Clayman, a member of the 1st Quartermaster Group of the US Army, completed on February 20, 1945. The report stated that Captain Sophian's body was buried by a "Frenchman who was passing thru and left vicinity" sometime in "July 1944." The source of this information was the "Mayor of Graignes" (Mr. Voydie). Tribehou is about three miles southwest of Graignes; one kilometer (0.6 mile) southwest of Graignes is in the vicinity of Le Mesnil-Angot. In addition, the report noted that the cause of Captain Sophian's death was "KIA" (killed in action). Captain Sophian was identified by his identification tag (Sophian, Abraham Jr. Rank (UNK) ASN 0-1700222). The report said that there were no other graves, unburied remains, or wrecked or abandoned vehicles or equipment in the immediate vicinity. SS troops had apparently executed Captain Sophian separately from the medics and wounded paratroopers.

The US Army generated a second document titled *Report of (Re) burial* on February 20, 1945, which recorded the transfer of Captain Sophian's remains from the isolated grave along the road near Le Mesnil-Angot to the US Military Cemetery #1 at Marigny, France. There they were reburied in Plot #R, Row #2, Grave #22. A Star of David marked Captain Sophian's grave. Marigny, France, is about ten miles south of Graignes and seven miles west of Saint-Lô. US Army Quartermaster Corps buried both American and German soldiers, each in their own field, at the US Military Cemetery of Marigny.

After the war, according to the information plaque at Marigny today:

The American war dead were moved to Saint-Laurent-sur-Mer whilst the German burial field remained. At the time of the handover of the land to the French administration, the number of German dead stood at 4,246. After reburial by the French burial service, this figure had reached 5,713. On the basis of the

Franco-German War Graves Agreement, the reburial service of the Volksbund was able to remove other German dead from smaller plots and rebury them at this cemetery in 1957, thus putting the total number there today at 11,169. The site was inaugurated on 20th September 1961.

Saint-Laurent-sur-Mer is about twenty-five miles northeast of Marigny. Today the cemetery at Marigny is called the German Military Cemetery Marigny. Contrary to the information on the plaque at Marigny, Captain Sophian's remains on June 23, 1948, were taken by truck from Marigny not to Saint-Laurent-sur-Mer, but southward to the US Military Cemetery of Saint-James, France, a distance of about forty miles.

Even though the US Army had documentation dated February 20, 1945, that Captain Sophian's remains were (re)buried in the US Military Cemetery of Marigny, it conveyed to his family on April 3, 1945, that his remains were buried in "Eastern France." After recovering from the initial shock of the telegram confirming the death of his son, Dr. Abraham Sophian on May 3, 1945, wrote the following letter, which he addressed to the Secretary of War, War Department, Washington, DC, asking for more specific information:

Dear Sir:
My son, Abraham Sophian, Jr. Serial No. 0-1700222, was reported killed by your department recently.

He was Captain in the 507th Paratroopers Infantry Regiment, 82nd Airborne Division; Colonel Millett, Senior Officer. Ten months ago [August 1, 1944] he was reported missing as of June 11th 1944 by your Department; we heard nothing further until the telegram and confirming letter advising us of his death, which we received about a month ago [April 3, 1945].

In view of the circumstances, namely: the fact that he was reported missing almost ten months before confirmation of his death, we feel very much concerned about the exact situation and I wish to know what definite information has been obtained on which was based the final report.

It seems very strange that confirmation could not be obtained at the time when one would expect confirmation much more possible, namely, on the date he was reported missing rather than ten months later when evidence of confirmation surely must be much more difficult to obtain.

I would appreciate an early answer. It is not fair, in a matter of this kind with the circumstances as explained, for your Department not to submit confirmatory evidence at an early date.

Yours very truly,

Dr. A. Sophian

On May 11, 1945, a frustrated Dr. Abraham Sophian wrote a second letter, which he addressed this time to the Quartermaster General in Washington, DC, requesting information about the exact location of his son's remains:

Sir:

My son, Captain Abraham Sophian, No. 0-1700222, 507th Parachute Infantry, Medical Detachment, was reported killed in France June 11, 1944. We have been advised by the War Department that he has been buried in an American Cemetery in the East of France.

Will you kindly advise us as to the exact location of the cemetery and all information usual for situations of this kind.

Very truly,

Dr. A. Sophian

On May 14, 1945, Dr. Abraham Sophian received a response to his first inquiry from a major general in the Office of the Adjutant General of the Army, who promised to forward Dr. Sophian's concerns to The

Quartermaster General in Washington, DC. The major general's letter read as follows:

Dear Dr. Sophian:

I have received for reply your letter of 3 May 1945, concerning your son, Captain Abraham Sophian, Jr., who was killed in action on 11 June 1944 in France.

It would be gratifying indeed to be able to encourage you in your hopes that Captain Sophian still survives. However, I must inform you that our theater commanders exercise every precaution to insure that casualty reports are thoroughly checked before they are forwarded to the War Department and no death reports are submitted unless conclusive evidence of death exists. In this connection, it may be stated that the commanding general of the various theaters of operations report as "missing in action" personnel whose whereabouts, due to enemy action, is unknown. In many of these cases our overseas commanders subsequently obtain conclusive evidence of death, such as the recovery of the remains and as soon as information of this nature is secured, a report is submitted to the War Department giving the data on which the evidence discloses that death occurred.

I fully realize the comfort you would derive in obtaining information concerning the burial of the remains of your son. I am forwarding a copy of your communication to The Quartermaster General, Washington 25, DC, who is charged with matters of this nature with the request that you be furnished data in this respect providing it is available.

You have my heartfelt sympathy in the great loss you have been called upon to bear.

Sincerely yours,

J. A. [unreadable]
Major General
The Adjutant General of the Army

When Dr. Abraham Sophian had not heard back from the quartermaster general in what he considered a timely manner (he sent the letter on May 11, 1945), he sent a third letter, this time addressed to General Edmund B. Gregory, the Quartermaster General, on June 27, 1945:

Dear General Gregory:

On May 11, 1945, I wrote you concerning my son, Captain Abraham Sophian, who was killed in France and requested information from your department such as it is customary to give. Up to this time I have had neither an answer to my question or the ordinary courtesy of an acknowledgement to my letter.

I am writing this letter to you personally because I cannot believe that you approve of actions of that kind; actions which are both callous and unkind.

I am fully aware that I am not the only one but I do feel that I have allowed enough time to at least have had an acknowledgement from your department.

I am writing this letter to request an early response to my letter.

Very truly yours,

Abraham Sophian, MD

E. B. Gregory, Lieutenant General in the Office of the Quartermaster General, responded on July 4, 1945, to Dr. Sophian's letter of June 27, 1945:

Dear Doctor Sophian:

Acknowledgment is made of your letter of 27 June 1945 requesting information concerning your son, the late Captain Abraham Sophian, Jr.

It is regretted that your original letter of 11 May 1945 was not acknowledged at the time of its receipt but reference to our files indicated a report of burial had not yet been received. As information has not as yet reached this office pertaining to the burial of your son, an investigation has been requested and upon its receipt you will be notified.

Sincerely yours,

E. B. Gregory

Lieutenant General

The Quartermaster General

The Office of the Quartermaster General sent that same day (July 4, 1945) a letter to the Commanding General, Comzone, European Theater of Operations, for the Chief Quartermaster, which read:

Information is desired as to whether or not the remains of the decedent named below have been recovered and interred, as to date a report covering the disposition of these remains has not been received in this office.

NAME: Sophian, Abraham, Jr. (Captain)

SERIAL NUMBER: 0-1 700 222

DATE OF DEATH: 11 June 1944

PLACE OF DEATH: European Area (France)

REMARKS: In a missing in action status from 11 June 1944 until such absence was terminated on 3 April 1945, when evidence considered sufficient to establish the fact of death was received by the Secretary of War from a commander in the European Area.

Information received in this office states that the remains of Captain Sophian were interred in Eastern France.

FOR THE QUARTERMASTER GENERAL,

ARTHUR L. WARREN

Colonel, QMC

Assistant

On August 25, 1945, Colonel Warren conveyed the desired information on the whereabouts of Captain Sophian's remains to Dr. Sophian:

Dear Doctor Sophian:
Reference is made to the letter from this office dated 4 July 1945, regarding the place of burial of your son, the late Captain Abraham Sophian, Jr.

The official report of interment received in this office reveals that the remains of your son were interred in the US Military Cemetery #1, Marigny, France, Plot R, Row 2, Grave 22. With reference to other larger cities the approximate location of Marigny, France is five miles west and south of Saint-Lô and ten miles east and north of Coutances, both in France.
FOR THE QUARTERMASTER GENERAL:
Sincerely yours,
ARTHUR L. WARREN
Colonel, QMC
Assistant

Dr. Sophian responded to Colonel Warren with the following note dated September 3, 1945:

Dear Colonel Warren:
Wish to acknowledge your letter of August 25th. It is my understanding that the Government has made arrangements to bring the remains of our boys back home.

Will you kindly advise me if that is the case so we may act accordingly.
Very sincerely yours,
Abraham Sophian, MD

Colonel Warren responded to Dr. Sophian on September 18, 1945:

Dear Dr. Sophian:

Acknowledgment is made of your recent letter requesting information concerning the return of the remains of your son, the late Captain Abraham Sophian, Jr.

Now that Japan has been defeated immediate plans are being formulated with a view to returning to the next of kin the remains of their loved ones. This sacred duty will be carried out by the Government at its expense and insofar as practicable in accordance with the expressed wishes of the legal next of kin, who will be notified by this office well in advance of the actual return of the remains. The mission as a whole is world wide in scope and of necessity time consuming, but you may rest assured that this office fully appreciates your desires and will do everything in its power to fulfill them at the earliest possible date.

It will not be necessary to make application for the return of the remains, as the Government, at the proper time will contact the legal next of kin requesting them to designate the place of final shipment.

FOR THE QUARTERMASTER GENERAL:

Sincerely yours,

Arthur L. Warren

Colonel, QMC

Assistant

Captain Sophian's widow Dorothy meanwhile had received the personal effects of her late husband from the Kansas City Quartermaster Depot on June 25, 1945. A letter to her on that date said:

Dear Mrs. Sophian:

The Army Effects Bureau has received from overseas some personal effects of your husband, Captain Abraham Sophian, Jr.

These effects are being forwarded to you in two cartons.

If, by any chance, the property has not reached you at the expiration of thirty days from this date, please notify me and tracer will be instituted.

The action of this Bureau in transmitting personal effects does not, of itself, vest title in the recipient. Such property is forwarded for distribution according to the laws of the state of the officer's legal residence.

I regret the circumstances prompting this letter, and wish to express my sympathy in the loss of your husband.

Yours very truly,

Harry Niemiec

2nd Lieutenant, Q.M.C.

Chief, Correspondence Branch

Captain Sophian's personal effects (as officially documented) consisted of:

- 1 book, fiction
- 1 envelope without insignia
- 1 bundle of envelopes
- 1 pad writing paper
- 1 pair binoculars
- 4 golf balls
- 2 boxes of bulbs, flashlight
- 2 pair sun glasses
- 1 stethoscope
- 1 watch chain
- 1 box of insignia
- 1 sewing kit
- 1 brush
- 1 ETO ribbon
- 1 miniature chess board
- 10 cards

- 10 photos
- 1 fountain pen (missing its top) [recall Bud writing in his final letter to Emily on May 25, 1944, that he had lost the top to his fountain pen]
- 14 shirts
- 9 pants
- 1 blouse
- 1 provings and background
- 1 belt
- 11 ties
- 2 jackets
- 5 hats
- 2 pr. shoes
- 2 pr. slippers
- 1 rain coat
- 1 overcoat
- 2 coveralls
- 1 housecoat
- 29 pieces of underwear
- 1 pr. trunks
- 2 pr. gloves
- 10 handkerchiefs
- 6 towels
- 10 pr. socks
- 4 bars

Captain Sophian's personal effects were delivered to the 82nd Airborne Division in the United States on August 6, 1944, and then forwarded to Kansas City Quartermaster Depot and to Dorothy Sophian around June 25, 1945.

On July 3, 1945, Mrs. Dorothy Sophian received another letter from the Kansas City Quartermaster Depot, which said a footlocker belonging to her late husband would soon be delivered to her:

Dear Mrs. Sophian:

The Army Effects Bureau has received some additional property of your husband, Captain Abraham Sophian, Jr.

These effects, contained in one footlocker are being forwarded to you. If delivery is not made within thirty days from this date, please notify me so that tracer action may be instituted.

As previously indicated, personal property is transmitted by the Bureau for distribution according to the laws of the state of the officer's legal residence.

Extending every sympathy, I am

Sincerely yours,

P.L. Koob

1st Lt. Q. K. C.

Officer-in-Charge

SJ Unit

The contents of this footlocker likely were a bugle, Briddell bolo knife, and Signal Corps field telephone (see photos at end of chapter).

Five months later, Dorothy Sophian remarried (early December 1945) and moved to another state. Her new husband, who was a US Navy colleague of her brother-in-law Ted O'Leary, initiated adoption proceedings for Bud's two-year-old child within two weeks of the wedding. The adoption was finalized in 1946.

Dr. Abraham Sophian had other problems in addition to trying to comprehend the finality of his son's death and facilitate transport of his son's remains back to the United States for permanent burial. His brother Harry Joseph Sophian, who had been hospitalized under his care at Menorah Hospital since December 1944 for chronic renal failure, succumbed to the disease on September 21, 1945.[32] Harry's wife Jane Felix Sophian, despondent since his death, committed suicide on October 8, 1945 by jumping out of the eighth-story window of her apartment in Sophian Plaza, as meticulously described with photo and diagram on the front page of the *Kansas City Star* on October 9, 1945.

Dr. Sophian's own health was also a growing concern. He was sixty-one years old when Bud died. In 1945, he hired two young brothers, Drs. Harry and Morris Statland, to help with his patient load, since Bud would not be coming to Kansas City to join his practice. Dr. Sophian composed a document that committed the Statland brothers to accepting either of Emily's young sons Dennis and Theodore, Jr. into the medical practice, should either of them become physicians. The Statland brothers eventually bought the practice from Dr. Sophian's widow Estelle and renamed it Statland Clinic, which continues to care for patients today at Menorah Medical Center in Overland Park, Kansas.

Seven months after Harry and Jane were buried in Kansas City, Dr. Abraham Sophian again wrote to the quartermaster general in Washington, DC, in a letter dated July 8, 1946:

Dear Sir:
Will you be kind enough to send me any available information regarding return of our war dead to their families. My son Capt. Abraham Sophian is buried in Eastern France.
Thanking you, I am,
Very truly yours,
Abraham Sophian, MD

On August 27, 1946, Dr. Sophian received a response from the quartermaster general:

Dear Dr. Sophian:
Your letter concerning your son, the late Captain Abraham Sophian, Junior, has been received in this office.
The War Department has now been authorized to remove, at Government expense, to the final resting place designated by the next of kin, the remains of those American citizens who died while serving overseas with our armed forces during this war.

When the necessary preliminaries have been completed, a letter with an information pamphlet and a "Request for Disposition" form attached will be sent to the next of kin of those American dead. The "Request for Disposition" form, when properly filled out, will constitute the formal expression of the next of kin's detailed desires. Since letters to the next of kin will be dispatched automatically and according to the records here, communications with this office regarding this subject will not be necessary.

As you probably know, the supply of steel for the manufacture of caskets is, at present, uncertain. Without this essential item, the movement of remains cannot properly be initiated. This fact and the necessity for complete coordination of movement in many parts of the world make it impossible, at this time, to estimate when these forms will be mailed. Responses to them will be acted upon with a minimum of delay.

FOR THE QUARTERMASTER GENERAL
Sincerely yours,
James L. Prenn
Major, QMC
Assistant

On September 3, 1946, one year after Dr. Sophian elicited the information about the location of his son's burial place in Marigny, the quartermaster general wrote the following to the former Dorothy Keck Sophian:

Dear Mrs. Sophian:
The War Department is most desirous that you be furnished information regarding the burial location of your husband, the late Captain Abraham Sophian, Jr., A.S.N. 0-1 700 222.

The records of this office disclose that his remains are interred in the US Military Cemetery Marigny, plot R, row 2, grave 22.

You may be assured that the identification and interment have been accomplished with fitting dignity and solemnity.

This cemetery is located nine miles west of Saint-Lô, France and is under the constant care and supervision of US military personnel.

The War Department has now been authorized to comply, at Government expense, with the feasible wishes of the next of kin regarding final interment, here or abroad, of the remains of your loved one. At a later date, this office will, without any action on your part, provide the next of kin with full information and solicit his detailed desires.

Please accept my sincere sympathy in your great loss.
Sincerely yours,
T.B. Larkin
Major General
The Quartermaster General

On October 28, 1947, the quartermaster general sent another letter to Dorothy, who had been remarried for almost two years:

Dear Mrs. Sophian:
The people of the United States, through the Congress have authorized the disinterment and final burial of the heroic dead of World War II. The Quartermaster General of the Army has been entrusted with this sacred responsibility to the honored dead. The records of the War Department indicate that you may be the nearest relative of the above-named deceased, who gave his life in the service of his country.

The enclosed pamphlets, "Disposition of World War II Armed Forces Dead," and "American Cemeteries," explain the disposition, options and services made available to you by your Government. If you are the next of kin according to the line of kinship as set forth in the enclosed pamphlet, "Disposition of World War II Armed Forces Dead," you are invited to express your wishes as to the disposition of the remains of the deceased by completing Part I of the enclosed form "Request for Disposition of Remains." Should you desire to relinquish your rights to the next in line of kinship, please complete Part II of the enclosed form. If you are not the next of kin, please complete Part III of the enclosed form.

If you should elect Option 2, it is advised that no funeral arrangement or other personal arrangement be made until you are further notified by this office.

Will you please complete the enclosed form, "Request for Disposition of Remains" and mail in the enclosed self-addressed envelope, which requires no postage, within 30 days after its receipt by you? Its prompt return will avoid unnecessary delays.

Sincerely,

Thomas B. Larkin

Major General

The Quartermaster General

Dorothy filled out part II (option 2) of the form, in which the army had classified her as the "decedent's widow (remarried)," thus relinquishing her disposition authority to Bud's father, Dr. Abraham Sophian. More months passed. On April 5, 1948, Dr. Sophian requested that his son's remains be returned to the United States for final burial in the national cemetery at Jefferson City, Missouri.[163]

On June 17, 1948, the US Army disinterred Captain Sophian's remains from his grave in Marigny, France, according to his Disinterment Directive form. He was still wearing his uniform. The condition of his remains was "advanced decomposition," according to the embalmer. Captain Sophian's religion on the Disinterment Directive form was identified as "H." for Hebrew. He was placed in a casket, which was officially sealed on July 2, 1948. A captain verified all tags, markings, and plates, and another soldier boxed and marked the casket that same day. The casket was then driven to Saint-James, France, as noted earlier.

On September 9, 1948, the remains of Captain Sophian, which had been resting at the US Military Cemetery of Saint-James, France, since June 23, 1948, once again got underway by truck, this time rumbling northward to Casketing Point A in Cherbourg, France, a distance of about eighty miles. On October 11, 1948, Captain Sophian's remains were moved from Casketing Point A, Cherbourg, to Port Unit, Cherbourg.

On October 29, 1948, Dr. Abraham Sophian changed his mind about where to bury his son. He sent a letter to Major General Larkin requesting that Captain Sophian's remains be interred at the Fort Leavenworth National Cemetery (Kansas) instead of the Jefferson City National Cemetery (Missouri). The letter read:

Dear Major General Thomas B. Larkin:
If it is not too late to make another selection of a United States National Cemetery as a final resting place for our son, we would like to have him buried at the Fort Leavenworth National Cemetery, Fort Leavenworth, Kansas instead of the Jefferson City National Cemetery at Jefferson City, Missouri—which place we elected a number of months ago when the form was sent us.
Will you be good enough to advise us if this can done?
Thank you for your kind consideration of our request.
Very truly yours,
Abraham Sophian, MD

The request was granted in a formal letter dated November 26, 1948:

Dear Dr. Sophian:
Your letter pertaining to the remains of your son, the late Captain Abraham Sophian, Jr., has come to my attention.

I wish to inform you that your previous request to have the remains of your son returned to the United States for final burial in the Jefferson City National Cemetery, Jefferson City Missouri, has been cancelled, and we will comply with your wishes to have his remains returned for final burial in the Fort Leavenworth National Cemetery, Fort Leavenworth, Kansas.

Please be assured of my continued sympathy in your great loss.

Sincerely yours,

James F. Smith

Major, QMC

Memorial Division

On November 27, 1948, the remains of Captain Sophian left the port of Cherbourg, France, and crossed the Atlantic Ocean on the USAT (transportation service) cargo ship *James E. Robinson* bound for the New York Port of Embarkation. The latter port was the same place Captain Sophian had boarded the *Strathnaver* five years earlier on December 5, 1943, bound for Liverpool and the European Theater of War. Captain Sophian's remains reached the New York Port of Embarkation on December 7, 1948. On December 9, 1948, Captain Sophian's casket was placed on Train Number 27, CB&Q RR (Chicago, Burlington & Quincy Railroad). This railroad operated in the Midwestern United States, including Kansas City. Captain Sophian's casketed remains were accompanied by military escort. His casket reached Beverly, Missouri, on January 3, 1949, at 9:40 in the morning. Beverly, Missouri, is three and a half miles due east across the Missouri River from Fort Leavenworth National Cemetery. From Beverly, his casketed remains were trucked to the cemetery for services held at 2:00 in the afternoon on the same day (January 3, 1949). Captain Sophian was laid to rest that day and has remained undisturbed ever since.

The re-interment initiative undertaken by the United States military after the Second World War was vast in scope. The number of Americans who died during the Second World War totaled around 359,000. Of these 359,000 fallen heroes, 281,000 (79 percent) were recovered and buried in more than 250 temporary military cemeteries around the globe. Of these 281,000 burials, some 171,000 casketed remains were delivered to next of kin in the United States by completion of the re-interment operation in 1951.[164]

In the European Theater, the remains of approximately 140,000 American soldiers were buried in thirty-six temporary US Military Cemeteries. Twenty-four of these cemeteries were in France. The US Military Cemeteries of Blosville and Marigny were two of the twenty-four cemeteries in France.[163]

As part of the re-interment process, the Army Graves Registration Service of the US Army Quartermaster Corps managed fifteen casketed remains distribution centers in the United States. Repatriated deceased servicemen arrived aboard US Army transport ships from their overseas locations. All mortuary preparations were completed prior to their transport from overseas to the United States.

Movement from the foreign port of debarkation to the US distribution center generally took about ten days. Upon arrival at the distribution center, each serviceman was assigned an escort from the Army Graves Registration Service Detachment. Generally, officers escorted officers and enlisted men escorted enlisted men. The escorts remained with the serviceman until the funeral or upon release by the family next-of-kin. As already noted, the Kansas City Quartermaster Depot in Kansas City, Missouri, was the distribution center for the casketed remains of Captain Abraham (Bud) Sophian, Jr.

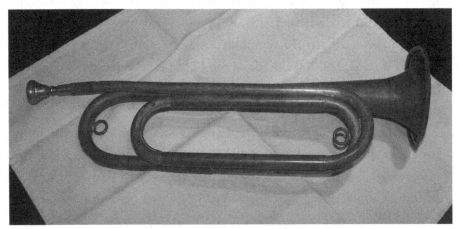

US Army bugle, personal effect of Captain Abraham
(Bud) Sophian, Jr. (1915–1944). *Sophian Archives.*

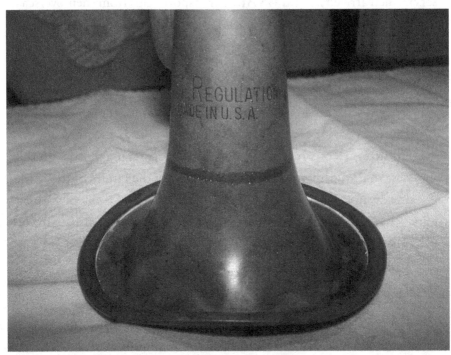

Close-up of US Army bugle, personal effect of Captain Abraham
(Bud) Sophian, Jr. (1915–1944). *Sophian Archives.*

Briddell bolo knife, personal effect of Captain Abraham
(Bud) Sophian, Jr. (1915–1944). *Sophian Archives.*

Signal Corps field telephone with the initial "M" scratched into its
leather carrying case, personal effect of Captain Abraham
(Bud) Sophian, Jr. 1915–1944). *Sophian Archives.*

Leavenworth National Cemetery, Kansas.
Photo by M.O'Leary, 2009. Sophian Archives.

Gravestone of Captain Abraham (Bud) Sophian, Jr.,
Leavenworth National Cemetery, Kansas.
Dr. Bud Sophian was laid to rest among thousands
of his fellow soldiers at Leavenworth National Cemetery on
January 3, 1949. *Photo by M.O'Leary, 2009. Sophian Archives.*

Epilogue

———◆◆◆———

Immediate Fate of 507th Parachute Infantry Regiment Graignes Survivors

Fortunately, most of the Americans in Graignes reached safety after they lost the village to the 17th Panzer Grenadier Division on the night of June 11–12, 1944. The survivors were allowed three days of rest after their ordeal, and then were ordered to rejoin their full regiments, either the 507th or the 501st Parachute Infantry Regiments. During the three days' rest, Captain Leroy Brummitt wrote and submitted his after-action report dated July 16, 1944, to the 82nd Airborne Division G-2.[165] The full 507th Parachute Infantry Regiment soon relieved the 90th Infantry Division and continued to attack westward toward Saint-Sauveur-le-Vicomte, which the Germans still held.[164]

After more than a month of fighting, the 507th Parachute Infantry Regiment was "relieved on the line and pulled back to the vicinity of Utah Beach" on July 12, 1944. Three days later, one landing ship tank (LST) transported all that was left of the regiment back to England for rest. The ravaged 507th regiment was detached from the 82nd Airborne Division temporarily on August 27, 1944, and then permanently attached in December 1944 to the 17th Airborne Division during the Battle of the Bulge (December 1944 to January 1945). The 507th Parachute Infantry Regiment continued to sustain heavy losses and required continuous paratrooper replacements. On March 24, 1945, it participated in the massive daytime Operation Varsity jump across the Rhine River—the final barrier separating the Allies from the heart of Germany. The 507th Parachute Infantry Regiment was occupying Essen when the war in Europe officially ended in May 1945.

In early September 1945, the 507th Parachute Infantry Regiment received orders to return to the United States where, on September 16, 1945, it was "unceremoniously disbanded," wrote Morgan, as follows:

> There was no fanfare, no inspiring farewell address and no great expression of appreciation for what the men had done. Paul Smith had been with the 507th from the beginning to the end and later rose to the rank of Major General in the US Army. He said, "Nobody called the men together and said, 'Guys, you did a great job—thank you.' Nothing. They said, 'Here's your ticket—goodbye.'"[166]

Graignes War Memorial

The history of the Graignes War Memorial is as convoluted as the whereabouts of Captain Sophian's remains before final interment at Fort Leavenworth National Cemetery. The original Graignes War Memorial was dedicated in 1947. One local French newspaper opined in 1947, "It will not be possible, alas, to inscribe on the great marble plaque fixed to the wall of the church's apse, where the names of 32 civilian victims and 12 dead Americans are brought together, the names of the dead paratroopers, because they are unknown: nor those who were drowned, nor those who were shot at Mesnil-Angot." In other words, in 1947, the names of only twelve Americans were on the plaque affixed to the wall of the church's apse, and it is likely that Captain Sophian's name was not among them, as he was shot and killed near Le Mesnil-Angot, not in Graignes.

On November 11, 1948, the French government awarded the military decoration *Le Croix de Guerre* ("Cross of War") with the Silver Star to the Graignes community for its resistance activities toward the

German occupiers. Ironically, the French military drew its inspiration for Le Croix de Guerre from Germany's Iron Cross military decoration, which Kaiser Wilhelm II proudly distributed beginning in 1914.[167]

As Captain Sophian's remains were being disinterred from their grave at Marigny, the French and American governments worked together to establish the Franco-American Memorial in Graignes. The memorial was constructed from the ruins of the Norman church and dedicated on June 12, 1949. The purpose of the memorial is to recall "for generations the great sacrifices of those who gave their lives for freedom" during the Battle of Graignes, June 6–11, 1944. US Ambassador to France (1949–1952) David K. E. Bruce represented the United States at the memorial's inaugural dedication ceremony.[168]

In 1956, the Graignes War Memorial listed an abbreviated list of the names of the dead. Fourteen American paratroopers' names were then on the plaque.[168]

In 1984, Graignes survivor Francis "Frank" E. Naughton returned to Graignes to celebrate the fortieth anniversary of D-day. During the forty-year interval since D-day, he had remained with the army, ascending to the rank of colonel. Colonel Naughton met with the citizens of Graignes he had last seen in the Rigault barn on the evening of June 12, 1944. He learned in 1984 that every paratrooper hidden in the Rigault's barn in 1944 had safely reached American lines. Recall that Naughton and Captain Brummitt had led seventy paratroopers from the Rigault barn to Carentan safely on Monday night June 12, 1944.

Colonel Naughton was deeply moved by his 1984 experience in Graignes and was determined to "see to it that the people of Graignes received some sort of official recognition from the US government for what they had done." Colonel Naughton and Earcle "Pip" Reed, another Graignes veteran who became a career army officer (attaining the rank of lieutenant colonel), developed an official army document "recommending several citizens of Graignes for awards." The secretary of the army approved this document in February 1986.

On July 6, 1986, Colonel Naughton and Lieutenant Colonel Reed handed out an Award for Distinguished Civilian Service to eleven villagers at a ceremony at the Graignes War Memorial. The awards recognized the villagers' roles in assisting the men of the 3rd Battalion/507th. Six of the awards were posthumous.[168-169] In addition, the French mounted a new Graignes War Memorial plaque that listed the names of thirty-four Americans and thirty-two Graignes residents. "The passage of thirty years had placed another twenty American names belonging to the fallen of the 507th and 501st Parachute Infantry Regiments on the Memorial," noted Bennett.[169] He opined, "Undoubtedly more than thirty-four Americans lost their lives at Graignes. With something like twenty Americans massacred at Graignes and Le Mesnil-Angot the loss of only fourteen American lives in the intense fighting around Graignes seems remarkably low. Perhaps the passage of another thirty years will be sufficient to place another handful of names on a new plaque at Graignes."[170]

Eighteen years later (2004) during the sixtieth anniversary of D-day, French and American authorities added an even newer plaque to the Graignes War Memorial. Gradually, the Battle of Graignes and the Graignes War Memorial were becoming better known to the world. What were the causes of the delay in recognition, according to Bennett?

> The men of the 507th and 501st parachute infantry regiments at Graignes [fell] too far away from any of the major centers of action on D-day to merit consideration in the official histories written after the war. The 507th itself, which transferred to the 17th Airborne Division after D-day, was itself largely overlooked by historians until the 1990s. The town of Graignes quietly rebuilt its houses and established a new church in the 1950s. It was not until over 50 years after D-day that the story of the 507th began to be reclaimed by French and American historians.[170]

Historians also may have overlooked the Battle of Graignes, according to Bennett, because "the heavy casualties sustained by the 82nd Airborne

Division in Normandy" caused "Graignes and a dozen other incidents [to be] swallowed in a wave of bleak statistics." Bennett noted that losses among battalion commanders were extremely heavy. Of the twelve battalion commanders who went into action with the 82nd Airborne Division in June 1944, only one was able to fight through to the end of the campaign. Of the rest, two were killed, five wounded, three injured, and one relieved of his command. Casualties among the ranks of the 507th Parachute Infantry Regiment dropped all over Normandy was heavy. Three hundred and three officers and men were killed in action, 354 were wounded, and 178 were classified as missing in action. By comparison, later fighting in the Ardennes and in the campaign to cross the Rhine to bring about German's defeat would cost the regiment fewer fatalities than its first combat jump over Normandy, according to Bennett.

Members of the 507th Parachute Infantry Regiment made up a large portion of overall losses of the 82nd Airborne Division, and many of those classified as missing in action in 1944 (including Captain Sophian) would later be determined to have been fatalities. For most families of the men categorized as missing in action from the 507th, the liberations from the German prisoner-of-war camps in 1945 would not produce a happy ending. Rather, it would be left to the army to make inquiries and, from 1945–1947, to quietly change the status of men listed as missing in action to killed in action, as was done for Captain Sophian.[170]

Criminal Prosecution of German War Atrocities

Were German commanders prosecuted for the atrocities they sanctioned in Normandy? After the war ended, there were few war crimes investigations among the mass of potential cases scattered across Normandy and elsewhere in Western Europe. Any war crimes trial had the "capacity to allow the accused to turn the spotlight on the behavior of their accusers ... The massacre at Graignes was not an isolated event. Rather it was part of a wider pattern of unlawful killing in Normandy that has largely been almost lost to history," averred Bennett.[170] He continued:

> The murder of Canadian prisoners of war by the Hitler Jugend SS Division on and after June 7 [1944, mentioned above] was the only high-profile case to be prosecuted. In the circumstances of the cold war, many wanted to forget the excesses of the old war. West Germany was suddenly a valuable friend against the communist enemy. There seemed to be little point in antagonizing German opinion with war crimes trials if they could be avoided. Even in the most high-profile public cases justice would singularly not be done. In 1945 SS Major-General Kurt Meyer was tried and convicted of involvement in the murder of Canadian prisoners of war at the Abbaye d'Ardenne. Eleven men had been executed and buried by the Hitler Jugend Division under Meyer's command on June 7. The division would go on to murder at least 156 Canadian prisoners at various locations over the forthcoming days. War crimes investigators held that Meyer was present at some of the executions and was an inspiration to his troops in their murderous behavior towards prisoners. An Allied court duly convicted him and he was sentenced to death. In 1946 the death sentence was commuted to life imprisonment. The sentence was commuted again in 1954, and he was a free man by the end of the year. Many felt that justice had not been done.
>
> In a further example of the near-total failure of the justice system, there was similarly little punishment for the men who, after the Ardennes offensive, had run a concentration camp for Jewish GI prisoners of war. Sixty or so GIs were mistreated to the point of death, or were murdered at the camp. Two Germans were sentenced to death for their crimes. Both would have their sentences commuted and would be freed by the mid-1950s. The families of the murdered GIs were not consulted.

Similarly those GIs who had suffered in the camp were not informed of the reductions in sentence. The silence indicated that the US military authorities at least felt a certain shame and embarrassment, even if they had forsaken the principles of justice and comradeship.[170]

Fate of Nazi Commander Werner Ostendorff

What happened to Nazi SS Commander Ostendorff after his troops burned Graignes to the ground on June 12, 1944? He led his division on to Carentan, where he was wounded badly during the assault on the town on June 15, 1944. He returned to duty four months later on October 21, 1944, and resumed command of the 17th SS Panzer Grenadier Division *Gotz von Berlichingen* until transferred again in mid-November 1944. He then became chief of staff for Heinrich Himmler's *Heeregruppe Oberrhein* ("Upper Rhine") from December 1, 1944 to January 22, 1945. Himmler was the Nazi head of the SS from 1929 to 1945 whose immoral innovation was to transform the race question from "a negative concept based on matter-of-course anti-Semitism" into "an organizational task for building up the SS ... It was Himmler's master stroke that he succeeded in indoctrinating the SS with an apocalyptic 'idealism' beyond all guilt and responsibility, which rationalized mass murder as a form of martyrdom and harshness towards oneself."[171]

Ostendorff's final posting was to *Das Reich* as division commander. He was grievously wounded by a shell on March 9, 1945, while fighting in Hungary, and died in a hospital in Bad Aussee from his wounds on May 4, 1945.[171] No officers in Commander Ostendorff's SS 17th Panzer Grenadier Division were ever tried for the atrocities they committed in Graignes.

Fate of Captain Brummitt

Captain Leroy David Brummitt became a career officer in the US Army and attained the rank of colonel. He retired from the military twenty-one years after the Battle of Graignes and died in 2002. He was buried in Arlington Cemetery. In lieu of flowers, his family requested that contributions be made to the 507th Parachute Infantry Regiment Memorial Fund, Inc., in Norcross, Georgia.[172]

American Jewish Soldiers in World War II

Researchers with the Bureau of War Records of the National Jewish Welfare Board spent four years (1942–1945) assembling data from war records to assess the contribution of American Jews to the Second World War effort to eradicate "the most powerful foe ever to confront mankind." In 1947, Louis I. Dublin and Samuel C. Kohs published *American Jews in World War II: The Story of 550,000 Fighters for Freedom* (Washington, DC: National Jewish Welfare Board, Dial Press, 1947) from which the following data has been drawn.[173]

Of the approximately sixteen million men and women who served in the US military during the Second World War, at least 550,000 (3½ percent) were Jews. The researchers used surnames and other available information to identify Jews from the lists of names of those who served during the Second World War. When in doubt, the researchers excluded people from the list. Thus, the number 550,000, they say, is probably an underestimate of the true number of Jews who served in the Second World War.

Of the approximately 550,000 Jews who served during the Second World War, an overwhelming proportion—about 81 percent—served in the US Army, as did Captain Sophian. Sixteen percent of American Jews served in the US Navy, about 1 percent in the US Coast Guard, and about 2 percent in the US Marine Corps.[174]

Of the Jewish servicemen in the US Army during the Second World War, slightly less than two thousand (less than ½ percent) served as parachute infantry, as did Captain Sophian.[175] These two thousand Jews made up about 15 percent of the approximately twelve to thirteen thousand paratroopers of the combined 82nd and 101st Airborne Divisions who jumped on D-day. Captain Sophian was one of these two thousand Jewish parachutists. Of the 550,000 Jewish servicemen who were involved in the Second World War, about 20 percent (more than one hundred thousand Jewish servicemen) served as military officers in the various service branches.[176]

Jewish physicians like Captain Bud Sophian were well represented in the armed forces during the Second World War. For example, religion was known for 92 percent of the 7,500 physicians listed in Brooklyn and the Bronx (New York State) in October 1943. In this group, 32 percent of the Jewish physicians were in military service in October 1943 versus 27½ percent of the non-Jewish group. Additional reports from twenty-two cities covering roughly three thousand physicians listed 20 percent as being Jewish and 80 percent as non-Jewish. Data show that of the Jewish and non-Jewish physicians, 44 percent and 25 percent, respectively, reported serving in the military. A New Jersey survey of male physicians under forty-five years of age found 63 percent and 51 percent of Jewish and non-Jewish physicians, respectively, served in the military during the Second World War.[177]

Of the half-million Jews who served in the military during World War II, around eight thousand died in combat (about 1½ percent of the total who served).[177]

Remembering Captain Bud Sophian

The news of Bud Sophian's untimely demise deeply stirred his relatives, colleagues, friends, and the medical community at the local, state, and national levels. Abraham, Estelle, and Dorothy

Sophian received many letters of condolence. One relative wrote in early April 1945:

Dear Doctor and Mrs. Sophian and Dorothy,

At least we know now that no German ever had the chance to torment or humiliate Bud [in a concentration camp]. He died in the first flush of that high adventure of D-day, I can believe with a smile on his face—for I never saw Bud without. His memory will become your dearest treasure. I hope your long tried courage can match his.

With love,
Mathilda H. O'Leary
Lawrence, Kansas

Some friends wrote:

Dr. and Mrs. A. Sophian
Mrs. Dorothy K. Sophian

Friends:
Ever since the coming of the unwelcome news that your Captain was reported missing, we have clung to the hope that he would "turn up" safe, as has been the happy experience of so many others.

There are no words that can be put together to express our deep regret at the loss of an outstanding young Doctor, well bred, schooled in the best Universities, with a fine sense of honor, prepared to follow in the footsteps of an honored and distinguished father.

Perhaps there is some comfort in that it is not how long we live to serve, it is rather how well we serve, and the greatness of the objective for which we give our all.

Accept our sympathy.

Isadore Anderson

Elizabeth H. Anderson

Major A. B. Anderson

April 4/1945

Captain Sophian's physical life ended near Graignes, France. However, his life's story endures and even grows six decades later, because he chose to stay with his medics and wounded comrades when he could have saved his own life (but not theirs) by fleeing with the rest of his peers the infamous night of June 11–12, 1944. In his empathic, principled, and selfless way, Captain Sophian stuck it out with his patients in the old Norman church in Graignes, hopeful of a good outcome, which in the end proved elusive. Captain Sophian lost his life but in death won honor and a measure of immortality.

Appendix

◆—◆—◆

My Father: A Veteran's Story
By Norman Costa (2008)
Reprinted by permission

Note from the authors: Norman Costa is the son of Frank P. Costa, Private First Class of the 507th Parachute Infantry Regiment during Operation Overlord. We found his story of his father's experience in Graignes online and recognized its beauty and importance (available at http://www.3quarksdaily.com/3quarksdaily/2008/12/my-.html; accessed October 9, 2010). The careful reader will note a few discrepancies between Norman Costa's report of his father's Graignes experience and this book's version of that reality. Norman Costa's colorful and touching remembrance of his father's experience enriches and furthers knowledge about the events that transpired during that unforgettable June week in Graignes in 1944. Thus, we have included it here, verbatim, with Mr. Costa's permission. MRO/DSO

* * *

Frank P. Costa, Sr. is ninety-one years old and resides in the Home Sweet Home assisted living residence in Kingston, New York. Quite by accident, I saw my father in a TV ad for Home Sweet Home on a local

TV station. I mentioned the TV ad to a cousin of mine and we talked about possible residuals that should go to his estate for the heirs to split. Of course, this was a ridiculous discussion, and we got a good laugh out of it. My father suffers from dementia and many of his memories of the past are no longer accessible to him in any detail. Having a discussion with him, of any consequence, is just about impossible now.

Dad was a paratrooper in the 82nd Airborne Division of the US Army during World War II. He was in the 507th Parachute Infantry Regiment. His first combat jump was on the night of June 5–6, 1944 into Normandy France—D-day, the allied invasion of Europe. The designated landing zone was the area around the small town of Sainte-Mère-Église. It was on the only main road to the fortified city and deep water port of Cherbourg, further west. Sainte-Mère-Église was the principal objective of the 82nd so that the Allied armies could prevent any German rescue or resupply of Cherbourg.

My father was positioned as the first soldier to exit the plane when the green light, the jump signal, was given. [On D-day, he jumped ninth of sixteen in his stick.[101]] On his training jumps, he was always faint and queasy in the aircraft. He couldn't wait to get out of the plane and into the fresh air. So the jump sergeant sat him next to the door of the C-47. The triple A flak (anti-aircraft artillery) was so heavy, the pilot veered to avoid the danger and gave the jump signal at a purely arbitrary moment. Many of the pilots in the following planes, with other 507th paratroopers, followed the lead pilot's right turn. They landed more than thirty kilometers [eighteen miles] from their intended drop zone.

Dad landed in a flooded field, up to his shoulders in water. He cut himself out of the risers on his parachute with his trench knife, but he lost his M1-A carbine. With the arrival of dawn, he spotted a church on high, dry ground and made his way out of the water. He regrouped with his regiment, part of it anyway, in the tiny hamlet of Graignes, maybe fifteen kilometers from Carentan. The village church with a tall bell tower was the most recognizable feature and occupied the highest elevation in generally flat terrain. The church was of typical medieval

Norman design, but I don't know how old it was. One hundred and seventy-six soldiers assembled, including a few from the 101st Airborne Division, the Screaming Eagles. There was one army air force fighter pilot. None of the surviving vets remember where the fighter pilot came from.

The 507th was a headquarters outfit. That meant they had mortars, 50 caliber "light" machine guns, and lots of explosives. They also had a lot of communications equipment, but they were too far away to contact any of the Allied units. They were completely cut off from all communications. They had some great officers with them: a Colonel ("Pip" Reed) [he was a First Lieutenant in 1944], a Captain, and number of Lieutenants. The first thing they did was ascertain where they were with the help of the locals. They were so far off the drop zone that their location was off their military map. After much deliberation and argument, Colonel [First Lieutenant] Reed decided to stay and set up a defense perimeter rather than try to get back to the friendly lines through unfamiliar terrain and mostly flooded fields [Major Johnson, not First Lieutenant Reed, made this decision].

The head of the French Resistance in the area was a Graignes farmer named Regault [Rigault]. His second in command was the Mayor of the hamlet [Acting Mayor Alphonse Voydie]. The trusted locals were instructed the night before, by Regault [Rigault] and the Mayor [Acting Mayor Alphonse Voydie], that the invasion was coming and that they were expected to do their duty when the time came. Regault [Rigault] had two daughters, Yvette [Odette] and Marthe. They were to become heroes in their own right and save the lives of many of the Americans. The first thing the locals did was to scour the area for the equipment and supplies that were parachuted with the soldiers. They smuggled the equipment in their horse carts and wagons. The proprietor of the local restaurant, Mme. Boursier, organized her suppliers to bring in large quantities of food stuffs to feed the paratroopers. They had to smuggle and be discreet so as not to attract the attention of the German soldiers in the area. The Germans soon learned of the existence of the

Americans, but did not know who they were, how many, or how they were equipped. Some of the young French girls ran off to alert their German soldier boyfriends.

Eventually, the 507th set up a defensive perimeter, dug in, zeroed in all the roads with their mortars, and then sent out patrols. The first advance by the German soldiers toward Graignes was a small patrol. They were dispatched very quickly by the mortars and machine guns. The next day it was a larger German patrol, but they were destroyed as well.

Colonel [First Lieutenant] Reed decided they had to destroy a concrete bridge, the only bridge on the only road, that led straight to Graignes and the Americans. My father was part of a platoon, led by [First] Lieutenant Frank Naughton, that was assigned to blow up the bridge. Naughton and his men set up defensive positions in the hedgerows while the demolition experts set the charges under the bridge. My father and one other soldier were sent across the bridge to set up a reconnaissance point to watch for any advancing Germans. They were positioned where the road made a 90 degree turn to the right. Among the hedgerows it was impossible to see more than about 50 meters in a straight line, at most. By this time my father had a Browning automatic rifle (BAR) instead of a carbine. Sure enough, he spotted a large German patrol comprised of several hundred soldiers and led by a half-track armored personnel carrier. He sent the other soldier back to the bridge to warn Naughton and tell them to hurry with the demolition charges.

The Germans continued a steady advance. At one point my father let go with a burst or two from the BAR. This served to scatter the Germans and slow them, temporarily. After a few more bursts, he left his concealed position and ran back to the bridge. The turn in the road and the hedgerows concealed my father from the Germans. Naughton and his platoon were concealed as well. The demolition charges were set and ready to go. Naughton and most of the platoon were to the right of the road, as they faced the oncoming Germans. My father and a few others were on the left and had a better view of the advancing Germans. My father, trying not to give away his position, hollered over to Naughton to blow the bridge. Naughton indicated he wanted to wait until the German soldiers were on the bridge. With several hundred German troops advancing, and my father having a better view of road ahead, he said again to Naughton to blow the bridge. Naughton still wanted to wait. It was very tense, all the way around. With the Germans just about on the bridge, my father YELLED to Naughton, "Goddamn it! Will you blow the fu***** bridge!"

BOOM! There were a couple of German soldiers on the bridge who were obliterated as concrete debris was blown sky high. A fire fight broke out. The Americans were concealed very well and inflicted a lot of casualties on the Germans. At least one German soldier tried to wade across the small river on my father's side of the blown bridge. That was the very first human being my father ever killed. It was always vivid in his memory over the many years he talked about it. He also talked about how he felt and that this was another soldier like himself doing his duty. Dad and his buddies, whom I met over the years, were always proud of the fighting they did, but not one of them ever took any satisfaction in the killing of another human being. When I accompanied him to the 50th anniversary of D-day he talked about the fact that he "killed a lot of guys." It was not a boast, but a conscious statement of what he had to do. What was unsaid, but understood, was the wish that it would never have happened.

Each successive day a larger force was sent against Graignes. From this point on, the American positions were shelled by artillery fire from a single German 88mm field piece. The Americans could see the field gun being positioned in the distance, outside the range of their mortars. Every night the artillery barrage from the '88' would last a straight hour. At daylight the German troops would advance directly on the American positions across an open field. In the words of a couple of my father's fellow soldiers (I also attended the 42nd anniversary in 1986), "The German's had to be green troops. They were inexperienced. They stood up and marched right at us and we slaughtered them with our mortars and machine guns." This predictable scene repeated itself for a couple more days. The people of the hamlet, those who tried to leave the area, were pressed into service by the Germans to retrieve the wounded and dead soldiers from the battlefield each day.

The Americans were starting to take casualties. The local priest and a priest friend of his from another region set up an infirmary in the small school house. They and a few other locals tended to the wounded. Each morning the priest offered mass and as many GIs that could be spared would attend. The woman who owned the restaurant continued to provide food for the soldiers, but with depleting stocks. Most of the time the soldiers were fed "on the guns," at their combat posts. One morning when my father was in church at mass, someone ran in and said, "The Germans are launching another attack." The church emptied in a matter of seconds. Everyone returned to their combat positions.

Food was getting low. What was once a very large supply of ammunition, mortar shells, and explosives was now getting to a critical level. The Colonel [First Lieutenant Reed] felt that the next assault might render their position uncertain. In fact, the Germans were reinforcing their existing soldiers with Panzer Grenadiers and a detachment of Waffen SS. The final assault on Graignes was about 4,000 German troops. To prepare for the expected heavy attack, Naughton sent my father and one other soldier, his name was Eddie Page, to dig in and create a defensive position near the flooded field on the back side of Graignes about 150 to 200 meters and down hill from the church. It was unlikely that the Germans would attack from the water, but he wanted to cover the possibility. The shelling started at night, as usual, only this time it would go on for two hours instead of one. Not long after the shelling started, Charlie joined Dad and Eddie in the fox hole by the water. Charlie had been directing mortar fire from the church bell tower, the highest point in the area. Minutes earlier Charlie was relieved by one of the Lieutenants. Dad, Eddie, and Charlie looked up as the bell tower took a direct hit from the "88".

This was probably the 7th [6th] night of the American occupation of Graignes. Unlike the prior sequence of night time artillery followed by a daytime assault, the Germans launched a nighttime infantry attack following the two-hour artillery barrage. The Americans put up a fierce and determined defense while under withering fire from the Germans, but they eventually ran out of ammunition. The order was given to abandon their positions, flee into the swamps and flooded fields, and it was every man for himself.

I spoke to one of the machine gunners on a 50 cal "light". His name was Hinchliff. Before I spoke to him, I spoke to a couple of his buddies who told me about Hinchliff's actions. They described a scene that could have inspired a Hollywood movie. The German bodies were piled high in front of his machine gun position. Hinchliff told me that the 50 cal machine gun, with its armor piercing bullets, was intended as an anti-vehicular weapon. Also, he was supposed to shoot in short bursts, only, of about 2 or 3 rounds. Otherwise, the barrel overheats and destroys the rifling inside the barrel. That night, as he described it, "You simply had no choice but to squeeze the trigger and keep up a continuous burst."

Well, Dad, Eddie, and Charlie were in their 6 x 6 x 6 foxhole, completely oblivious to the outcome of the nighttime assault. In the morning it was all quiet. Dad got out of the foxhole and took a deep stretch to squeeze out the sleep and tiredness. As he did, he saw three soldiers digging a foxhole about 50 meters from his position. At least one was wearing a German army helmet. His reaction was as instantaneous as it was instinctive. He jumped back into his foxhole and woke Eddie and Charlie and hushed them at the same time. He had not been seen by the Germans. They were dug in next to a hedgerow. So, he sent Eddie into the hedgerow to make his way toward the center of the hamlet and see what was going on. (I've been to the hedgerows. Although the hedgerows are dense, they actually are two dense, parallel rows with a walkable path between them.) Eddie came back and said the place was crawling with Germans. Also, he saw the Captain [Sophian?] being led away with his hands raised.

Dad got the three of them into the hedgerow where they had very good concealment. Of course they talked about what to do next. Eddie said, "We ought to stay here and fight to the last man!" Dad and Charlie gave a surprised look at each other and then turned to Eddie and said, a due "What for?" They were unimpressed with Eddie's reasoning based on the fact that they were paratroopers. So they hid for two days in the hedgerow. Dad was getting light-headed from a lack of food. Eddie wanted to stay and wait for relief, if it would ever come. Dad and Charlie decided to try to make their way back to friendly lines. Eventually, they convinced Eddie to come along. On a road they met a farmer and held him at gun point. The farmer gestured to follow him. They had no choice, but they kept a rifle on him at all times. He knocked on a farm house door; a frightened woman opened and let in the soldiers. She gave each of the soldiers a crepe, which seemed to be the only food they had in the house. The farmer and woman spoke briefly, then they were led to another farm house. It was the farm of the Regault [Rigault] family. The twelve year old daughter, Marthe, was there and led the three into the barn where 11 other paratroopers were hiding in the hayloft.

The night of the final attack, the Americans were wandering aimlessly in the dark trying to flee the Germans. Regault [Rigault] and his two daughters went out into the night to find the American soldiers and lead them back to his farm. They did not go together as a trio. Instead, Regault [Rigault] sent each of his daughters in different directions, and he covered a third area, himself. They would find the soldiers, hide the soldiers in their barn, and then sneak them out of the area at night on a canal boat. My father, Eddie, and Charlie were the last ones to be found and hid in the barn. The Germans were patrolling the area. Young Marthe and Yvette had to go about their farm chores in as normal a way as possible so as not to arouse any suspicions. As they could, they passed a little food and drink to the soldiers. At one point two German soldiers came into the barn to inspect it. The Americans had their weapons trained on them the whole time. Fortunately, they did not go further than inside the door and then left to resume their patrolling.

That night a canal boat was brought up to get the soldiers out. The French felt it was too dangerous to accompany the Americans so they tried to give them directions and let them pilot the boat themselves. After a short way out, the Americans were lost. So my father had them return, to the horror of the locals, and begged for a guide. A young man agreed to pilot the boat. He safely navigated the canals and let the Americans off on a road and pointed in the direction of the allied lines. Before they left the boatman, my father collected all the French Franc money the soldiers had and gave it to the young man who piloted them to safety. The young man refused, but my father was insistent on his taking the gift of appreciation. They made it back [to American lines]. The first thing they did was eat pork and beans from a can and then slept, propped against a small house, for 12 hours straight. After getting a hot shower, new clothes, and weapons they were united with the rest of their regiment, the 507th. They went right back into combat for a total of 39 straight days "on the line."

After the war, it was determined that members of the 507th Parachute Infantry Regiment killed at least 800 and possibly as many as 1,200 German soldiers in the Battle of Graignes. The local priest and the visiting priest stayed with the wounded soldiers in the school house infirmary. They intended to minister to their wounds and plea for them with the Germans. When the Germans secured the small hamlet, they went into the school [the church] and bayoneted the wounded Americans. A number of the captured Americans were shot. The two priests were singled out, shot inside the ruins of their church, and their bodies dowsed with petrol and burned on the spot. Eventually, Regault [Rigault], the Mayor, and other members of the resistance were captured and executed by the Germans. [?] The boatman who piloted my father and thirteen others to safety was found with all of the money my father insisted he take. The Germans put two and two together and shot the hero who saved their lives. You can imagine how my father felt about this when he found out more than forty years later. More of the locals were scheduled to be executed, including Marthe, Yvette, and the restaurant owner, Mme. Boursier. Without explanation, a German officer said there had been enough killing and ended the reprisal executions.

Lieutenant Frank Naughton stayed in the military and retired after a distinguished career as a full "Bird" Colonel. He returned to Normandy and Graignes in 1984, on the 40th anniversary of D-day. He realized that the local farmers of the hamlet of Graignes were never thanked nor shown any other appreciation for what they did, fighting side-by-side with the American paratroopers, in the Battle for Normandy. So Colonel Naughton spent the next two years researching and documenting the actions of the residents of Graignes. The Department of Defense, led by John Maher, Secretary of the Army, returned to Graignes in 1986 to recognize the people of that hamlet. A number of the surviving residents, including Marthe, Yvette, and the restaurant owner, were given the highest award that the DOD, Department of Defense, can bestow on a civilian. Others received their medals posthumously. Many other medals were awarded to the people of Graignes, as well as to the surviving American soldiers. I accompanied my father on his return to Graignes in 1986, along with many of his surviving buddies from the 507th. I had the honor of serving as interpreter for the GIs with the locals. Armed with my high school and college French and a pocket dictionary, we managed to communicate quite well. I had to invent a few terms (*fusile automatique* Browning) but everyone got the gist of my stories. We learned that one year after the war, Yvette was married. She sewed her wedding dress from the white nylon fabric of a parachute she salvaged from the Battle of Graignes. She showed us the pictures of her wedding. She still has the wedding dress.

Notes

1. Mark Wischnitzer: *To Dwell in Safety: The Story of Jewish Migration Since 1800*. Philadelphia, Pennsylvania: The Jewish Publication Society of America, 1949, p. 78.

2. Robert Francis Byrnes: *Pobedonostsev: His Life and Thought*. Bloomington, Indiana: Indiana University Press, 1968.

3. Konstantin Pobedonostsev: *Reflections of a Russian Statesman*. Ann Arbor, Michigan: University of Michigan Press, 1965.

4. Mark Wischnitzer: *To Dwell in Safety: The Story of Jewish Migration Since 1800*. Philadelphia, Pennsylvania: The Jewish Publication Society of America, 1949, pp. 67–70.

5. Michael Stanislawski: *Tsar Nicholas I and the Jews: The Transformation of Jewish Society in Russia 1825–1855*. Philadelphia, Pennsylvania: The Jewish Publication Society of America, 1983.

6. John Doyle Klier: *Russia Gathers her Jews: The Origins of the "Jewish Question" in Russia, 1772–1825*. DeKalb, Illinois: Northern Illinois University Press, 1986.

7. Richard G. Robbins, Jr.: *Famine in Russia, 1891–1892*. New York, New York: Columbia University Press, 1975.

8. John D. Klier and Shlomo Lambroza: *Pogroms: Anti-Jewish Violence in Modern Russian History*. Cambridge, England: Cambridge University Press, 1992.

9. John Doyle Klier: *Imperial Russia's Jewish Question 1855–1881*. Cambridge, England: Cambridge University Press, 1995.

10. "New York (Manhattan) Wards: Population & Density 1800–1910." *Demographia*. Available at http://www.demographia.com/db-nyc-ward1800.htm; accessed March 14, 2010.

11. Robert J. Brym: *The Jews of Moscow, Kiev and Minsk: Identity, Antisemitism, Emigration*. Washington Square, New York, New York: New York University Press, 1994.

12. Michael F. Hamm: *Kiev: A Portrait, 1800–1917*. Princeton, New Jersey: Princeton University Press, 1993.

13. Michael F. Hamm: *The City in Russian History*. Lexington, Kentucky: University Press of Kentucky, 1976.

14. "Prizes for Hebrew orphans: Annual distribution before many visitors at the asylum in Amsterdam Avenue." *New York Times*, June 2, 1902.

15. "New York Incorporations: Independent Lumbar Company, New York Directors—Michael Sophian, VI East 10th Street, Hyman Leventhal, 5 West 114th Street; Morris Sophian, 45 West 112th Street, New York." *New York Times*, October 27, 1908.

16. US Census: "United States—Places and (in selected states) County Subdivision with 50,000 or More Population." GCT-PH1-R. Census 2000. Available at http://factfinder.census.gov/servlet/GCTTable?_bm=y&-geo_id=&-ds_name=DEC_2000_SF1_U&-_lang=en&-mt_name=DEC_2000_SF1_U_GCTPH1R_US13S&-format=US-13; accessed March 12, 2010.

17. Lillian D. Wald: "The nurses' settlement in New York." *American Journal of Nursing*, May 1902, Volume 2, Number 8, pp. 567–575.

18. Lillian D. Wald: *Windows on Henry Street*. Boston, Massachusetts: Little, Brown and Company, 1934.

19. Jacob A. Riis: *How the Other Half Lives*. New York, New York: Penguin Books, 1997. First published by Charles Scribner's Sons, 1890.

20. Naomi Wiener Cohen: *Jacob H. Schiff: A Study in American Jewish Leadership (Brandeis Series in American Jewish History, Culture, and Life*. Hanover, New Hampshire: University Press of New England, 1999, pp. 91–92.

21. Abraham Sophian: *Epidemic Cerebral Meningitis*. Saint Louis, Missouri: CV Mosby, 1913.

22. Margaret R. O'Leary: "Texas cerebrospinal meningitis epidemic of 1911–1912: Saving lives with New York City horse immune serum." *SEMP Biot Report #389*, August 22, 2006. Available at http://www.semp.us/publications/biot_reader.php?BiotID=389; accessed March 12, 2010.

23. "Texas Gifts to Dr. Sophian: Grateful to Rockefeller Institute Specialist for Fighting Meningitis." *New York Times*, Feb. 4, 1912, p. 14.

24. "Back from Winning War on Meningitis: Dr. Sophian Reports Epidemic in Dallas and Other Texas Cities Practically Stamped Out." *New York Times*, February 15, 1912.

25. "Dr. Abraham Sophian, retired Kansas City physician dies at 71, since October the authority on infectious diseases had lived in Miami." *Kansas City Times*, Friday, September 20, 1957.

26. For example, in 1910 only 1,500 Jews lived in Nassau County, Long Island, whose total population was about eighty-four thousand people. Joann P. Krieg and Natalie A. Naylor:

Nassau County: From Rural Hinterland to Suburban Metropolis. Interlaken, New York: Empire State Books, 2000, p. 190, 265–271.

27. Bill Hemp: *A Sketchbook of Long Beach Island, New York.* Victoria, British Columbia: Trafford Publishing, 2007.

28. Robert E. Adams: "Research Hospital and how it grew." *Jackson County Medical Society Commemorative Section, Weekly Bulletin Golden Anniversary,* June 30, 1957.

29. Robert A. Long was a millionaire lumbar baron and Kansas City father who was a driving force behind creation of Kansas City's Liberty Memorial, a World War I museum and monument, and founder of Longview, a planned community in Washington State dedicated in 1923. See "Robert Alexander Long" in William E. Connelley: *A Standard History of Kansas and Kansans.* Chicago, Illinois: Lewis Publishing Company, 1918. Available at http://skyways.lib.ks.us/genweb/archives/1918ks/biol/longra.html; accessed March 24, 2010.

30. Thomas Pendergast was a Kansas City and Jackson County (Missouri) Democratic political boss who eventually served time for income tax evasion at the US Penitentiary in Leavenworth, Kansas. Many books have been written about him, including 1) Lawrence H. Larsen: *Pendergast!* Columbia, Missouri: University of Missouri Press, 1997; 2) William M. Reddig: *Toms' Town: Kansas City and the Pendergast Legend.* Raleigh, North Carolina: C and M Online, 1986; 3) Frank R. Hayde: *The Mafia and the Machine: The Story of the Kansas City Mob.* Fort Lee, New Jersey: Barricade Books, 2008; 4) Rudolph H. Hartmann and Robert H. Ferrell: *The Kansas City Investigation: Pendergast's Downfall, 1938–1939.* Columbia, Missouri: University of Missouri Press, 1999; and 5) Robert H. Ferrell: *Truman and Pendergast.* Columbia, Missouri: University of Missouri Press, 1999.

31. "R. F. Kilpatrick, 73, realty executive." *New York Times*, November 4, 1955.

32. "Harry J. Sophian: Brother of Dr. A. Sophian had been ill ten months." *Kansas City Times*, September 22, 1945.

33. US Department of the Interior, National Park Service, National Register of Historic Places Inventory: Historic Sophian Plaza, 4618 Warwick Blvd, Kansas City." Available at http://dnr. mo.gov/shpo/nps-nr/83001019.pdf; accessed March 14, 2010.

34. "New million dollar apartment building to be an imposing structure of Italian architecture." *Kansas City Star*, April 9, 1922, p. 2B.

35. Nodia Case: "The Sophian Plaza: Enduring elegance in apartment living." *Historic Kansas City News*, August 1978, Volume 3, Issue 1. See http://www.kchistory.org/cdm4/item_ viewer.php?CISOROOT=/Local&CISOPTR=11304&CISOBO X=1&REC=13; accessed March 14, 2010.

36. Diagram of Sophian Plaza, designed by Shepard and Wiser architects. Available at http://www.kcmo.org/idc/groups/cityplanningplanningdiv/ documents/cityplanninganddevelopment/017987.pdf; accessed March 14, 2010.

37. Harry J. Sophian built the Georgian Court Apartments at 400 E. Armour Boulevard in the Hyde Park neighborhood of Kansas City, Missouri, at a cost of $300,000 around 1917–1918. By the early 1970s, the Georgian Court Apartments had become unfashionable and were designated Section 8 low-income housing. In June 2006, the Maine-based firm Eagle Point Enterprises LLC announced plans to renovate and upgrade the Georgian Court. The project consisted of complete interior demolition and historic restoration of some interior and exterior features. The architect for the historic renovation was Rosemann & Associates and the contractor was Straub

Construction Company. The building reopened in 2007. Source: Beth Paulsen: "Georgian Court Apartments grand opening." *Kansas City Star.* September 12, 2007. Available at http://pressreleases.kcstar.com/?q=node/3368; accessed April 3, 2010.

38. Julie Kalman: *Rethinking Antisemitism in Nineteenth Century France.* Cambridge, England: Cambridge University Press, 2010, pp. 24, 172–173.

39. Michael Meyer: *Response to Modernity: A History of the Reform Movement in Judaism.* Detroit, Michigan: Wayne State University Press, 1988, p. vii.

40. Cydney Millstein and Carol Grove: *Houses of Missouri.* New York, New York: Acanthus Press, 2008, p. 13.

41. Frank J. Adler: *Roots in a Moving Stream: The Centennial History of Congregation B'nai Jehudah of Kansas City 1870–1970.* Kansas City, Missouri: The Temple, Congregation B'nai Jehudah, 1972. See also Samuel S. Mayerberg: *Chronicle of an American Crusader.* Kansas City, Missouri: Mayerberg Press, 2007.

42. Nathan Glazer: *American Judaism: An Historical Survey of the Jewish Religion in America.* Chicago, Illinois: University of Chicago Press, 1957, pp. 46–48, 60–61. See also David Philipson: *The Reform Movement in Judaism* was first published in 1903 and was revised by Philipson in 1931 (New York, New York: MacMillan). It covers the reform movement from its beginnings up until 1930. See also Michael A. Meyer: *Response to Modernity: A History of the Reform Movement in Judaism.* Detroit, Michigan: Wayne State University Press, 1988. It covers the reform movement from 1931 to the 1970s.

43. Yohanan Petrovsky-Shtern: *Jews in the Russian Army, 1827–1917: Drafted into Modernity.* Cambridge, England: Cambridge University Press, 2009. For a review, see http://www.cambridge.

org/us/catalogue/catalogue.asp?isbn=9780521515733&ss=exc; accessed March 19, 2010.

44. George Q. Flynn: *Conscription and Democracy: The Draft in France, Great Britain, and the United States.* Westport, Connecticut: Greenwood Press, 2002. See also Frederick Palmer: *Newton D. Baker: America at War*, Volume I. New York, New York: Dodd, Mead, & Company, 1931, pp. 185–219.

45. Nathan Glazer: *American Judaism: An Historical Survey of the Jewish Religion in America.* Chicago, Illinois: University of Chicago Press, 1957, pp. 82–83.

46. Lenore K. Bradley: *Robert Alexander Long: A Lumberman of the Gilded Age.* Durham, North Carolina, Forest History Society, 1989, pp. 110–111, 209-Note #31.

47. Sister Marie Ida de Sion: *Sion! Long May Her Banner Wave! Memories of Notre Dame de Sion in Kansas City 1912–1965 and the Fifty Golden Years of Sister Marie Ida de Sion 1915–1965.* Kansas City, Missouri: April 22, 1965. For more information on the Ratisbonne brothers see Theodore Ratisbonne: *Answers to a Jewish Enquirer.* London, England: Catholic Truth Society, 1920; Marie-Alphonse Ratisbonne: *The Conversion of M. Marie-Alphonse Ratisbonne.* W. Lockhart (ed), 1842. Facsimile by Kessinger Press, 2008.

48. "A. Sophian, Jr., dead: Medical corps captain killed in action last June." *Kansas City Star, Times.* April 4, 1945.

49. "Pembroke Hill: History/Archives." Available at http://www. pembrokehill.org/page.cfm?p=8; accessed March 14, 2010.

50. A copy of the Pembroke School *Blue and White Magazine*, Christmas 1926, is available at Pembroke Hill Archives located at 400 West 51st Street, Kansas City, Missouri.

51. "Morrow sets pace at golf with 78: Choate player leads for first qualifying round of Eastern Interscholastic Test." *New York Times*, June 28, 1932.

52. 1932 Phillips Academy yearbook *Pot Pourri*, pp. 76, 81–85.

53. Karen Bartholomew: "The bad boys of Encina Hall." *Stanford Magazine. September/October 1998*. Available at http://www. stanfordalumni.org/news/magazine/1998/sepoct/articles/encina. html; accessed May 15, 2010.

54. Medical Center Archives: "Establishment of New York Hospital-Cornell Medical Center," 2007. Available at http:// www.med.cornell.edu/archives/75years/site/pdf/historical_ timeline.pdf; accessed March 17, 2010.

55. "Procedure smooth; answering the registration call in America's first peacetime draft." *New York Times*, October 17, 1940, p. 1.

56. Helene Jamieson Jordan: *Cornell University—New York Hospital School of Nursing, 1877–1952*. Society of the New York Hospital. New York, New York: Lenz & Riecker, 1952, pp. 59–73.

57. "Text of proclamation." Associated Press, Washington, DC, May 27, 1941. *New York Times*, May 28, 1941.

58. "Medical Preparedness: The 1940–1941 Military Training Program, Participation of the Medical Department of the Army." Committee on Medical Preparedness of the American Medical Association. *Journal of the American Medical Association*, Volume 115, Number 23, December 7, 1940, pp. 2003–2009.

59. "Mt. Sinai Medical Center." *The Encyclopedia of Cleveland History*. Web page maintained by Case Western Reserve University. Last modified 25 Dec 2009. Available at http://ech. cwru.edu/ech-cgi/article.pl?id=MSMC; accessed May 15, 2010.

60. Center for Military History, Lineage and Honors, Headquarters and Headquarters Detachment 421st Medical Battalion. Washington, DC, Center for Military History, 27 August 1996, as quoted in "421st Medical Evacuation Battalion history and accolades." *The Free Library by Farlex*. Available at http://www.thefreelibrary.com/421st+Medical+Evacuation+Battalion+history+and+accolades.-a0147669354; accessed May 15, 2010.

61. Graham Cosmas and Albert E. Cowdrey: *US Army in World War II: The Medical Department: Medical Service in the European Theater of Operations*. Washington, DC, Center of Military History, US Army, 1992, pp. 131–132.

62. Phil Nordyke: *All American All the Way: The Combat History of the 82nd Airborne Division in World War II*. St. Paul, Minnesota: Zenith Press, 2005, pp. 6–9.

63. First observer: Clay Blair: *Ridgway's Paratroopers: The American Airborne in World War II*. Annapolis, Maryland: Naval Institute Press, 1985, p. 27. Second observer: James M. Gavin: *Airborne Warfare*. Washington, DC: Infantry Journal Press, 1947, p. 61.

64. Ibid, p. 29. Dwight D. Eisenhower: *Crusade in Europe*. Garden City, New York: Doubleday and Co., 1948, p. 517. See also Gerald M. Devlin: *Paratrooper! The Saga of US and Marine Parachute and Glider Combat Troops during World War II*. New York, New York: St. Martin's Press, 1979, pp. 32–33, and Chris McNab: *German Paratroopers: The Illustrated History of the Fallschirmjager in World War II*. Osceola, Wisconsin: MBI Publishing, 2000.

65. Gerald M. Devlin: *Paratrooper! The Saga of US and Marine Parachute and Glider Combat Troops during World War II*. New York, New York: St. Martin's Press, 1979, pp. 35–38.

66. Clay Blair: *Ridgway's Paratroopers: The American Airborne in World War II*. Annapolis, Maryland: Naval Institute Press, 1985, p. 30.

67. Gerald M. Devlin: *Paratrooper! The Saga of US and Marine Parachute and Glider Combat Troops during World War II*. New York, New York: St. Martin's Press, 1979, pp. 48–49.

68. Ibid, p. 108.

69. Ibid, p. 111.

70. Ibid, p. 113. See also: Eisenhower Foundation: *D-day: The Normandy Invasion in Retrospect*. Lawrence, Kansas: University of Kansas Press, 1971, p. 106.

71. Phil Nordyke: *All American All the Way: The Combat History of the 82nd Airborne Division in World War II*. St. Paul, Minnesota: Zenith Press, 2005, pp. 8–9.

72. Ibid, 10–11.

73. First quote is from Martin K. A. Morgan: *Down to Earth: The 507th Parachute Infantry Regiment in Normandy, June 6–July 15, 1944*. Atglen, Pennsylvania: 2004, p. 19. Second quote is from F. O. Miksche: *Paratroops*. New York, New York: Random House, 1943, p. v.

74. Graham Cosmas and Albert E. Cowdrey: *US Army in World War II: The Medical Department: Medical Service in the European Theater of Operations*. Washington, DC, Center of Military History, US Army, 1992, p. 203.

75. Martin K. A. Morgan: *Down to Earth: The 507th Parachute Infantry Regiment in Normandy, June 6–July 15, 1944*. Atglen, Pennsylvania: 2004, p. 15.

76. Private Keith Winston (combat medic, World War II): "Evacuation of the wounded during World War II." Available at http://home.att.net/~steinert/; accessed March 19, 2010.

77. Martin K. A. Morgan: *Down to Earth: The 507th Parachute Infantry Regiment in Normandy, June 6–July 15, 1944*. Atglen, Pennsylvania: 2004, pp. 35–36.

78. Edward M. Isbell: "Paratrooper: My World War II story, April 15, 1942 to December 14, 1946." 507th Parachute Infantry Regiment, 1997. Available at http://pages.prodigy.net/jabeckpearce/poor_town/eds/isbell01.htm; accessed March 20, 2010.

79. Martin K. A. Morgan: *Down to Earth: The 507th Parachute Infantry Regiment in Normandy, June 6–July 15, 1944*. Atglen, Pennsylvania: 2004, p. 44.

80. Clay Blair: *Ridgway's Paratroopers: The American Airborne in World War II*. Annapolis, Maryland: Naval Institute Press, 1985, pp. 26–27.

81. Martin K. A. Morgan: *Down to Earth: The 507th Parachute Infantry Regiment in Normandy, June 6–July 15, 1944*. Atglen, Pennsylvania: 2004, pp. 44–71.

82. Clay Blair: *Ridgway's Paratroopers: The American Airborne in World War II*. Annapolis, Maryland: Naval Institute Press, 1985, pp. 17–32. See also Phil Nordyke: *All American All the Way: The Combat History of the 82nd Airborne Division in World War II*. St. Paul, Minnesota: Zenith Press, 2005, p. 18.

83. Phil Nordyke: *All American All the Way: The Combat History of the 82nd Airborne Division in World War II*. St. Paul, Minnesota: Zenith Press, 2005, p. 163.

84. Martin K. A. Morgan: *Down to Earth: The 507th Parachute Infantry Regiment in Normandy, June 6–July 15, 1944*. Atglen, Pennsylvania: 2004, p. 74.

85. Historic marker at Camp Shanks. Available at http://www.skylighters.org/forts/images/mason-sh3.jpg; accessed March 21, 2010.

86. For further description of the difficult cross-Atlantic voyage of *Strathnaver*, see John P. McCann: *Passing Through: The 82nd Airborne Division in Northern Ireland 1943–44*. Newtownards, Northern Ireland: Colourpoint Books, 2005, pp. 42–45, and Martin K. A. Morgan: *Down to Earth: The 507yth Parachute Infantry Regiment in Normandy, June 6–July 15, 1944*. Atglen, Pennsylvania: 2004, p. 73–78.

87. James M. Gavin: *Airborne Warfare*. Washington, DC: Infantry Journal Press, 1947, pp. 39, 57–58, 61.

88. Clay Blair: *Ridgway's Paratroopers: The American Airborne in World War II*. Annapolis, Maryland: Naval Institute Press, 1985, p. 198.

89. Martin K. A. Morgan: *Down to Earth: The 507th Parachute Infantry Regiment in Normandy, June 6–July 15, 1944*. Atglen, Pennsylvania: 2004, pp. 78–79, 82.

90. Dwight D. Eisenhower: *Crusade in Europe*. Garden City, New York: Doubleday and Co., 1948, pp. 220, 240, 246–247.

91. "V-Mail." Smithsonian National Postal Museum Permanent Exhibit. Available at http://www.postalmuseum.si.edu/exhibits/2d2a_vmail.html; accessed May 15, 2010. See also James Wesley Hudson: *Victory Mail of World War II: V-Mail, the Funny Mail*. Bloomington, Indiana: XLibris, 2007.

92. Clay Blair: *Ridgway's Paratroopers: The American Airborne in World War II*. Annapolis, Maryland: Naval Institute Press, 1985, pp. 70–71.

93. Ibid, pp. 201–204.

94. Gerald M. Devlin: *Paratrooper! The Saga of US and Marine Parachute and Glider Combat Troops during World War II*. New York: St. Martin's Press, 1979, pp. 366–367.

95. Thomas M. Rice: *Trial by Combat: A Paratrooper of the 101st Airborne Division Remembers the 1944 Battle of Normandy.* Bloomington, Indiana: Author House, 2004, p. 78.

96. Clay Blair: *Ridgway's Paratroopers: The American Airborne in World War II.* Annapolis, Maryland: Naval Institute Press, 1985, pp. 206–207.

97. Christopher Chant: *Hitler's Generals and their Battles.* New York City, New York: Chartwell Books, 1976, pp. 60–65.

98. Gerald M. Devlin: *Paratrooper! The Saga of US and Marine Parachute and Glider Combat Troops during World War II.* New York: St. Martin's Press, 1979, p. 368.

99. Martin K. A. Morgan: *Down to Earth: The 507th Parachute Infantry Regiment in Normandy, June 6–July 15, 1944.* Atglen, Pennsylvania: 2004, pp. 103–104.

100. Ibid, pp. 107–109.

101. Brian N. Siddell: *507th in Normandy and Germany: The Complete Jump Rosters & Aircrew for Operations Neptune and Varsity.* Ithaca, New York: EQS Press, 2007, pp. i, 25.

102. Robert P. Anzuoni: *"I'm the 82nd Airborne Division!" A History of the All American Division in World War II After Action Reports.* Atglen, Pennsylvania: Schiffer Military History Book, 2005, p. 171.

103. Martin K. A. Morgan: *Down to Earth: The 507th Parachute Infantry Regiment in Normandy, June 6–July 15, 1944.* Atglen, Pennsylvania: 2004, p. 131.

104. Gerald M. Devlin: *Paratrooper! The Saga of US and Marine Parachute and Glider Combat Troops during World War II.* New York, New York: St. Martin's Press, 1979, pp. 379–382.

105. The Ridgway quote is from Matthew Ridgway: *Soldier: The Memoirs of Matthew Ridgway: As Told to Harold H. Martin.* New York, New York: Harper & Brothers, 1956, pp. 3–4. The

second quote is from Clay Blair: *Ridgway's Paratroopers: The American Airborne in World War II*. Annapolis, Maryland: Naval Institute Press, 1985, pp. 226–235.

106. Martin K. A. Morgan: *Down to Earth: The 507th Parachute Infantry Regiment in Normandy, June 6–July 15, 1944*. Atglen, Pennsylvania: 2004, p. 138.

107. Ibid, pp. 140–141.

108. Gary N. Fox: *Graignes*. Fostoria, Ohio: Gray Printing Co., 1990, p. 24.

109. Martin K. A. Morgan: *Down to Earth: The 507th Parachute Infantry Regiment in Normandy, June 6–July 15, 1944*. Atglen, Pennsylvania: 2004, pp. 144–145.

110. Ibid, p. 151.

111. Ibid, p. 147.

112. Clay Blair: *Ridgway's Paratroopers: The American Airborne in World War II*. Annapolis, Maryland: Naval Institute Press, 1985, pp. 236–237.

113. Gary N. Fox: *Graignes*. Fostoria, Ohio: Gray Printing Co., 1990, p. 18.

114. Matthew Ridgway: *Soldier: The Memoirs of Matthew Ridgway: As Told to Harold H. Martin*. New York, New York: Harper & Brothers, 1956, p. 7.

115. Gary N. Fox: *Graignes*. Fostoria, Ohio: Gray Printing Co., 1990, p. 23.

116. G. H. Bennett: *Destination Normandy: Three American Regiments on D-day*. Mechanicsburg, Pennsylvania: Stackpole Books, 2007, p. 106.

117. Francis E. Naughton: "Narrative, Interaction of United States Forces and French Citizens during the Battle of Graignes, 6–12 June, 1944," courtesy of Lieutenant Francis E. Naughton, as quoted in Phil Nordyke: *All American All the Way: The Combat*

History of the 82nd Airborne Division in World War II. St. Paul, Minnesota: Zenith Press, 2005, p. 359.

118. G. H. Bennett: *Destination Normandy: Three American Regiments on D-day.* Mechanicsburg, Pennsylvania: Stackpole Books, 2007, pp. 119–124.

119. Gary N. Fox: *Graignes.* Fostoria, Ohio: Gray Printing Co., 1990, p. 28. Gary Fox's lists indicate fourteen officers. See pp. 58, 73–75.

120. Martin K.A. Morgan: *Down to Earth: The 507th Parachute Infantry Regiment in Normandy, June 6–July 15, 1944.* Atglen, Pennsylvania: 2004, p. 237.

121. Gary N. Fox: *Graignes.* Fostoria, Ohio: Gray Printing Co., 1990, p. 29.

122. "The Battle For Carentan (8–15 June)." In US Army Center for Military History: *Utah Beach to Cherbourg (6 June–27 June 1944).* Washington, DC: US Government Printing Office, 1948, pp. 76–93. Available at http://www.army.mil/cmh-pg/ BOOKS/WWII/utah/utah5.htm; accessed March 22, 2010.

123. Dwight D. Eisenhower: *Crusade in Europe.* Garden City, New York: Doubleday and Co., 1948, p. 516. Eisenhower wrote that the two other main types of German combat divisions were "infantry divisions, consisting after D-day of three infantry regiments of two battalions each, with an authorized strength of approximately 12,000 officers and men, and Panzer divisions, corresponding to US Army armored divisions, consisting of two Panzer Grenadier regiments, a tank regiment, a Panzer artillery regiment, and five battalions of supporting troops, plus service troops, a personnel total of 14,000 officers and men."

124. George H. Stein: *Waffen SS: Hitler's Elite Guard at War 1939–1945.* Ithaca, New York: Cornell University Press, 1966, pp. 137–138, 143, 168, 274, 282, 296.

125. Antonio J. Munoz: *Iron Fist: A Combat History of the 17.SS Panzergrenadier Division "Gotz von Berlichingen" 1943–1945.* New York City: Axis Europa Books, 1999, p. 5.

126. Mark C. Yerger: "Werner Ostendorff." In *Waffen SS Commanders: The Army, Corps and Division Leaders of Legend, Kruger to Zimmermann.* Atglen, Pennsylvania: Schiffer Military History, 1999, pp. 136–142.

127. Antonio J. Munoz: *Iron Fist: A Combat History of the 17.SS-Panzergrenadier-Division "Gotz von Berlichingen"1943–1945.* New York City: Axis Europa Books, 1999, p. 82.

128. G. H. Bennett: *Destination Normandy: Three American Regiments on D-day.* Mechanicsburg, Pennsylvania: Stackpole Books, 2007, p. 120.

129. Dwight D. Eisenhower: *Crusade in Europe.* Garden City, New York: Doubleday and Co., 1948, p. 238.

130. Gary N. Fox: *Graignes.* Fostoria, Ohio: Gray Printing Co., 1990, p. 32.

131. E. C. Daniel: "Allied line erupts; Germans expend men and rams in futile blows at British; recapture Maltot; U.S. troops smash on junction—advance down west coast." *New York Times,* July 12, 1944.

132. Martin K. A. Morgan: *Down to Earth: The 507th Parachute Infantry Regiment in Normandy, June 6–July 15, 1944.* Atglen, Pennsylvania: 2004, pp. 240–241.

133. Gary N. Fox: *Graignes.* Fostoria, Ohio: Gray Printing Co., 1990, p. 37.

134. G. H. Bennett wrote: "In 1917 the Virgin Mary had appeared to three children at the village of Fatima in Portugal. The children had proceeded to relay the message she brought. War, said the Virgin Mary, was a punishment for sin. War, famine, and persecution of the church were God's way of punishing

the world. As well as a message, *The Appearances at Fatima* contained a prophecy of a world engulfed by war unless it returned to faith. *The Appearances* was officially endorsed by the Catholic Church in the 1930s." Source: G. H. Bennett: *Destination Normandy: Three American Regiments on D-day.* Mechanicsburg, Pennsylvania: Stackpole Books, 2007, p. 121.

135. Dominique Francois: *507th Parachute Infantry Regiment.* Bayeux, France: Heimdal, 2002, p. 55.

136. G. H. Bennett: *Destination Normandy: Three American Regiments on D-day.* Mechanicsburg, Pennsylvania: Stackpole Books, 2007, p. 123.

137. Gary N. Fox: *Graignes.* Fostoria, Ohio: Gray Printing Co., 1990, p. 38.

138. Janusz Piekalkiewicz: *The German 88 Gun in Combat.* Atglen, Pennsylvania: Schiffer Publishing, 1992.

139. Terry Gander: *The German 88: The Most Famous Gun of the Second World War.* Barnsley, England: Pen and Sword, 2009.

140. Gary N. Fox: *Graignes.* Fostoria, Ohio: Gray Printing Co., 1990, p. 39.

141. Martin K. A. Morgan: *Down to Earth: The 507th Parachute Infantry Regiment in Normandy, June 6–July 15, 1944.* Atglen, Pennsylvania: 2004, p. 247.

142. Gary N. Fox: *Graignes.* Fostoria, Ohio: Gray Printing Co., 1990, p. 40.

143. Martin K. A. Morgan: *Down to Earth: The 507th Parachute Infantry Regiment in Normandy, June 6–July 15, 1944.* Atglen, Pennsylvania: 2004, pp. 250–251.

144. Gary N. Fox: *Graignes.* Fostoria, Ohio: Gray Printing Co., 1990, pp. 43–44.

145. Ibid, pp. 58, 73–75.

146. Martin K.A. Morgan: *Down to Earth: The 507th Parachute Infantry Regiment in Normandy, June 6–July 15, 1944*. Atglen, Pennsylvania: 2004, pp. 248, 254–256.

147. Phil Nordyke: *All American All the Way: The Combat History of the 82nd Airborne Division in World War II*. St. Paul, Minnesota: Zenith Press, 2005, pp. 366, 368.

148. G. H. Bennett: *Destination Normandy: Three American Regiments on D-day*. Mechanicsburg, Pennsylvania: Stackpole Books, 2007, p. 126.

149. Martin K.A. Morgan: *Down to Earth: The 507th Parachute Infantry Regiment in Normandy, June 6–July 15, 1944*. Atglen, Pennsylvania: 2004, p. 257.

150. Antonio J. Munoz: *Iron Fist: A Combat History of the 17.SS Panzergrenadier Division "Gotz von Berlichingen" 1943–1945*. New York City: Axis Europa Books, 1999, p. 7.

151. G. H. Bennett: *Destination Normandy: Three American Regiments on D-day*. Mechanicsburg, Pennsylvania: Stackpole Books, 2007, p. 123.

152. Colonel B. L. Davis: "Appendix: Instructions for Officers and Men of the Eighth Air Force in the Event of Capture." AGS AF No.1, 21 July 1942. Available at *World War I– Prisoners of War Stalag Luft I: Documents*. Available at http://www.merkki.com/images/eoc1.gif, http://www.merkki.com/images/eoc2.gif, http://www.merkki.com/images/eoc3.gif; accessed April 24, 2010.

153. Ian J. Campbell: *Murder at the Abbaye: The Story of Twenty Canadian Soldiers Murdered at the Abbaye D'Ardenne*. Kemptville, Ontario, Canada: Golden Dog Press, 2000.

154. Martin K. A. Morgan: *Down to Earth: The 507th Parachute Infantry Regiment in Normandy, June 6–July 15, 1944*. Atglen, Pennsylvania: 2004, pp. 256–257.

155. Testimony given by Mayor Voydie, Mayor Poullain, Miss Meunier, and Mrs. Lareculey in June 1947 during the investigation of the Graignes battle and massacre. Source: Martin K. A. Morgan: *Down to Earth: The 507th Parachute Infantry Regiment in Normandy, June 6–July 15, 1944*. Atglen, Pennsylvania: 2004, p. 258.

156. Gary N. Fox: *Graignes*. Fostoria, Ohio: Gray Printing Co., 1990, pp. 51–52.

157. Martin K. A. Morgan: *Down to Earth: The 507th Parachute Infantry Regiment in Normandy, June 6–July 15, 1944*. Atglen, Pennsylvania: 2004, p. 259.

158. The number thirty-one comes from the American paratrooper names listed on the memorial plaque at Graignes, France, as of March 2010. Author Gary N. Fox, however, lists thirty-five American paratroopers dead in his book *Graignes* (Fostoria, Ohio: Gray Printing Co., 1990), pp. 58, 73–74.

159. E. C. Daniel: "Drive nears Orne; Second Army threatens to cut off Germans." *New York Times*, July 11, 1944.

160. Col Elbert E. Legg: "Crosses at Normandy, June 1944." *Quartermaster Professional Bulletin*, Autumn/Winter 1994. Available at http://www.qmfound.com/crosses.htm; accessed March 28, 2010.

161. "Graves Registration Service." FM 10-63 War Department Field Manual, War Department, January 1945. Posted by Alain Batens and Ben Major at their website "WW2 US Medical Research Centre." Available at http://med-dept.com/grs.php; accessed March 28, 2010.

162. US Army Quartermaster Foundation: *Tell me About My Boy...*: 1946 Pamphlet produced by the Quartermaster Corps for Next of Kin of Deceased Service Personnel from World War II. December 1, 1946, Fort Lee, Virginia. The text of the pamphlet

is available at http://www.qmfound.com/mortuary-affairs. htm#World War II; accessed April 2, 2010.

163. Steven Anders: "With all due honors." *Quartermaster Professional Bulletin*. Autumn/Winter 1994. US Army Quartermaster Foundation, Fort Lee, Virginia. Available at http://www.qmfound.com/honors.htm; accessed April 2, 2010.

164. Martin K. A. Morgan: *Down to Earth: The 507th Parachute Infantry Regiment in Normandy, June 6–July 15, 1944*. Atglen, Pennsylvania: 2004, p. 263.

165. Gary N. Fox: *Graignes*. Fostoria, Ohio: Gray Printing Co., 1990, p. ii.

166. Martin K. A. Morgan: *Down to Earth: The 507th Parachute Infantry Regiment in Normandy, June 6–July 15, 1944*. Atglen, Pennsylvania: 2004, pp. 271–272.

167. "Iron Cross inspired Croix de Guerre." *New York Times*, March 18, 1928.

168. Gary N. Fox: *Graignes*. Fostoria, Ohio: Gray Printing Co., 1990, pp. 55–56.

169. Martin K. A. Morgan: *Down to Earth: The 507th Parachute Infantry Regiment in Normandy, June 6–July 15, 1944*. Atglen, Pennsylvania: 2004, pp. 279, 281.

170. G. H. Bennett: *Destination Normandy: Three American Regiments on D-day*. Mechanicsburg, Pennsylvania: Stackpole Books, 2007, pp. 133–138.

171. Robert S. Wistrich: *Who's Who in Nazi Germany*. London, England: Routledge, 2001.

172. "Leroy D. Brummitt, Colonel, US Army." Arlington National Cemetery website, January 11, 2002. Available at http://www. arlingtoncemetery.net/ldbrummitt.htm; accessed April 23, 2010.

173. Gary N. Fox: *Graignes*. Fostoria, Ohio: Gray Printing Co., 1990, p. i.

174. Louis I. Dublin and Samuel C. Kohs: *American Jews in World War II: The Story of 550,000 Fighters for Freedom*. Two Volumes. Washington, DC: National Jewish Welfare Board, Dial Press, 1947. Available at http://www.archive.org/stream/americanjewsinwo000267mbp#page/n11/mode/2up; accessed April 24, 2010.

175. Ibid, p. 25.

176. Ibid, p. 26.

177. Ibid, pp. 22–23, 27.

References

Books

- Frank J. Adler: *Roots in a Moving Stream: The Centennial History of Congregation B'nai Jehudah of Kansas City 1870–1970*. Kansas City, Missouri: The Temple, Congregation B'nai Jehudah, 1972.
- Stephen E. Ambrose: *D Day: June 6, 1944: The Climactic Battle of World War II*. New York, New York: Touchstone, 1994.
- *American Hospital of Paris: A Century of Adventure, 1906–2006*. New York, New York: The American Hospital of Paris Foundation, 2006.
- *The American Hospital of Paris: Annual Report 1925*. 63, Boulevard Victor-Hugo, Neuilly-Sur-Seine, 1925.
- Robert P. Anzuoni: *"I'm the 82nd Airborne Division!" A History of the All American Division in World War II After Action Reports*. Atglen, Pennsylvania: Schiffer Military History Book, 2005.
- Caroline Arnold: *Children of the Settlement Houses*. Minneapolis, Minnesota: Carolrhode Books, Inc., 1998.
- Arthur H. Aufses, Jr. and Barbara J. Niss: *This House of Noble Deeds: The Mount Sinai Hospital, 1852–2002*. New York, New York: New York University Press, 2002.
- Mark Bando: *101st Airborne: The Screaming Eagles at Normandy*. St. Paul, Minnesota: Zenith Press, 2001.

- G. H. Bennett: *Destination Normandy: Three American Regiments on D-day*. Mechanicsburg, Pennsylvania: Stackpole Books, 2007.

- Morris Bishop: *A History of Cornell*. Ithaca, New York: Cornell University Press, 1962.

- Clay Blair: *Ridgway's Paratroopers: The American Airborne in World War II*. Annapolis, Maryland: Naval Institute Press, 1985.

- Hyman Bogen: *The Luckiest Orphan: A History of the Hebrew Orphan Asylum of New York*. Urbana, Illinois: University of Illinois Press, 1992.

- Lenore K. Bradley: *Robert Alexander Long: A Lumberman of the Gilded Age*. Durham, North Carolina: Forest History Society, 1989.

- E. Richard Brown: *Rockefeller Medicine Men: Medicine & Capitalism in America*. Berkeley, California: University of California Press, 1979.

- Robert J. Brym: *The Jews of Moscow, Kiev and Minsk: Identity, Antisemitism, Emigration*. New York, New York: New York University Press, 1994.

- Robert Francis Byrnes: *Pobedonostsev: His Life and Thought*. Bloomington, Indiana: Indiana University Press, 1968.

- Christopher Chant: *Hitler's Generals and their Battles*. New York City, New York: Chartwell Books, 1976.

- Winton Churchill: *The World Crisis, 1911–1918*. New York: Free Press, 2005.

- Winston Churchill: *The Second World War* (Volumes I–VI). Boston, Massachusetts: Houghton Mifflin, 1948–1953.

- Naomi Wiener Cohen: *Jacob H. Schiff: A Study in American Jewish Leadership (Brandeis Series in American Jewish History, Culture, and Life)*. Hanover, New Hampshire: University Press of New England, 1999.

- Graham Cosmas and Albert E. Cowdrey: *US Army in World War II: The Medical Department: Medical Service in the European*

Theater of Operations. Washington, DC, Center of Military History, US Army, 1992, pp. 131–132.

- Michel De Trez: *At the Point of No Return*. Wezembeek-Oppem, Belgium: D-day Publishing, 1994.

- Gerald M. Devlin: *Paratrooper! The Saga of US and Marine Parachute and Glider Combat Troops during World War II*. New York, New York: St. Martin's Press, 1979.

- Louis I. Dublin and Samuel C. Kohs: *American Jews in World War II: The Story of 550,000 Fighters for Freedom*. Two Volumes. Washington, DC: National Jewish Welfare Board, Dial Press, 1947.

- Genevieve Dubosq: *My Longest Night*. New York, New York: Arcade Books, 1994.

- Dwight D. Eisenhower: *Crusade in Europe*. Garden City, New York: Doubleday and Co., 1948.

- Eisenhower Foundation: *D-day: The Normandy Invasion in Retrospect*. Lawrence, Kansas: University of Kansas Press, 1971.

- Bernard Fergusson: *The Watery Maze: The Story of Combined Operations*. New York, New York: Holt, Rinehart and Winston, 1961.

- Mark Fiege: *Irrigated Eden: The Making of an Agricultural Landscape in the American West*. Seattle, Washington: University of Washington Press, 1999.

- George Q. Flynn: *Conscription and Democracy: The Draft in France, Great Britain, and the United States*. Westport, Connecticut: Greenwood Press, 2002.

- Gary N. Fox: *Graignes*. Fostoria, Ohio: Gray Printing Co., 1990.

- Dominique François: *507th Parachute Infantry Regiment: Normandie, Ardennes, Allemagne: A Forgotten Regiment*. Bayeux, France: Heimdal, 2006.

- Barry Gregory: *United States Airborne Forces*. London, England: Brian Trodd Publishing House Limited, 1990.

- Terry Gander: *The German 88: The Most Famous Gun of the Second World War*. Barnsley, England: Pen and Sword, 2009.
- James M. Gavin: *Airborne Warfare*. Washington, DC: Infantry Journal Press, 1947.
- Nathan Glazer: *American Judaism: An Historical Survey of the Jewish Religion in America*. Chicago, Illinois: University of Chicago Press, 1957.
- David Goldstein: *Letters Hebrew-Catholic to Mr. Isaacs*. St. Paul, Minnesota: Radio Replies Press, 1943.
- Michael F. Hamm: *Kiev: A Portrait, 1800–1917*. Princeton, New Jersey: Princeton University Press, 1993.
- Michael F. Hamm: *The City in Russian History*. Lexington, Kentucky: University Press of Kentucky, 1976.
- Richard Hargreaves: *The Germans in Normandy*. Mechanicsburg, Pennsylvania: Stackpole Books, 2006.
- Gordon A. Harrison: *US Army in World War II: The European Theater of Operations: Cross-Channel Attack*. Washington, DC: Department of the Army, Center of Military History, 1951.
- Heinrich Hoffman: *Storm Trooper: Pictorial History of the S.A. in Germany 1932*. German original: 1932, English language reissue: 1976. No city, no press mentioned. Hoffmann was the official photographer of the National-Socialist German Workers' Party.
- John Keegan: *The Battle for History: Re-Fighting World War II*. New York, New York: Vintage Books, 1995.
- John Doyle Klier: *Imperial Russia's Jewish Question 1855–1881*. Cambridge, England: Cambridge University Press, 1995.
- John Doyle Klier: *Russia Gathers her Jews: The Origins of the "Jewish Question" in Russia, 1772–1825*. DeKalb, Illinois: Northern Illinois University Press, 1986.
- John D. Klier and Shlomo Lambroza: *Pograms: Anti-Jewish Violence in Modern Russian History*. Cambridge, England: Cambridge University Press, 1992.

- George E. Koskimaki: *D-day with the Screaming Eagles*. New York, New York: Ballantine Books, 2006.
- Arthur S. Link: *Struggle for Neutrality*. Princeton, New Jersey: Princeton University Press, 1960.
- S. L. A. Marshall: *Night Drop: The American Airborne Invasion of Normandy*. Boston, Massachusetts: Little, Brown and Company, 1962.
- John P. McCann: *Passing Through: the 82nd Airborne Division in Northern Ireland 1943–1944*. Countydown, Northern Ireland: Colourpoint Books, Newtownards, 2005.
- Chris McNab: *German Paratroopers: The Illustrated History of the Fallschirmjager in World War II*. Osceola, Wisconsin: MBI Publishing, 2000.
- Allan A. Michi: *The Invasion of Europe: The Story Behind D-day*. London: George Allen & Unwin, 1964.
- F.O. Miksche: *Paratroops*. New York, New York: Random House, 1943.
- Cydney Millstein and Carol Grove: *Houses of Missouri*. New York, New York: Acanthus Press, 2008.
- Lucy Moore: *Anything Goes: A Biography of the Roaring Twenties*. New York, New York: Overlook Press, 2010.
- Martin K. A. Morgan: *Down to Earth: The 507th Parachute Infantry Regiment in Normandy*. Atglen, Pennsylvania: Schiffer Publishing, 2004.
- Antonio J. Munoz: *Iron Fist: A Combat History of the 17.SS Panzergrenadier Division "Gotz von Berlichingen" 1943–1945*. New York, New York: Axis Europa Books, 1999.
- Phil Nordyke: *All American All the Way: The Combat History of the 82nd Airborne Division in World War II*. St. Paul, Minnesota: Zenith Press, 2005.
- Wade W. Oliver: *The Man Who Lived for Tomorrow*. New York, New York: E.P. Dutton & Co., 1941.

- Frederick Palmer: *Newton D. Baker: America at War*, Volume I. New York, New York: Dodd, Mead, & Company, 1931.

- Yohanan Petrovsky-Shtern: *Jews in the Russian Army, 1827–1917: Drafted into Modernity*. Cambridge, England: Cambridge University Press, 2009.

- Janusz Piekalkiewicz: *The German 88 Gun in Combat*. Atglen, Pennsylvania: Schiffer Publishing, 1992.

- Konstantin Pobedonostsev: *Reflections of a Russian Statesman*. Ann Arbor, Michigan: University of Michigan Press, 1965.

- Forrest C. Pogue: *The US Army in World War II: European Theater of Operations: The Supreme Command*. Washington, DC: Department of the Army, Office of the Chief of Military History, 1954.

- Pontifical Biblical Commission: *The Jewish People and their Sacred Scriptures in the Christian Bible*. Boston, Massachusetts: Pauline Books & Media, 2002.

- Edson Raff: *We Jumped to Fight*. New York, New York: Eagle Books, 1944.

- Thomas M. Rice: *Trial by Combat: A Paratrooper of the 101st Airborne Division Remembers the 1944 Battle of Normandy*. Bloomington, Indiana: AuthorHouse, 2004.

- Matthew Ridgway: *Soldier: The Memoirs of Matthew Ridgway: As told to Harold H. Martin*. New York, New York: Harper & Brothers, 1956.

- Jacob A. Riis: *How the Other Half Lives*. New York, New York: Penguin Books, 1997. First published by Charles Scribner's Sons, 1890.

- Richard G. Robbins, Jr.: *Famine in Russia, 1891–1892*. New York, New York: Columbia University Press, 1975.

- Cornelius Ryan: *The Longest Day: June 6, 1944*. New York, New York: Simon and Schuster, 1959.

- Dietrich Schindler and Jiri Toman: *The Laws of Armed Conflicts*. Leiden, Netherlands: Hotei, 2004. (The full texts of the Geneva

Convention of 1929 and related resolutions and documents are available in this book.)

- Joseph P. Schultz (Ed.): *Mid-America's Promise: a Profile of Kansas City Jewry*. Kansas City, Missouri: Jewish Community Foundation of Greater Kansas City and the American Jewish Historical Society, 1982.
- Brian N. Siddell: *507th in Normandy and Germany: The Complete Jump Rosters & Aircrew for Operations Neptune and Varsity*. Ithaca, New York: EQS Press, 2007.
- Ken Small: *The Forgotten Dead*. London, England: Bloomsbury Publishing, 1988.
- Abraham Sophian: *Epidemic Cerebral Meningitis*. Saint Louis, Missouri: CV Mosby, 1913.
- Lawrence Sophian: *The Sulfapyrimidines*. New York, New York: A. Colish Press, 1952.
- Michael Stanislawski: *Tsar Nicholas I and the Jews: The Transformation of Jewish Society in Russia 1825–1855*. Philadelphia, Pennsylvania: Jewish Publication Society of America, 1983.
- George H. Stein: *Waffen SS: Hitler's Elite Guard at War 1939–1945*. Ithaca, New York: Cornell University Press, 1966.
- David Kenyon Webster: *Parachute Infantry*. New York, New York: Delta Book, 2002.
- George Weller: *The Story of the Paratroops*. New York, New York: Random House, 1958 (for youths).
- Chester Wilmot: The Struggle for Europe. New York, New York: Harper & Brothers, 1950.
- John Charles Wonsetler: *Yanks in Action: The Story of Paratroops and Gliders and Tanks and Mechanized Warfare*. Artists and Writers Guild, New York, New York: Grosset and Dunlap, 1943 (for youths).

- Mark C. Yerger: *Waffen SS Commanders: The Army, Corps and Division Leaders of Legend, Kruger to Zimmermann.* Atglen, Pennsylvania: Schiffer Military History, 1999.

Movies

- Johnny Marr, Edward D. Barnes, Dick Carr, and Bob Davis: *D-day: Down to Earth: Return of the 507th.* Phil Walker and David Druckenmiller, directors and editors. Chief historical consultant: Martin K. A. Morgan. PBS Home Video, 2004.
- *D-day: The Secret Massacre.* Produced by Bill Kurtis. History, A&E Television Networks, 2008.
- *The Holy Terror.* Starring Jane Withers, Leah Ray. Directed by James Tinling, 1937. Available from Turner Classic Movies.
- *The Longest Day.* Starring John Wayne, Henry Fonda, Robert Mitchum, Sean Connery and Richard Burton. Directed by Andrew Marton and Bernhard Wicki. Produced by Darryl F. Zanuck, 1962.
- *Parachute Battalion.* Historical Fort Benning parachuting movie, starring Robert Preston, Edmond O'Brien, Nancy Kelly, Harry Carey, and Bud Ebsen. Directed by Leslie Goodwins, 1941. This film is available for download free of charge at http://www.archive.org/details/parachute_battalion; accessed April 4, 2010.
- *Saving Private Ryan.* Starring Tom Hanks and Matt Damon. Directed by Steven Spielberg. Produced by Allison Lyon Segan and others, 1999.

Index

—◆·❖·◆—